Howard J. Macgregor

Donald Macgregor

Running My Life

One man's lifelong run in search of contentment

Pinetree Press

The author gratefully acknowledges a Culture Grant from Fife Council.

Images have been acknowledged with thanks.
Where there is no attribution the image is private.
I will be happy to correct any omissions.

ISBN: 978-0-9548741-0-0

Ithaca

When you set out on your journey to Ithaca,
pray that the road is long,
full of adventure, full of knowledge.
The Lestrygonians and the Cyclops,
the angry Poseidon -- do not fear them:
You will never find such as these on your path,
if your thoughts remain lofty, if a fine
emotion touches your spirit and your body.
The Lestrygonians and the Cyclops,
the fierce Poseidon you will never encounter,
if you do not carry them within your soul,
if your soul does not set them up before you.

Pray that the road is long.
That the summer mornings are many, when,
with such pleasure, with such joy
you will enter ports seen for the first time;
stop at Phoenician markets,
and purchase fine merchandise,
mother-of-pearl and coral, amber and ebony,
and sensual perfumes of all kinds,
as many sensual perfumes as you can;
visit many Egyptian cities,
to learn and learn from scholars.

Always keep Ithaca in your mind.
To arrive there is your ultimate goal.
But do not hurry the voyage at all.
It is better to let it last for many years;
and to anchor at the island when you are old,
rich with all you have gained on the way,
not expecting that Ithaca will offer you riches.

Ithaca has given you the beautiful voyage.
Without her you would have never set out on the road.
She has nothing more to give you.

And if you find her poor, Ithaca has not deceived you.
Wise as you have become, with so much experience,
you must already have understood what Ithacas mean.

Constantine P. Cavafy (1911)
Translation © by George Barbanis, Athens, with kind permission.

For my
family and friends

Foreword

If memory serves me right, I first met Donald Macgregor in 1965 at the Edinburgh to Glasgow road relay race. He ran for Edinburgh Southern, I for Edinburgh AC. There was no love lost between the club officials but most of the athletes got on reasonably well.

Donald was a tall well spoken man with a sharp wit and good company to train with on long runs where his humorous observations on officials, politicians and other runners kept us all amused.

At the time British distance runners were dominant, with ten men winning every European or Commonwealth marathon title over 16 years from 1968 to 1974. Donald was on the fringe of this elite group through the sixties but could always be relied on to challenge the best when leading.

I recall at least two marathons: the first was the AAA championship 1967 at Tamworth where three Scots broke away from the field – Donald, Alastair Wood and myself, on a scorching hot summer's day. Donald forced the pace and I thought as he and I opened a huge gap that we would pay dearly for those suicidal tactics. Sure enough Donald tired, then I tired and Alastair roped the two of us in, passing Donald late on and finishing only yards behind me – I cursed Donald.

The second was the Scottish marathon selection race in May 1970 in Edinburgh. The race was being filmed for BBC tv for a documentary. As usual Donald forced the pace and he and I were clear at 20 miles where I suffered an embarrassing bout of diarrhoea. I held on to win by three seconds from Don who said to me on the rostrum that he would have won if he had not been slipping!

An interesting aside from those Games was the identity of the "mystery runner" who would carry the baton on the final lap of its long relay journey round every Commonwealth country. Inaugural Empire Games 1930 winner Dunky Wright checked out with his doctor and started training again in his mid 70s hoping to "get the nod". He didn't get it, and the honour came to me.

In the 1970s most British elite stars were on the wane, whereas Donald's star was on the rise. He made the British team for the 1972 Games in Munich and finished an excellent seventh as second Briton. To put that into context, no British marathon runner has made the top 12 in the Olympics in the last 25 years! Donald in his mid-thirties was now at the top table with the world's elite.

Despite this elevation Donald was still in awe of his father and forebears whom he rates as much better than himself – I think not, Donald, you have achieved as much as any of them.

Jim Alder, M.B.E.
Commonwealth Marathon Champion 1966

On the Terrace

Most sporting biographies begin with a chapter in which the atmosphere of the subject's greatest triumph is built up and the crucial line crossed or goal scored. Then the ghost-writer rewinds to the favelas or sad streets and the future sporting hero being born to a father who worked on a rubber plantation and to a mother who was not quite on the game, and recounts how he grew up in an ambiance of underworld thuggery, until one day the coach spotted him as he played with his pals.

My sporting triumphs are all relatively insignificant and completely unknown to the general public, so why did I decide to write all this stuff down? It was to see if I could manage to do it. My father Forbes Macgregor, as well as being a better and greater man than me, was a prolific author, and in several articles or essays touched on aspects of his own long life (1904-1991); but he did not leave more than fragments of an account. This book will thus hopefully be some interest to my children, friends and fellow-runners.

My great-great grandfather James Macgregor, born in 1789, did record his life's main events until 1836 - the events that had framed and conditioned his existence and progress through the sometimes very wild and rough sea of life.

The manuscripts of those accounts are in the National Library on George IV Bridge, Edinburgh, together with most of my father's papers, though I have the MS of an unpublished novel by my father about the troubled period around 1820, *Such as Adam*, that is deserving of publication.

By comparison mine has been an easy passage, at least so far. Like most people, I have experienced highs and lows: episodes of unforeseen tragedy, times of great happiness or deep misery, as well as long periods when general contentment has alternated with the opposite. This book is laid out more or less chronologically. It describes growing up long ago in suburban Edinburgh, then getting out of the capital to study at the University of St Andrews. It outlines a long career in education and touches on la vie en famille from 1980 onwards. However running forms the backbone of the book, because it was through running that I first came to develop self-confidence and through successes and failures in running that I worked my way up to a small measure of celebrity.

Edwardians at play: HRH May of Teck, Princess of Wales, awaits the marathon start on the East Terrace, Windsor on 24th July 1908. Prince Albert (the future George VI), Prince Henry, and Princess Mary look on. Runners 17. 18 and 53 are G.J.M. Buff (NL), F.Celis (BEL) and J.G. Beale (GBR). Beale was 17th, the others dropped out.

This introductory section precedes 26 chapters, reflecting the marathon race with its 26 miles 385 yards, plus a short section with maxims for readers to reflect on while walking back to the changing room. The distance was established in 1908, when the start of the Olympic Marathon was pulled back to the East Terrace of Windsor Castle so that the royal children, including the future George VI, could watch the start. If there are mistakes in the book, that too is reflected in the event, as it has been established by John Disley, co-founder with Chris Brasher of the London Marathon, that the distance was incorrectly measured and was 174 yards short.

A painting by William Hogarth, ca. 1755, called An Election Entertainment, includes the famous Give us our Eleven days protest slogan against the introduction in Britain and the British Empire in 1752 of the Gregorian calendar. The painting shows a Whig banquet, and Give us our Eleven Days is a stolen Tory campaign banner. Unlike the 1752 protests there is no great clamour among marathon runners to "Give us back our 174 yards".

I am indebted to my lifelong friend and running companion John Bryant, father of my godson Matthew and his brother William, and husband to Carol. John's books, especially *3:59.4* (Random House 2004) and *The Marathon Makers* (John Blake 2008), both of which I helped research, should be on every runner's shelf. I must also thank especially my friend Ron Morrison who devoted much time to editing the text before it was ready for the printers. More help came from others, notably from Ron Hilditch, Alistair Blamire, Volker and Gabi Kluge and Tim Johnston, Peter Mason and Brian Scobie. I am also grateful to that great marathon runner Jim Alder, who without hesitation consented to write a foreword to this book. Thanks also to David Roche, Margaret Smith and Duncan Stewart at Print & Design, University of St Andrews for scanning, repair and layout. I have mentioned many people in the book, but will no doubt have omitted some who deserve thanks. I hope they will forgive me.

This is not a kiss-and-tell memoir, so that private aspects of my relationships have been kept private. I feel however that it is fair to speak openly about many other people whose lives have crossed with or run parallel to mine, even if I do not always write uncritically in praise of them. I have been, or tried to be, at least equally hard on myself.

On Sunday April 25th 2010 two significant things in the world of running happened: Alan Sillitoe, the author of "The Loneliness of the Long-Distance Runner", died aged 82; and eighth place in the London Marathon was taken by Andrew Lemoncello, first Briton home, who was at school at Madras College and started running with Fife AC. There was a huge field: today's runners are never lonely.

Donald Macgregor
St Andrews
Summer 2010

Chapter 1

Over the Treetops

Somehow in dreams it's easy to take off
And let your weightless feet carry you through the air
Skimming the feathery treetops as you run.
At night in bed when I lay fast asleep
My dreaming self would canter down Kaimes Road,
Take off and, gaining height, veer over lofty walls
To gaze into the private worlds below. (written 2010)

Playing street tennis on late summer evenings in Gordon Road; stumping through deep snow in wellies along to the Maybury Roadhouse and back by East Craigs with my dad in the fierce winter of 1946-7; walking fearlessly in procession with a few pals, despite occasional cries of indignation from householders, along the top of the ten foot high wall that separates Kaimes Road back gardens from Edinburgh Zoo; riding the roundabout in Victoria Park between Corstorphine High Street and genteel Dovecot Road; late evening fish suppers from Tarry's after the film at the Astoria; roaming Corstorphine Woods with our "gang" or going up there in winter to sledge or in summer, under greater supervision, with the Cubs; being chased, forced to dismount from my bike, threatened by a gang of youths, and ignored by passing adults in the western suburbs near Cammo, scene of some of the action in *Kidnapped*: such are just a few of the memories of growing up in quiet Corstorphine in the 1940s and 50s.

When I was 11 or 12, my dad gave me an ancient bike that was far too big for me. He had attached wooden blocks to the pedals, strictly illegally, so that my feet could reach them. One spring afternoon the front brake pads came unscrewed just as I was gaining speed down the steep hill of Barony Terrace. The rear brakes did not have much grip on the rims either. If a Standard Vanguard, Triumph Mayflower, Austin A30 or indeed any vehicle had been coming along the street, Forrester Road, at the bottom of the hill, as I desperately tried to get the bike round the 90 degree corner with no functioning brakes, I would probably not be here now. As so often through my life, I was lucky. In the early 1990s during an October holiday with the family plus Whisper the gentle rough collie I was out for a solitary stroll near

My mother Rosemary Crerar around 1930.

Dunsinane and sheltered from the rain behind a station halt, when the Birnam train nearly got me. In 1953 in the new Elizabethan Age I didn't panic (nor did I in the Birnam incident), and somehow got round the corner. It was frightening at the time and alive in my mind for years after.

From July 1939 until mid-March 1945, I lived with my mother and father in a cosy world of grannies, aunties, hens, chicks, cats, snowmen and rabbits. That world was shattered by death, first of my mother who died giving birth to twins on March 18th 1945. The twins were named Forbes and Rosemary after our parents. I do not know, nor did I ever ask, if those names had been decided before the twins were born, or whether my father chose the names after our mother's death.

Neither of the babies ever saw our mother. The tragedy was compounded when Rosemary died suddenly just six months later. This devastating double bereavement was felt most keenly and immediately by our father, who thus lost half his family within six months. In his essay on Scottish education, published twenty-five years later, he quoted three lines of Dante's "Divina Commedia" to describe how he felt:

"Nessun maggior dolore
Che ricordarsi del tempo felice
Nella miseria."

[No greater pain
Than to remember the happy time
In misery.]

For a mere nine years our parents had enjoyed a blissfully happy marriage, the culmination, long delayed by lack of money through most of the Thirties, of a close relationship that had lasted a good fifteen years before that.

Of course I too missed my mother badly, though at this distance it is hard to recall much of what I felt. The last I remember was that I sat up in my bed and asked my Granny where Mummy was, and was told she was "away to the hospital".

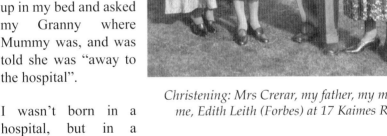

Christening: Mrs Crerar, my father, my mother with me, Edith Leith (Forbes) at 17 Kaimes Road, 1939.

I wasn't born in a hospital, but in a nursing home at 20 Chester Street, just off Palmerston Place towards the West End of Edinburgh. It's offices now. Strangely enough, I was in my fifties before I went to see exactly where 20 Chester Street was – for some reason I had confused it with Blenheim Place or Royal Terrace just above London Road off Leith Walk. That was perhaps because London Road was the area where my father had spent his teenage years in the household of his rather strict maternal grandfather William Forbes, as recounted earlier. My paternal grandfather David Macgregor, a third generation engineer, died of a heart attack in 1910 after helping a woman carry in a heavy sack of coal, when my future dad was just six. His mother, Edith Macgregor (née Edith Forbes) brought her two children – Forbes and his younger sister Margaret, known as Peggy, back to her family home in Edinburgh. A few years later she married George Leith, a tall quiet civil servant who wore his grey hair cut very short "en brosse", and moved with him to a bungalow, 76 Meadowhouse Road, Corstorphine – rather like my present house in St Andrews. As a child I spent a lot of time at my Granny's, although I saw little of Mr Leith.

Both my parents were primary teachers. My dad was deputy head at Leith Walk Primary School during the war years. He was in a reserved occupation and became a member of the Home Guard and did fire-watching. In 1951 he was promoted to headmaster of South Morningside Primary. As he later wrote, Edinburgh Corporation had thought South Morningside would have to be closed for lack of numbers. However, my father revived the school and increased the roll. No longer did S.M. stand for Salt Mines, for its headmaster became for a time a minor Edinburgh celebrity through the daily newspaper column A Scotsman's Log written by Wilfred Taylor. The journalist had sent his two sons to South Morningside rather than to one of Edinburgh's numerous fee-paying schools and featured the school frequently in the column, nearly always in a positive light, and it prospered. However in 1965 my father decided to retire aged 61, despite the efforts of Edinburgh's Director of Education to retain him. By this time he was valued by the service, but remembered the level of gratitude shown by Edinburgh Corporation in 1937 when he had finally achieved an external BA Honours degree from the University of London, mainly by correspondence, studying in the evening after his day job in David Kilpatrick ("D.K.") Primary School. In recognition the Edinburgh Corporation were pleased to offer him an increase in salary of 3 shillings and eightpence per week, a derisory amount even then.

A footnote in filial piety: When I ran at the Olympics in 1972, I was still a member of Edinburgh Southern Harriers. All Olympians with an Edinburgh connection were invited to a post-Games reception to be hosted by the Lord Provost of the time. I had just taken up a job at Dunoon Grammar School, and had started by being granted a very generous 4 weeks paid leave of absence by Argyll County Council's Director of Education, Charles Edward Stewart. I therefore wrote to the Lord Provost's secretary that I was sorry, but I could not attend a midweek reception. But that was not enough for the Edinburgh Toun Cooncil, who wrote back to ask me to think again, as "this is, after all, a very important occasion". Not so important for me.

In March 1945 my poor father wasn't sure what to do with three motherless bairns. He contemplated giving us over to the Orphanage at the foot of Kaimes Road, an imitation Tudor building painted white with black mock half-timbers. I'm glad he didn't, though the first year of my mother's absence does not bring back very pleasant memories. Auntie Peggy, a professional nanny, came to live with us. The two adults did not get on well. My father must have been in a terrible emotional state and Peggy could not resist bringing up old family arguments. A recurrent theme was the money that Granny had lent my parents to buy their new house.

The loan had been a few hundred pounds in a time when the total cost of the house in Kaimes Road, the first one to be built, was £800. Peggy perhaps felt the loan was money that could have come to her, but I don't know. What I do know is that when it comes to thieves of time, recrimination runs a good second to procrastination. From the perspective of a five-year-old, Peggy was no replacement for my mother, of whom I had few memories and those exclusively fond ones. Under the Peggy regime, I broke the top off a Scots pine sapling my father had planted, just so that I could stick it in a sandcastle. Happily the tree survived and now is taller than the house, but you can still see the kink in the trunk. I also broke a green Timpo Toy car in 1946 while Peggy and I were on holiday at Aberdour on the Fife coast, where I dug up some garnets at the beach known as Ruby Bay. At home I deliberately smashed a toy badminton racquet whose striking surfaces were made of celluloid material, so that I could get to use a new one that I knew was in the cupboard. Such are the trivial incidents that have stuck in my memory from that unhappy time.

Soon after I was born, the doctor told my father I would never walk. I'm not sure what deformity he thought he had spotted in my feet, but he saw fit to modify his judgment later, saying that I would have to wear boots all my childhood. The great Czech Emil Zatopek trained in military boots for a time because he said that when he put on spikes the contrast made him run faster. Some may think the doctor's opinion was a portent. In fact I did wear tackety boots for a while as a schoolboy. The tackets were blueish-silver. Quite a lot of children (mainly boys) had similar boots, which were good for sliding on the pavement, though I wasn't very skilled at that, being afraid of falling over.

Things like wall-bars, gym horses, indeed obstacles of any sort were not for me. Later I was the butt of jokes from members of the cross-country teams that I ran in for my hesitancy at crossing fences and other barriers. Only once did I perform well "over the sticks" and that was at the international San

Sebastian cross-country in the early 1970s where out of pure fear I managed to clear all the barriers on the race-course. Gareth Bryan-Jones, who had been an Olympic steeplechaser in Mexico City, was one of my Scotland team-mates and I wasn't anxious to make a fool of myself.

With Forbes Macgregor, 17 Kaimes Road.

To return to my father's dilemma in his deep distress in 1945: he decided that Auntie Peggy would take on the role of housekeeper and mother-substitute. She was one of those women for whom the word 'spinster' was devised. The babies, Forbes and Rosemary, were to be looked after by two nurses, Miss Anne Chamberlayne and Miss Phyllis Bennett, who lived, along with their terrier Kerry, in Dovecot Road on the south side of Corstorphine.

Auntie Anne (Chamberlayne) originated from Gloucestershire where several of her relatives were farmers. She was an open, friendly and motherly woman. Auntie Phyl (Bennett) was also friendly, but more reserved. In the absence of his real mother, Forbes could not have wished for a more caring home, though because he lived at Dovecot Road, I didn't see much of him when he was an infant. In any event he was two and a bit when he came to live with us at Kaimes Road, and by that time (July 1947) my father had re-married. Our new stepmother, Jean Combey, was in her mid-thirties and had lived all her adult life up till then in an all-female household across in Greenbank, close to the Braid Burn. Her father had been a professional cricketer and his widow, a white-haired old lady known to us as "Commie", had stayed in Edinburgh rather than return to her native County Durham.

Our stepmother had a rather corpulent and allegedly witty – seven year olds don't notice - elder sister called Nancy, who taught in the primary department of the Royal High School and was a well-known clarsach player, and a considerably younger sister, Marguerite, known mostly by her middle name of Gordon, who was a talented cellist and painter who later taught French and German at Tynecastle Secondary School in Gorgie, before retiring first to the West Indies and then to Anstruther where she and her sisters owned the Old Manse at Anstruther Wester. Its stone stable has been several times destroyed by storms, most recently in March 2010. It was there that Forbes and I spent summer holidays paddling around in the mouth of the Dreel Burn in a green canvas boat built by our father, and in that outhouse that he wrote most of his 48 page view of Anstruther, *Salt-Sprayed Burgh* (1979), reflecting among much else on the storm of the previous year.

It was very difficult for my stepmother, who had to look after not only a widower but also two boys of 7 and 2. It was difficult for me to accept a new and intrusive presence in the house. In addition, little Forbes was considerably cuter than me. I was entering a "difficult stage" that lasted a long time. It was harder for our father, who had to adjust to this new wife while keeping the peace as best he could between the resentful seven year-old and the woman he refused to call Mum. I never really accepted her, though my brother did.

With Forbes I got on very well, the usual brotherly arguments apart, and I don't think we have ever seriously fallen out about anything. When we meet or talk on the phone it's as if we had never been apart, even though we don't see each other all that often.

Our family house is a rather attractive two-storey building: Forbes still lives there. It stands at the apex of a 45-degree angle formed by Gordon Road and Kaimes Road, Corstorphine. My parents chose the site carefully in 1937 when the development was being planned by James Miller the builder. The view across to the Pentland Hills is stunning, and it would be impossible ever to obscure that view by any building, so steeply does Kaimes Road plunge in its descent from the edge of Corstorphine Woods to the A8 Glasgow road some 600 yards away.

A triangular sloping front garden thickly hedged on the Kaimes and Gordon Road sides contributes to the seclusion of number 17. As a very small boy I once poked my head through the Gordon Road beech hedging to yell at a lady called Mrs Butters "You're a beaty old woman!", for which I was rightly told off by my parents. "Beaty" was a derogatory word I had invented and I have no idea what it was supposed to mean.

There is an almost identical house to ours at the corner of Gordon Road and Belgrave Gardens, about 200 yards to the west, but that has much inferior views, and in addition was painted white at some later stage, in contrast to our house which still has its original pebble harling. The other house was dubbed "the whited sepulchre" by my father, who as a child had had the benefit of having even more exposure to Scripture than I did.

On the grass, which might have been justifiably called a lawn when I was a child, my brother and I used in the early 1950s to play "badminpong", a game in which we used tennis rackets and a shuttlecock. It was also possible to play it in the road, as there weren't many cars. The rules were simple: the smaller person (Forbes) stood higher up the grass or street, the taller (Donald) lower down. A point was won as in badminton, but there was no net.

Early memories are usually suspect, as they may be just versions of what older people have told you rather than what you remember yourself. I have a memory of playing with Glitterwax on the rug in front of the fire in the living room. I think I remember the almost daily visits I made to the Zoo around 1942-44 with a nanny. The word "nanny" was what was said in the 1940s for a person who today would be a childminder. The fact I had a nanny should thus not be taken as a sign that we were well off, because we certainly weren't. My parents needed someone to look after me during the day because they both had full time jobs as teachers. I know there was a succession of nannies, one of whom got the sack for nipping me regularly. My dad, a keen and knowledgeable naturalist, had, for a small subscription, become a Fellow of the Zoological Park, which meant that he and his family could visit the Zoo whenever it was open. On several mornings a week my nanny and I would make our way down to the Glasgow Road, turn left past the nursing home - it was along that stretch of pavement that the famous Sunday afternoon Penguin Parade was held, unbelievable as it seems today - and enter the majestic gates. It was not yet forbidden to feed the animals and birds, and I regularly had bits of bread or biscuits to throw to the Polar bears or to the ostriches. Unfortunately this practice came to an end when I decided to toss a hippopotamus a large bone, which stuck in its throat. The uniformed keeper had to stick his hand in and retrieve it, a rather risky procedure, and of course afterwards the man had a few serious pieces of advice for my nanny and me.

Edinburgh Zoo, constructed on the animal-friendly model of Hagenbecks Tierpark in Hamburg, lies on the steep southern slopes of Corstorphine Hill. We would wend our way gradually upwards, calling at the parrot-house, perhaps the Aquarium, looking in on the giraffes, elephants, penguins, storks, cranes and the big cat enclosures and emerging into bourgeois Corstorphine again via a turnstile, which is still there, and down the hill to our house, just in time for "elevenses".

The turnstile was adjacent to the studio and garden of a painter, John Hunter, and his wife, who were friends of my father. I liked the studio with its strong, attractive smells of paint and turpentine, and the canvases stacked round the walls. At the back of the Hunters' garden a few years later my pals and I would jump or clamber down off the long wall we had walked daringly up for about 600 yards to the horror, real or assumed, of the good folk of the eastern side of Kaimes Road, among them the Grants, the Stobbses, the Russells, the Lamberts, and the Tainshes, all now "vanished under the cover of night, as if they had never been" (Beowulf). Or at least vanished from Kaimes Road, where my brother can claim to be the resident who has by far the longest tenure. If Frances Grant, who was the only girl in our "gang", Robert Tainsh, Michael Cook, and Malcolm Mechie are around to read these words, I wish them all well. Robert had been affected by the 1946-7 "infantile paralysis" (polio) epidemic as had Norman Grant, Frances's elder brother, and the disease had killed the eldest of the Mechie children, Andrew, at the manse – one death and two partly paralysed in just one street.

I have so far said nothing about my mother's family. The version I have is from my father, who was naturally not unbiased in his views. Donald Crerar, originally from Perth, worked around 1900 in the administration of the Post Office in Edinburgh. He was sent to Shetland on business, and billeted on the postmaster in Lerwick, a Mr Laurenson, who had three daughters. These ladies were supposedly all a-flutter to have a young chap from the capital, in a suit, bowler hat, and kid gloves staying, and he took advantage of the situation to indulge in a bit of flirting. Now, at least according to my father's account, two of the daughters were comely and attractive, and the third less so. Donald Crerar was caught by the postmaster on the sofa one evening, but as ill luck would have it with the least attractive daughter. Threatened with denunciation to the Postmaster-General, he returned to Edinburgh with a blushing bride. My future grandmother proceeded to nag him literally to death, for after a number of years of marriage, he took a long Sunday walk out to Threipmuir Reservoir in the Pentlands, laid down his bowler hat, walking stick and gloves, and walked into the water. His body was found two days later.

When my future father visited my future mother for the first time at her mother's home, an upper flat in Roseburn, near the Water of Leith, in the early 1920s, the photographs in the living room were bordered in crape. "Has someone died?" Forbes asked Rosemary in hushed tones. "Yes, that's my dad, he died about ten years ago." I have a photograph taken at my christening showing me, my parents and both paternal and maternal grandmothers, and it appears as if my mother, brother and I were lucky not to have inherited old Mrs Crerar's looks.

The story becomes even darker. Following the death of our mother in March 1945, Mrs Crerar held my father responsible for the death, because if he had not impregnated her, she would not have died. This spiteful if understandable attack did not go down well, and our visits to Mrs Crerar, already rare, diminished even more in frequency. I don't know how or when she died. The only connection that persisted was my father's acquaintanceship with Laurinda Cowe, who had been a neighbour as well as my mother's bridesmaid, and remained a friend of my aunt Peggy. I know we have relatives on Shetland but have never met them.

I have few other close relatives. My paternal grandmother had a sister, Auntie Lila (Booth), who lived down in Portobello, and whom we occasionally saw at Granny's bungalow in Meadowhouse Road. Lila's son Gavin became an expert on buses and has published books about them.

Edinburgh in the 1940s was not a very exciting place, at least I didn't think so. On Sundays, it was frowned upon to play in the street –like that scene in the film "Chariots of Fire" where the Eric Liddell character tells a boy God doesn't want him to play football on the Sabbath. We didn't play football on the Sabbath either, but I think it had more to do with the pressure of convention than with God. Our Sunday afternoons were spent at my Granny's. In the early war years a large stone, flung up in the air by a discarded German bomb that had made a huge crater in Corstorphine Hill, fell through our roof and landed on the rug before the fireplace where little Donald Forbes would normally have lain in his cot – had he not been at his Granny's. Maybe God had a hand in that.

Sunday afternoon visits to Granny's were the tradition, and once I could read I joined the others in digesting

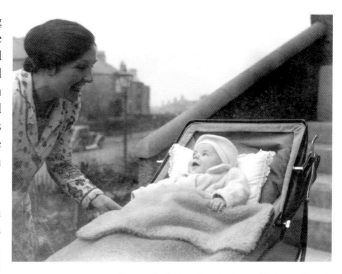

Perambulator, front steps, Kaimes Road.

the Sunday Post and as the years passed read my way through Dickens, Hardy, Scott, Stevenson and a few others. The editions my grandparents had were very thin-leaved so that the pages were fiddly to turn. In the background the pendulum clock ticked away the afternoon. Whenever I think of Hardy's sentence "The President of the Immortals had finished his sport with Tess", it takes me back to that otherwise silent living room with the dust motes caught in the sunshine and the ticking of the clock. In the living room also was a blue-green mother-of-pearl shell ashtray. It showed an oasis with palm trees and shimmered as you held the dish at varying angles.

In the kitchen Granny had a set of labelled semi-transparent glass containers set out in shelves that held tapioca, rice, flour, sugar etc. I used to enjoy pulling these out and rearranging them. The back garden had a stone birdbath and where the fields began a James Grieve apple tree which produced much yellow-green fruit.

As a child I had recurrent dreams. One or two were sufficiently vivid for me to recall them still. A favourite dream had me able to fly, so that I could run and take off up Kaimes Road and reach the other side of Corstorphine Hill with the treetops beneath me. In another rather similar dream – which I have had on and off all my life - I am able to take a couple of strides, then somehow keep moving forward at a fastish running pace but without my feet touching the ground, rather like the loung-gom-pa runners of Tibet, who are said to be able to run long distances at high speed in a meditation-induced trance. A famous account of a couple of these is given by the French explorer and mystic Alexandra David-Néel in her 1929 memoir *Mystiques et Magiciens du Tibet*, a country she crossed disguised as a Buddhist monk.

I used also to dream that one of the tigers from the Zoo was chasing me through the garden, into the house, and up the stair. In the dream I rushed into the "boxroom" where I slept as a teenager, and closed the door with its hook. I always woke up just as the beast was tearing the wooden panels to bits with its claws.

The wicked stepmother from Snow-White and the Seven Dwarfs (Disney version) also featured in some dreams. That was the first film I ever saw. I am not sure whether my own stepmother was incorporated in this dream character, but I don't think so, certainly not explicitly.

But there was no question that we didn't get on. It must have been very hard for her. Once I saw her weeping at the kitchen door, my dad trying to console her; but it was also hard for me. She may have felt as much of an outsider as I often did. One of our conflicts was about swimming, which I hated because I got cold so quickly in the water. Our weekly visits to Drumsheugh Baths, where I also went with my school class for a while, turned into a battle of wills. On one occasion she was getting so angry at my stubbornness that she struck out at me. I dodged the intended blow or slap but hit my eyebrow on the back of one of the mahogany chairs we had in our living room, so that it swelled up. My stepmother then asked rather aghast : "Did I do that?" At least I was honest enough to say it had just been the chair. But there was no swimming that day.

My dad was an extremely well-educated man, with a wide range of interests and knowledge – birds, animals, plants, gardening (especially vegetables), trees, history, geography, agriculture, religion. His literary tastes were also wide, but he was steeped in writers of an earlier era, such as Thomas Carlyle, for example, who are little read today. From him and no doubt my mother I inherited a keen interest in books. At a very young age I had read the Jungle Books in a 1943 Macmillan crown quarto edition called "All the Mowgli Stories", beautifully illustrated with line drawings and full colour plates by Stuart Tresilian. Almost all the images in that book I carry around in my head.

One in particular is vivid still, a colour picture of Mowgli running barefoot across the hillside in spring, as two sambhur lock horns just below him. That was in the chapter entitled "The Spring Running". Several others have coalesced in my memory: I see myself lying on warm summer afternoons on the short grass of Corstorphine Hill, not far from the WWII radar masts – an area now overgrown with bushes – gazing like Mowgli far across to the West, or looking up into the depths of the cloudless azure wondering what is up there, or lying back with eyes closed to listen to the rich hum of bees close by and to the warm drone of a small aeroplane lazily crossing the distant blue.

I have kept quite a few of the books of my childhood – for example the Mumfie books by Katharine Tozer, now barely remembered, and sadly reduced, like Rupert Bear, by being made into TV cartoons devoid of any intellectual or artistic merit. At the age of 7, the earliest possible in those days, I joined the public library, and spent many weekday evenings sitting until 8 pm reading in the children's alcove of Corstorphine Library opposite the medieval Auld Kirk, before walking home through the shadowy streets, imagining that one of the witches or monsters I had been reading about would jump out on me. For those who believe in the spirit world, let me say: none ever did.

Much later I was told by a friend and colleague at Madras College, Donald Mackenzie, that Corstorphine was socially divided by the main road, the A8. Historic Corstorphine lay around the Auld Kirk but according to Donald, who grew up in that area, those who lived south of the main road were the real people and those who lived in the hillslope streets up Drum Brae or Clermiston Hill and towards the Zoo were social climbers and snobs.

My favourite shop as a child was Miss Dickson's sweetie shop at the corner of Clermiston Road and St John's Road, part of the A8. Every week my father or mother would take me to exchange my Saturday penny, plus the ration coupons, for some sweeties. I often bought a bar of Fry's Peppermint Cream, or possibly Crème, which was divisible into five segments, or Rowntree's Gums or Pastilles. Miss Dickson was the sister of the garage owner whose property extended about 50 yards in either direction. The shop itself was like the one described by Roald Dahl so brilliantly in *Boy*. As you entered, a bell tinkled, and you found yourself in front of row upon row of bottles of drops and toffees and allsorts and barley sugar and so on. There was a high counter, and behind it stood the diminutive Miss Dickson, looking benevolently

Under the awning: father, nurse with me, Auntie Peggy, 1940

(unlike Roald Dahl's moustached and grimy sweetie-wife) at her customers. Alas! Miss Dickson, her shop, Dickson's Garage – all swept away by the broom of time, along with Corstorphine Railway Station (terminus of the suburban line from Haymarket and points east), and numerous other shops that formed my childhood streetscape. The Three Kays, opposite the Post Office, which is still there, by a miracle, was a confectioner's and ice-cream shop with one assistant I remember, a black-haired and Brylcreemed Italian-looking man who sold Famous Five-style ices, either as cones or sliders (wafers). After rationing ended the Three Kays sold chocolate-covered ices wrapped in gold paper.

More or less every Tuesday I got the Dandy, and on Thursday the Beano, but I'm not sure if my dad brought the comics home or if I went to the newsagent's to collect them. When the Eagle started in 1952 I read it from issue one. Like thousands of others I was a fan of Dan Dare and cheered him mentally on in his struggles to defeat his evil adversaries the Treens led by the green, big-brained megalomaniac Mekon of Mekonta. I am sure the Mekon and the Treens were later the models for Davros and the Daleks. Dan Dare could also be heard in the early evening on Radio Luxembourg.

As a young man my father had hiked and cycled the country roads and the moors of the whole area of the Pentlands, the Lammermuirs and the Moorfoots, either with his troop of 1920s Boy Scouts from the Cowgate or with a band of brothers like George Brown, who ended his days in New Zealand's North Island, Ned Barnie, who was in 1951 the oldest man to swim the Channel, and some others. Barnie's chosen cross-Channel route was from Cap Gris Nez to Dover, and when he came to visit my father afterwards I obtained his autograph, and still have the book somewhere. He was a man of medium height, but barrel-chested and balding. He worked as a physics teacher at Leith Academy, prefacing each day, even in winter, with a bracing dip in the briny off Portobello beach. Brrr!

Around 1952 my father acquired for a small rent two terraced cottages at the foot of a hill in the parish of Heriot, Midlothian. I am positive that the rent was nominal, as my dad's salary in real terms did not exceed by a huge amount that of Goldsmith's village schoolmaster who was "passing rich on forty pounds a year". From 1951 we had however become car-owners, for a 1934 Standard 8 had been bought, and it was succeeded by another pre-war car, a Lanchester which possessed a "fluid flywheel", whatever that was. My father was very proud of that fluid flywheel, or at least mentioned it a lot to acquaintances.

Public transport to Heriot was irregular, and having a car made it possible for us to get near enough to unload and carry our food, drink, and bits and pieces down the hill to "Sunnyside" from the top of the hill some distance away. We could also park on a farm track near the road that led to the Heriot Water, at about half a mile's distance where it flowed under the shade of trees.

The cottage had no toilet, no electricity or gas, and water had to be hand-pumped from a well at the foot of the garden. About 200 yards away, in the direction of the burn, lay another cottage, Kirklandhill, which was uninhabited, but could be entered. It had a cement floor on which Forbes and I raced our model Grand Prix cars round chalked or painted circuits by pulling them on threads attached with Plasticine to the underside. We could choose between models including HWM, 2 litre Maserati, Alfa-Romeo 151, Gordini and 2 litre Ferrari.

In the burn we found trout, as well as minnows, caddis fly larvae clad in small stones, water boatmen, mallows and other flora and fauna. I once managed to guddle a trout, but my father was an expert. He would lie on the bank and slowly slide his hands and arms as far apart as possible into the water. Then inch by inch he would narrow the distance between his hands, and if he was lucky he would find himself touching a trout. Even more slowly he would "tickle" the fish until he was able to grab it and throw it in a single movement behind him on to the bank, where it could be despatched with a blow on the head. By such methods he procured trout for our supper, but that was not all. He was very skilful with a catapult. He made each one himself from a Y-shaped piece of willow.

Strong lengths of rubber were attached to the arms of the Y, joined by a piece of leather which held the missile – a stone or a piece of lead shot. With pretty unerring aim he could soundlessly stun or kill rabbits or pheasants, though an alternative way of catching young pheasants was to shake the conifers in which they lay in the family nest, and chase them through the undergrowth as they ran squawking over the pine needles, unable to fly. If you deplore this slaughter of the innocents, please remember that this was still the period of meat rationing, and even with coupons often next to nothing was available. There was much talk about goods being available "under the counter", i.e. on the Black Market. Thus if my father could catch his own meat, so much the better. At home we had poultry, kept in an air-raid shelter under the front steps, and we were always excited when the chicks hatched out and ran around chirping in a big cardboard box on the hearth. When the hens no longer laid eggs, they were converted into Christmas dinner.

Dad was also a very good gardener, having grown fruit and vegetables for the best part of his life. He was friendly with many Borders farmers, and also with some of the people who worked at the potato seed-testing station at East Craigs in western Corstorphine. Among his favourites were Sharp's Express and Duke of York. Peas, runner beans, broad beans, cabbages, broccoli, sprouts, carrots, parsley, artichokes, radishes, lettuce, tomatoes, radishes, curly kale, and turnips were regularly served up to us during the entire period of rationing and beyond, as well as a range of fruit that included apples, pears, currants red, black and white, strawberries, raspberries, and gooseberries of several varieties. Much jam and jelly was made, as well as Seville orange marmalade, at the appropriate time of year, in a copper jeely pan.

Back to Heriot Water: On the far side grew dense stands of a species of orange raspberry, called by my father "Jerusalem Jews", though I'm not sure why. There were also trees which bore enormous elephant ear fungi that could be carved with a pen-knife into even weirder shapes.

It sounds like Paradise, but I am afraid I didn't think so. I resented being taken away from Corstorphine for the weekend or for weeks on end in the holidays. Pumping water with a wooden handle, collecting firewood, the uncomfortable iron bedsteads, reading in the glow of an oil lamp were not my cup of tea, though I did like lying in bed talking to my brother when the fire in the bedroom cast its shadows on the wall and scented the air with pine resin.

After I acquired the bike with the built up pedals, on which I had my near-fatal swoop down Forrester Road, it was not long before I started to cycle out to Heriot, which was a ride of about 20 miles. Looking back, I wonder that my father and stepmother didn't think it too risky, though traffic in the 1950s was relatively light. I would be loth to attempt it now. My route took me up across Edinburgh via Fairmilehead to Gilmerton, Eskbank, Newtongrange, Gorebridge and along the A7 across the moors to Heriot. The village lay on the Borders railway line, though I think we only went there once by train.

The cycle ride must have taken me well over two hours, as there were quite a few hills, and it was not infrequently windy or wet. It may well be that the effort gave me some stamina which would be useful later in life. Apart from the first few miles across the open moorland, the journey back, though often into the wind, was easier. There was a long drag up from Eskbank to Gilmerton, but after that I could swoop down to Morningside and zig-zag my way through the city to Corstorphine. Sometimes I was there before the other three arrived in the car, and then, as often on other occasions, I had to wait for them coming before I could get into the house.

My stepmother did not trust me with a key, so that I wasn't even a latchkey kid. One of her favourite phrases was "we'll be back at the darkening'", an indefinite time, especially in summer. I resented having to hang around and get cold. "At the darkening" was one of a number of phrases that I classified as "Greenbank", that being the district near the Braid Burn in South Edinburgh where the Combey family had their home. We did not tend to visit the house in Greenbank Park very often, but I recall it had a garage, a damson tree and an extensive back garden. The two households made duty visits to each other on Christmas Day and on New Year's Day. Commie, Nancy and

Gordon, usually swathed in fur coats, would arrive at Kaimes Road in the late forenoon and then chatted with the other adults until Christmas dinner was served. Forbes and I had opened our presents much earlier, and escaped into the lounge, which had its annual fire lit in the grate, to play with them. The short day passed into night and the Greenbankers headed off in their taxi.

On January 1st it was our turn to drive over to Greenbank. In my memory it was always frosty, and inside in the hall with its polished wooden floor hardly above freezing. To add to that impression a mirror-topped table was set out like an icy lake, with tinsel and artificial snow on it, plus a scattering of miniature Santas, reindeer and similar seasonal fauna. The main attraction as far as toys went was a pre-war set of building bricks with which Forbes and I could construct houses, as well as a marble-shooting game like a hand-operated version of pinball, with a painted map showing the northern and southern hemispheres. It had beautiful painted animals on it, each in a cage of nails offering the players anything from 5 to 100 points if their marble whirled up the firing corridor and landed in the appropriate cage.

Exciting though these activities were, I think we were never unhappy to be able to go home through the streets of Edinburgh after the last bit of Christmas cake had been eaten.

The years of childhood and of growing up followed a similar pattern to that of thousands of others, no doubt. The week was dominated by school routine, the weekends by not being sure what to do on Saturdays – going out to play, sweeties, going into town maybe – and Sundays by the dead hand of Scottish Presbyterianism which sucked the excitement out of anything. I attended Sunday school at the bottom of the road in St Anne's Church Hall. My stepmother was no doubt pleased to get me out of the house, for I found it difficult in those growing up years to occupy myself meaningfully. Forbes somehow avoided getting into the tentacles of religion, probably because he was always busy with something and wasn't moping around like me.

The Superintendent was Mr Nicol, a tall beanpole of a man who looked like a drawn-out version of Pa Broon. Among my Sunday school teachers was W.K.L. Relph, who had played for Scotland as a rugby forward and was a Stewart's FP. It must be admitted that my knowledge of Scripture, which is well above today's average, derives mainly from attendance at Sunday School – so getting me out of the house had longer term benefits, I suppose.

Auntie Peggy, as might have been expected, was a pillar of the Kirk and of the Women's Guild. In the year she stayed with us she was always at her most argumentative after attendance at church. That gave me to think what the advantages of church membership in reality were.

When I was too old for Sunday school I went for a while to Bible Class, which was taken by the minister, Mr James Macmillan. I remember little about it, except that it was held in the church itself, and that I once embarrassed myself, when asked what the 'in-' of 'incarnate' meant in Latin, replied "Not".

In 1954 a boy who lived up the hill bribed me into coming with him to the Crusaders, a very middle-class evangelistic group who met on Sunday afternoons in a hall down Manse Road in Corstorphine village. The boy who had acted as recruiter shared a bar of chocolate, which was then hard to obtain, with any new recruit. The leader of the group was a Dr Boyd, a small, earnest and enthusiastic man who with his pious disciples preached Godliness and Cleanliness. I heard one of them talk about his days in the RAF on National Service when one fellow in the hut – from the lower classes, versteht sich – actually slept in his underwear! Can you imagine it, boys? Jesus would have had a blue fit!

My father's first trip abroad was to Paris in about 1970, where my stepmother photographed him sitting at a picnic table near the Eiffel Tower. He had however a good reading knowledge of French, and taught himself to understand and translate Dutch. Our family holidays however were taken in Scotland. I can recall going to Cullen in a grey August about 1948. We travelled by train via Dundee and Aberdeen, where I was impressed by the ships in the harbour. After the acquisition of our first car, it was possible to be more adventurous. In 1951 my father took us all to Gigha, where we stayed with a farmer and his wife, Angus and Babs McNeil on the "North Island". The McNeils were cattle farmers but were "diversifying", as would be said nowadays, by taking in paying guests. I loved the farm, and I was allowed to help with the milking and feed cattle cake, which tasted quite nice, to the beasts. Most days we hiked up the grassy track across the damp machair to a narrow isthmus of silver sand. There were lightly sloping beaches on both sides of the isthmus, and on its northern side was a rocky island covered in deep bracken. My brother and I went adventuring up on the island, and I recall us singing a ditty that repeated the line "There a hole I couldn't get through", referring to a narrow place between two rocks. In the rock pools by the shore Forbes and I caught crabs and poked sea anemones, and if we walked carefully in the shallows of cool green water we could feel and sometimes catch baby flounders under the soles of our feet. We had a rowing boat too, and my father placed lobster pots and left them overnight. The next day there was sometimes a scaly occupant, who ended up in a billy can of boiling water, in which its shell turned from steely blue to dull red. Mackerel, saithe and lithe were not hard to catch either. All my father had to do was to trail a line with a number of baited hooks out of the boat for a while.

To get to Gigha we left the car at West Loch Tarbert, boarded a Caledonian MacBrayne ferry, and disembarked near the island of Gigha into a heavily laden rowing boat. The Atlantic lapped round the gunwhales and sides of the boat only a few inches from the top.

We went twice to Gigha, but when Forbes and my parents some other summer went to the most westerly point of the British mainland, Ardnamurchan, I did not arrive until half way through the holiday as I had been at a cadet camp on the east coast. Ardnamurchan possessed magnificent expanses of beach, and no doubt still does, and a bay from which the sea recedes at low tide so that at high tide in summer it was possible to wade or splash around in quite shallow and pleasantly warm water. That is a nice place to end this brief account of my childhood en famille, and move on to the strange world that we humans impose on our young by sending them to school.

Chapter 2

A Most Peculiar Boy (1945-1957)

I reached school attendance age in 1944, and my parents decided to send me for that first experience of education to a PNEU nursery school run by a Mrs Fisher in Belgrave Road, opposite tennis courts. The school had a badge – a kingfisher – and all I can recall of the establishment is that at morning interval we played in the rockery. I assume that one of my parents or my nanny took me along and brought me back. I never asked why I wasn't sent to Corstorphine Primary School. It may be that it was farther away and my parents wanted to be sure I could get home quickly or that they could get me if there was some emergency. It was after all wartime.

My mother had attended the all-girl Mary Erskine School, or "Queen Street", one of the four Merchant Company schools – the others at the time being Daniel Stewart's College (boys), George Watson's College (Boys), and George Watson's College (Ladies). Edinburgh was and indeed remains a hotbed of school snobbery, and the "Edinburgh Question" is "What school did you go to?" The same question is asked in Glasgow, but there it is to determine whether you are Catholic or Protestant. In Edinburgh the reply has little to do with religion but defines your social status, at least in the mind of the questioner. Fettes, Loretto, Merchiston, Edinburgh Academy, George Heriot's, the Merchant Company Schools, Melville College, John Watson's (whose building off Belford Road is now the Royal Scottish Gallery of Modern Art), St George's…there were lots more fee-paying establishments, though the fees in 1945 were relatively low in real terms compared to what is charged today. Some of the lesser "Saint" schools were described by my dad in his 1970 essay on Education in Scotland as "All the saints that from their labours rest". Then there were the Edinburgh Corporation schools such as Boroughmuir or Broughton. My father attended Broughton in the late 1910s when it had some outstanding teachers. Edinburgh society is infested with FP (Former Pupil) activities and connections, a sort of Freemasonry, but one in which everyone is classified and has his or her pigeon-hole. Many inter-marry within the circumference of their school connections, so that the tradition is perpetuated.

My mother had wanted me to attend Daniel Stewart's, which is in a rather splendid mid-Victorian turreted building facing Queensferry Road and high above the spire of Fettes down in the valley to the north. My father made considerable financial sacrifices to ensure that I could become a Stewart's boy, and I was enrolled in Class 2 of the Primary School in the summer of 1945.

Aged 6, in Daniel Stewart's uniform, 1945.

I have a clear memory of arrival on the first day of term that September. Mr John A. Baird, who lived in Forrester Road in Corstorphine, had been my father's Home Guard sergeant. He was head of mathematics at "DSC" and offered to take me there for those first weeks and months. So I stood with this tall, stolid, slow-spoken man who smoked a pipe at the foot of Kaimes Road for the first of hundreds of times. We were waiting for a service 12, 25, 26 or 31 tram which would convey us past the Murrayfield rugby ground and as far as Roseburn, where the Water of Leith flows under the main road. Traffic was still very light on the A8 in 1945, for few people had a car. Those waiting sometimes walked out into the road to see if a tram was coming round the distant bend from the direction of Clermiston.

The old Edinburgh trams should, like the suburban railway, never have been scrapped. They rattled and shook all the way to their terminus, where the conductor turned the seat backs the other way, and the driver moved to the opposite end where there was also a space for him to spark it up and set off back towards the place whence he had just come. Once I saw a fatal accident at the Princes Street junction with Lothian Road, where an inspector was crushed under a tramcar, but in general trams were safe, cheap to travel on and to my eyes beautiful.

So on that bright, sunny morning in September 1945, Mr Baird and I disembarked at the Roseburn bridge over the river, walked up Coltbridge Terrace, through the lane past St George's girls' school to Crarae Avenue and down Ravelston Dykes as far as its junction with Belford Road. We crossed the road and entered the rear gate of DSC. A rough pebble-strewn earthen playground extended far to the right, and as we walked down the slope to the left hundreds of seagulls rose from their search for worms and took to the skies.

Missing Primary 1 had its disadvantages. I knew no-one in Miss Wilson's class, and, much worse, I had never played football and didn't know the rules. That first morning all the boys started a game on the playground, and when the tennis ball we played with went out of play, it was a "shy" (throw-in). Ignorant little chap that I was, I knew neither what a shy was nor how to take it. The others responded with scorn. As a mark of initiation (perhaps) one or two of them decided to put me in an empty dustbin. I kept quiet about this treatment, as "clyping" or telling the teacher was as even I realised the deadliest of sins against the spirit of pupil solidarity.

I don't intend to go into every detail of the 12 years I spent as a pupil at Daniel Stewart's. Most of it was bearable, and from an academic point of view I did quite well, save in Mathematics and Science. In Primary I scored very highly until P7, when the teacher, George "Bandy" Forsyth whose nickname derived from the configuration of his legs, tried to teach us algebra. By Class Ic I was lost. Our form master Mr Campbell would read out the test results and shake his head when he came to my name. Only with great efforts did I eventually achieve a Lower certificate in Maths and manage to pass Arithmetic.

My strong areas were language – English, French, German, Latin – and I gave up Science to take up German as a third language. Thus I was no longer taught by a chemistry teacher called Dr James C. Milligan, or (by pupils) "Spike". He was a much imitated teacher with a round face and a little moustache and spoke out of the corner of his mouth. In class I he made me write out a very long definition of a catalyst 25 times. Spike was also the Adjutant (whatever that meant) of the Combined Cadet Force (CCF) with the rank, earned or not, of Captain.

The Headmaster during my period at DSC was Dr Herbert J.L. Robbie, MA PhD (Cantab). A prominent educationist, Dr Robbie had various hobby-horses including spelling. He was wont to come into a classroom and ask pupils at random such questions as "How do you spell 'across'? 'Across'? ' Hmm? Hmm?" His habit of repeating – repeating – made him the target – target! of frequent imitation – imitation!

Primary 7, DSC, with George W. "Bandy" Forsyth, 1949. DFM 2nd back row, 5th from left.

We all have our idiosyncrasies, but Dr Robbie had more than most. As he spoke, or repeated his questions, he would bring his right index finger firmly across the tip of his nose, intoning 'Hmmpph! Hmmpph!'as he did so. During a craze for collecting autographs some third year boys approached him as he was conducting some visitors round the school: "No! No! Remember your manners!"

All the years I was at Stewart's I never had school dinners, perhaps because my father regularly complained of indigestion after the mince and tatties he was given at Leith Walk primary. Instead I brought a "piece", consisting of a large cheese, beef dripping (my favourite) or jam sandwich plus an apple or orange. At the morning interval we could buy a bun or other bakery from the

Dr Herbert JL Robbie 1951 (Yerburys and Co, Edinburgh).

school canteen next to the vestibule, which lay between the gymnasium and the cloakroom and dining hall. I liked iced buns or the sugar-topped ones that you pulled away from a circle of six. In my first senior year there was an innovation in the "fine dining" offer available, when soup and a roll were on sale in a kitchen downstairs on the western side of the building. I tried this compromise between "piece" and school dinners. Dr Robbie appeared on the second or third day of the soup experiment, as I was slurping away in my usual style. He took the spoon from me. "No, Donald, no! That's not the way to drink soup! Do it like this! Like this!" and he demonstrated how to charge the spoon with nourishing soup and then move it away from your mouth rather than towards it. I was unconvinced by the demonstration but did my best to absorb the soup in that way until he and his gown had swept away upstairs.

When my father and stepmother came to the last parents' evening before I left school in 1957, when I was 17, Dr Robbie remarked to my father that I was "a most peculiar boy! A most peculiar boy!" All I can retort to that is "Hmm! Look who's talking!" My daughter on the other hand just laughs and says: "And...?"

The CCF had an Army section, an RAF section and a Signals Section. It was not strictly compulsory for all boys from Class III onwards, but it would in 1952 have taken a more determined lad than me to insist on being treated as a conscientious objector. In those days all pupils who walked past the War Memorial in the school grounds were expected to salute it. The CCF was officered by teachers, from Lt Col "Bandy" Forsyth through Flt Lieut. "Eddie" Hyndman (gym teacher) who had been in the Fleet Air Arm in the war, and the ineffable "Spike" Milligan with his blancoed gaiters and brown boots. The under-janitor, RSM J Sim, was master of the parade ground. He really enjoyed shouting at the top of his voice in front of the headmaster's window: "That Robbie – he's either a mistayhke or a pinprick!". My brother tells me that Sim was once summoned to help a French teacher, who had a stuck window in his classroom. Sim entered the room in silver-buttoned splendour, yanked the window open with a mighty heave on the cord, and exclaimed scathingly in his regimental sergeant-major tones as he left: "It doesn't take an M A [an Emm Aaaay!] to open a window!"

We cadets were intended to achieve Certificate A Part 1. At least in theory if there were another war we could be officers, God help us all. After Cert A Part 1 we could choose to enter either the RAF section, mainly plane-spotters, or the Signals Section, mainly skivers. I did the latter. Mr Sim was in charge of administering the Cert A exams, which were sometimes held at Redford Barracks. On one occasion a pupil had been asked how far away a target was, having been given a hint by Sim : "How far awaaay would you say that bushy-topped tree was? I'd saaay about 200 yaaards." The pupil, trusting his own judgment, answered : "300 yards", whereupon Sim rolled his eyes and said in a slow, emphatic voice: "I would say that tree was TWO HUNDRED YAAARDS away – what do YOU think?". The pupil caught on that time.

Apart from the NCOs, who included some of the school bullies, the worst thing about the CCF was that Monday and Friday were parade days and you had to come to school in your prickly uniform, change out of and back into it before and after the Gym periods, which always seemed to be on Monday and Friday first period. You also had to spend some time on Sunday nights covering your belt and gaiters with a greeny-yellowish "Blanco" and, when the Blanco mixture had dried, polishing the brass bits. A complete waste of time! My dislike of the military undoubtedly dates from those three long years of experience of the well-intentioned teachers who ran the CCF. I was able to postpone doing national service by going to university, and by the time I had graduated it had been abolished. If I had gone, it would probably have involved taking part in the Suez adventure, of which I was one of only three boys in Class VI to disapprove, a judgment on DSC attitudes.

My time at school was not particularly happy. I was not a confident child, and suffered from bed-wetting, probably psychologically induced because of the suppressed trauma of losing my mother and the constant resentment I felt at not getting on with my stepmother. I spent a week under observation at the Deaconess Hospital without anyone ever telling me why I was there, but it seems nothing was found. The best thing about that week was that I was introduced to Superman and Batman comics of which another child had a quantity.

At school I had few real friends. As a defence mechanism I transformed myself in my teenage years into a class joker, for example offering would-be witty versions of the sentences we were asked to translate into Latin. The teacher, David Sked, was one of the most sympathetic members of staff, but warned me once that I was sailing rather close to the wind with a would-be joke about the geese defending the citadel from the barbarians.

Enuresis had plagued me from the age of seven or eight, and in primary school occasioned frequent requests to leave the room and visit the insanitary toilet block at the other side of the playground. My Class 4 teacher Miss Jean Rendall eventually asked another pupil to accompany me in case I was skiving.

One incident in particular plunged me for years into misery, when I suffered a bout of bed-wetting on a school trip to Belgium in Class I of the secondary school. Children can be very cruel. The use of a silly nickname by other pupils made three years of my school life pretty wretched. I should have confided in my father or stepmother but did not trust myself to do so. Happily, at least as far as I know, none of my own children ever suffered, from bullying or any worse name-calling than the accurate if hardly penetrating observation "Hey! Your dad's a teacher!"

Until its use was banned in the 1970s "the belt" or leather tawse was used for corporal punishment, though not terribly often. Scotland had moved on some way from the days recounted by my father when primary school children were severely strapped, as he was by a woman described by him as "that

DSC athletics team outside school, 1957. DFM front row right.

old harridan" for forgetting parts of the Shorter Catechism. "What does God do?" – "Don't know, Miss." – "Come out here, boy!" Whack – "God loves us!" Whack! Whack!

I had the belt three times in my school career. The first time was in Primary 5, when I helped another boy in a spelling test. For that Miss Sandilands, or "Sandbags", decided I should be belted. The next time was in Class IIIm of the Senior School, when our new form teacher, an strict disciplinarian called "Trot" Hardy, so named because he had been caught short during a cricket match and had had to trot off the field, called me out to the front when he saw me glancing across the room. That was what Maupassant would have called "une belle injustice bien saignante".

The third time was in Class IV when I was caught passing the answer to an item of a French vocabulary test to a pupil in the next row. The teacher this time was Mr Murdo MacRae. I have to say I still think these teachers behaved in a brutal and unnecessary manner, though I suppose the Zeitgeist was responsible.

Although in Primary 2 I had known nothing about football, I was quick to learn, and for many years enjoyed the games we played in the playground during intervals, lunchtimes, and often until 5 o'clock or so, before walking or cycling home up Ravelston Dykes and along the main Glasgow Road, or through Corstorphine Woods – where at the age of about 12 I was once followed by a man until I started running and got away from him.

Although I enjoyed playground football I was not aggressive enough to play well, but liked playing. I was even worse at cricket and tennis, and at rugby worse than useless. I hated having to play rugby at windy, chilly, wet Inverleith, where Bandy Forsyth, who fancied himself as a rugby buff, remarked during an early practice in Primary 6: "There's a boy who wants to learn to play rugby with his hands in his pockets". Wrong! I didn't want to play rugby, and I had my hands inside my shorts to keep them from freezing. It was Bandy who was in charge of the 6th Juniors (lower one could not go) one Saturday morning when we were due to play a George Heriot's junior team. They had 15 players, but we were missing two, and had to be lent one of theirs. You would think high treason had been committed! At half-time Bandy started foaming at the mouth (metaphorically) as he told us what a disgrace we were. None of us dared to point out that he should have been addressing his remonstrations to the absentees rather than to us. Poor old Bandy! He met a sudden end at an FP dinner, falling over with a smile on his face and a glass of whisky in his hand.

Segregation of pupils by gender is unnatural. At DSC there were no female pupils and indeed only a very few female members of staff. Nearly all of those ladies were of mature age and employed in either the primary department or as secretaries or "dinner-ladies". Only in later fiction such as Brian Aldiss's *The Hand-Reared Boy* [1970] could any of them have possibly been an object of desire for even the oldest pupils. Out of school, I knew hardly any girls of my own age. It is therefore not surprising that like many others who attended boys-only schools I entered adult life without much idea of how to behave in female company, and it took years to catch up. The school motto was "Never Unprepared" – what a joke!

Like all the rest, I spent those twelve years in uniform. Primary boys, as in all those Edinburgh boys' schools, wore a cap, and short trousers were the norm until we were about 14. Around that time, Dr Robbie decided to define the school colours more precisely as Adam Gold, Cardinal Red and black, or Robbie Black, as some of us called it. Previously they had simply been red, black and yellow, as listed in the jolly old school song: "Forward the col-ours, the red, black and yel-low/Emblems that hon-our the winds of the West/Hail to the Col-lege that floats them above her/Mo-ther the dearest, the kindest and best!"

One of H.J.L. Robbie's favourite phrases, delivered at assemblies in the school chapel, was "Stewart's maketh mannered men", a dubious assertion in respect of quite a lot of my contemporaries. The chapel was a dark, wood-panelled hall presided over normally in my time by "the Rev Chis", a Mr James Chisholm so called to distinguish him from Ronald H.E. Chisholm, an Aberdonian French teacher who was more distinguished for his batting, for he played for Scotland for a long time, than for his knowledge of French grammar and syntax. He was an amiable man, who could easily be distracted on a sunny afternoon into recounting some tale of derring-do at the wicket. He favoured the pronunciations "auunt, dunkey, and johter" (aunt, donkey and jotter), which we juveniles found amusing. I watched him play against the Australian touring side in 1955 at Edinburgh Academy's ground, where he made quite a good score. My own favourite cricket position was long-stop, and I would have liked the game much better if they used a tennis ball.

Our schoolteachers were all eccentric. Some would argue that all teachers are eccentric, or become so because of the stresses and strains of the job. I cling nonetheless to the view that our teachers were seriously eccentric. From Mr Neill (popping eyes), through Bandy Forsyth (full of himself, just as he had been at Moray House in the 1920s when my dad had known him), to Willie Craig (mathemahtics, boys) a douce wee man from Eyemouth whose son Ian was in my class, and of course Dr Robbie, le Grand Schtroumpf himself.

Mr Craig had a habit of starting a sentence and allowing the pupils to finish it: "And tomorrow we'll be moving to alge…bra, boys, thaht's correct.' On one occasion (according to my brother), a scream was heard somewhere outside. Mr Craig responded: "David Thom David, go and see who's screaming. If it's in the playground, tell the jahnitor – if it's out in the street, just come baack here." If pupils misbehaved till Mr Craig's face turned red, that was OK – but if it then turned white, they had gone too far. But Mr Craig was a kind and gentle man.

Mr Eric Reid, the music teacher, was a fine musician, but sadly put upon by pupils. Once his belt was cut up by someone and the bits scattered inside the piano. I felt really sorry for him, especially as he lived a few houses along from where I had attended Mrs Fisher's kindergarten and was thus a sort of neighbour. In 1953, it was arranged that Benjamin Britten would come up and conduct our junior choir in a performance of The Spring Symphony. Britten fell ill and had to cancel. Instead, the music staff took us all to see "Genevieve" with Kenneth More at the Cameo. Much better – at least I thought so, uncultured as I was.

In 1955 it was the school's centenary. The Duke of Edinburgh, poor soul, came to visit and to inspect the CCF, of which I had the misfortune still to be a member. We were instructed to line up in front of the War Memorial to be inspected, and told that as the ducal Daimler was purring its stately way towards the front gates of the school grounds we were to wave our Tam o'Shanters and shout "Hurrah!". Not "Hurray!" which would have been non-U, to use the idiom of the time. During the inspection, Prince Philip spoke with the boy to my right, and with the boy on my left, but ignored me. Too bad! Later that afternoon – or maybe it was another half-remembered occasion when some big-wig inspected us, we had a parade with rifles – "Present…arms!!! Hup two three! Hup two three!" – and a hundred khaki-clad schoolboys presented their ancient .303 rifles just in front of their noses.

Why do the military do this? We were lined up in three ranks on the grass at Inverleith, and I fainted, cutting my brow on the rifle butt of the boy in front of me. That incident had a good result, as I was allowed to go home for the rest of the day.

The traditional games that were played at DSC were rugby from September to March and cricket from Easter to July, though there was a chance to do athletics and tennis in the summer term. My French teacher, Murdo MacRae, suggested in the staffroom that it might be a good idea for boys who found rugby an ordeal to be allowed to go cross-country running on Wednesday afternoons instead. The suggestion, as he told me much later, was initially treated by his colleagues as heretical, but in the end gained acceptance, so that from Class III onwards 15 or 20 of us were permitted to run round a road circuit, which could be two or three miles depending on route, from Inverleith to Crewe Toll, then along Crewe Road, Carrington Road, Inverleith Place, Inverleith Row past Goldenacre, Heriot's sports ground, and back along Ferry Road. For some reason we never thought of running round Inverleith Park, where I used to train quite often later in my running career. We were creatures of habit. Mr David Sked, the Latin teacher who ran the Scripture Union, was the only member of staff I ever saw running this circuit with us.

Among the members of the group were Renton Laidlaw, later a prolific golf correspondent, and Andrew Hood, who became a well-known journalist on the Scotsman and the Herald.

The effect of these weekly runs, though we didn't run any other time, was to get me reasonably fit by comparison to most. I was probably the most promising runner among the non-rugby pupils. When I was in Class IV, in March 1955, a school cross-country championship was instigated, run on "house" lines. There were four "houses" on the English public school model, aped so willingly by the Scottish bourgeoisie: Ravelston, Drumsheugh, Belford, and Dean, all named for parts of Edinburgh close to the school. Ravelston's house captain did not initially select me for our house team, until persuaded by other runners that a specky skinnymalinky like me was worth a place. I finished 9th, to the surprise of all the rugger-buggers, and in Class VI I won the race - I think I was ill on race day in Class V – my first victory at any sporting event.

44

Encouraged by this, I took up track athletics that summer, using as manuals *Teach Yourself Athletics* by FNS Creek and *First Four Minutes* by Roger Bannister. Track is tough. In the first two trials for the mile team, I ran 5:25 and 5:20 on our 352 yards grass track at Inverleith, just scraping in as third string for the match versus George Heriot's School and Trinity Academy at Goldenacre, which had a 440 yard grass track. And on that glorious May evening, something transformed me. With just over a lap to go, I passed all the rest, surged into the lead and broke the tape in 4:57.2. It was unbelievable, and I basked in the unaccustomed praise. Even better, the next day in the sixth year English class, held in one of the turret classrooms, I was complimented by Dr David Rintoul, co-editor with James Skinner of *The Poet's Quair*, the standard poetry textbook for Higher English in most Scottish schools.

"Ah, Macgregor", he said in his usual benevolent and lively way. "Not only intelligent, but an athlete as well." That's the sort of remark you never forget, and made up for so much of the bad stuff.

In 1956 pupils sat their SCE Leaving Certificate (Highers or Lowers) in March, and the results were sent to the presenting schools in May. Most pupils did the exams in Class 5, at around 16, but it was possible to add more qualifications in Class 6. University entry was available if you had three or more Highers – grades were not yet a part of the system, so it was Pass or Fail – and I had a rather unbalanced range: H English, Latin, French and German, plus Lower History and Mathematics, and Arithmetic, which was the same for Lower and Higher candidates.

At DSC the usage was that candidates assembled in Room 18, a History Room which had been the room in which the kindly and popular Dr John Thompson had taught until 1955 when he was appointed Rector of Madras College, St Andrews.

There can't have been a huge number of expectant candidates, even though it was quite a large room. A hush fell on us all as "Herb", catching up the folds of his black gown in one hand and holding the sheets of results in the other (so that his customary nose-flicking was difficult), went through the names in alphabetical order. "Hmmph! Ian Andrews! - Excellent results, Ian!" or it might be "James Brown! Oh! Oh! You've come down in Physics,

James!" After each comment the pupil named would come out to receive his certificate and study the type-written results. I still have mine somewhere.

The summer term didn't end until late July, and there was no attempt made that I can recall to curb the indolence that most of us demonstrated through those summery days. I had decided that in Sixth Year I would study English, French and German, with a view to entering one of the "Bursary Comps" that the four Universities held in the spring term of our Sixth Year, in this case March/April 1957. As I had been so unhappy among my contemporaries, at least most of them, I decided not to attempt to win a bursary for Edinburgh University, but to try for one at St Andrews.

I should mention that at that time, hardly believably, I had only a vague notion where St Andrews was, although when I was 12 we had spent an Easter holiday at a rented house in Elie called "Sunterville", which I have been only been able to trace at the time of writing by the coincidence of meeting the builder's grand-daughter at Hogmanay 2009. It was a solid stone house constructed by a local builder, Mr Sunter, whose wife owned quite large parts of the burgh.

Elie is only about 12 miles from St Andrews, and so that doesn't say much for my sense of geography. The highlights of the fortnight in Elie were digging up garnets, and being allowed to go off to Kirkcaldy for the day in a lorry with whose driver I had formed a sort of friendship. It was totally innocent, but if such a thing were suggested now, the newspapers would have a field day!

Field Days at school were one-day manoeuvres which the CCF used to organise in places like Cultybraggan in Angus so that the cadets could practise the skills they were supposed to have learned over the preceding months. Like the CCF camps, which were similar to Field Days but longer and hence worse, there was the usual cast of teachers masquerading as officers, with RSM Sim shouting the odds in his usual sarcastic way: "You baoys! You're crawling through that grahss as if you were with your young laaydy – keep your bottoms down". We travelled around in rattly army trucks and endured parades and map-reading exercises ad nauseam.

The trip I made to St Andrews acted as a caesura in my life. Although I had done very little academic work in Sixth Year, I was so arrogantly confident that I would win a bursary that, when I didn't, I speculated that the university authorities might have made a mistake, an opinion rightly pooh-poohed by one of our English teachers, Mr Mackinnon. He sat on a desk with his feet on a chair and puffed his cheeks out while considering, then let the air out – Pfffff! - as from a balloon: "That is extremely unlikely, Macgregor!"

However in St Andrews, for the first time, I was treated like an adult. For the three or four days of the competition I stayed in St Regulus Hall in Queen's Gardens, where I was addressed as "Mr Macgregor". This was an agreeable novelty, as I remarked to Mr Mackinnon on return to school.

I made some new friends in St Andrews, whom I later re-encountered when we had been transmuted from bursary rivals to bejants, as first-year students were traditionally called. The only part of the exams I can remember was the essay title that all candidates had to expand on; "To travel hopefully is better than to arrive. R L Stevenson. Discuss."

The last term I spent at school was made enjoyable by my new success at running, though that first track victory was a false dawn – anti-climax followed. At the annual sports (where in previous years I had regularly finished last in events like the obstacle race) two other boys beat me in the mile. In a race against the Former Pupils I reduced my time to 4:52.1 and beat Scottish rugby international winger T G (Grant) Weatherstone. I had watched the Scottish team that included his brother D G in the 1951 season when after a long fallow period Scotland at last had a home win against Wales. After the match lots of us mocked the losing supporters as the crowd thronged from Murrayfield along past Roseburn towards town. Entry to the stadium was very cheap for schoolboys in those days, perhaps 1/6 or so, a complete contrast to today's over-priced corporate charging. Are the teams any better? I went regularly to Murrayfield right up to university days because Kaimes Road was only about a mile and a half at most from the ground.

Among the features of the last weeks of term were the annual concert and prize-giving held in the Usher Hall off Lothian Road. Rehearsals were necessary, not just for the concert, which included vocal as well as instrumental items, but also for the prize-giving. Because I was a fairly regular recipient of prizes, invariably books, I had to go in the morning of the ceremony to the Usher Hall to be lined up and practise the whole rigmarole: rising from the seats in front of the stage, mounting the steps, walking across from left to right, pausing where the wife of the Master of the Merchant Company (substituted for by a teacher) would stand. The drill was to extend the right hand, shake that of the wMMC, take the book or books in the left hand, say "Thank you, ma'am", bow, and walk off to the left side and descend to the appropriate row. During the actual evening, white shirts, tie, grey trousers, grey socks and black shoes were standard gear, and as each of the many prize winners crossed the platform, each was submerged under a wave of applause.

There was a sixth year parents' evening, a less majestic affair held in the school gym. It was there that Dr Robbie said to my father that I was a most peculiar boy.

The peculiar boy bridged that last vacation with a summer job in a rural hotel near Cockermouth, run by a couple who employed several students as bar and general staff, among them a girl from Aberdeen with whom I fell hopelessly in love, unreciprocated as may be imagined in view of my previous total lack of experience of girls. When it rained, I walked around yelling "Singin' in the Rain" to the unresponsive hedgerows. As soon as the job stopped, I forgot her.

In contrast to today's 18 year-olds, I had never been in a pub before reaching the age of permitted consumption. We students walked the mile or so down the road to the local, where we drank beer and played darts every night, then wended our unsteady way up again. About 11 the hotel was locked and we had to sleep in the barn across the yard – not that we noticed very much. I have never been quite so good at darts as I was by the end of that summer.

The hotel proprietor was a keen fisherman, and regularly headed off with his long waders and his rod and basket to the local river. Not long after I had left his employ I saw in the papers that he had been tragically drowned when he got out of his depth.

Chapter 3

Over to Fife

And so I left Edinburgh and came to St Andrews, desperate to make a fresh start, away from the contemporaries who had made aspects of my life so wretched at school. The two or three who were also to be at St Andrews were not among those. The domestic situation where I always felt put in the wrong by my stepmother, though I don't suppose she intended that, was also left behind.

In 1957 steam trains still ran from Leuchars Junction to the town station. Indeed it was possible to get from St Andrews to Glasgow, if you weren't in a hurry, via the East Neuk countryside route opened in the 1860s: through Mount Melville, Stravithie, Boarhills, Kingsbarns, Crail, Anstruther, Pittenweem, St Monans, and so on. That October afternoon, or possibly evening, because the many arrivals in St Andrews in early autumn have merged into a composite picture, the train puffed its way over the river Eden at Guardbridge, where the pilgrims landed until the Reformation ruined the local economy. It then headed east across the golf courses, bathed in warm October sunshine that put the hollows and bunkers in dark relief and gilded the greens and fairways. We were approaching a Holy City with its seven towers. It was far from being an Auld Grey Toun, rather it was a mysterious golden one, and despite all the years that have passed, and all the changes over that half-century, St Andrews remains so for me.

The train pulled into the neat little station, between high stone walls, and we disembarked on to one of the two platforms between which stood the ticket office, waiting room and toilets. On either side of the station were well-tended flower-beds. Of the two ways out, one was up a wooden stairway past the news stand up to the main exit in front of the bus station, and the other up a longer set of metal stairs to a lane to Doubledykes Road. Most of that has been lost except the bus station, and it has been modernised. The station is now a car park, and the flower-beds too are long gone. It's not quite "change and decay in all around I see", but like many others I regret the departure of the railway.

St Andrews Univ. CCC National Junior Champions, Hamilton 1958.

I had been unsuccessful in getting a room in St Regulus Hall, where I had stayed in April. Instead I was to share a "bunk" (digs) with another bejant called David Woolley, in Mrs Paton's council house at 84 Langlands Road. Eventually I managed to hoick my heavy suitcase through the town centre, down across the Kinness Burn, and right to the back of the "new town". That was the term used for all the post-First World War housing "south of the burn". The burn flows west to east along the valley of the Lade Braes south of the town centre and through the inner and outer harbours into St Andrews Bay.

Langlands Road leads past the St Andrews United football ground, Recreation Park, and numbers 82 and 84 form one half of a four apartment block, set at an angle to the rest of Langlands Road on the south side of the main distributor road, Lamond Drive, on which the adjoining half of the block has its postal address. Council house building was started at the eastern end, near the East Sands, by St Andrews Town Council in the 1920s as part of the Homes Fit for Heroes programme and was driven locally by the Liberal provost of the time. The houses in Langlands Road were built in the 1930s, and although the block where I stayed has a different style of roof and pebble-dash harling, unlike the other houses around, it is clearly of similar vintage.

David Woolley proved to be a science student, I think from the Midlands, and we had little in common, but we did not get on badly. However, my occupancy only lasted two terms, for in April of 1958 I was offered a room in "Regs"and said goodbye to Langlands Road. Those first days in St Andrews were spent finding my way around, matriculating and doing all the things that newcomers have to do. At the Societies' Fair I joined the cross-country club, St AUCCC, formed in the 1940s as an offshoot of the Athletic Club, itself one of the founder members in 1883 of the Scottish Amateur Athletic Association.

Although I had done little training over the summer, I intended to build on my school performances, though those offered little foundation. I had decided that running was to be my sport for three main reasons: I was pretty useless at any other sport; I enjoyed running; and the modest successes I had achieved had brought me a much-needed increase in self-esteem.

St Andrews in 1957 was in many respects different from St Andrews today. The University was much smaller. There were about 1200 students when I arrived, as opposed to the 7400 or so now. Most students came from Scotland or England, and there were relatively few from abroad. We were a privileged minority, as only around 3% of Scottish school pupils went on to university education in those days, and a local authority grants system operated. Living and tuition costs were paid for us, and there was a theoretical parental contribution. Extremely few students could have afforded a car; indeed the same applied to the general population. As the University was concentrated in the centre of town, we walked or cycled. Drivers still parked in the centre of North Street. To travel to Dundee, for Queen's College was still a constituent part of St Andrews University, or to venture farther afield, we used the train, or hired a coach if we were travelling in a large group.

St Andrews had a lot of shops but no supermarket. Bakers, butchers, newsagents, grocers and so on had their separate establishments. If you wanted to buy food on Sunday you went either to Mr Di Folco's general store in South Street next to Central Motors garage or to Ma Brown's in North

Street near the ruined Cathedral. The town boasted quite a number of pubs and bars, but few restaurants. Drinking hours were restricted. One of the few pubs to have television, black-and-white of course, was the Central, where I remember going with friends on Monday evenings to watch "Quatermass and the Pit".

Most undergraduate students could be accommodated in the halls of residence, strictly segregated by gender: St Salvator's ("Sallies"), Hamilton Hall, Hepburn Hall and Regs for the boys, and "Chattan" (MacIntosh Hall), University Hall ("Hall"), and Linden Lea for the girls. Male visitors were only permitted on Sunday afternoons. In some girls' halls the room doors had to be left open, or so it was said. As I was very shy and indeed retarded socially, I never found out. I was a sad case, very romantic by inclination but without a clue how to advance my cause.

A much tighter control of students' comings and goings was exerted than would be considered acceptable today. The voting age was 21, so that few students had the vote. We were expected to behave as "ingenui adolescentes", the phrase used in the document we had signed at matriculation. A considerable number of students lived in rooms in people's houses, known as bunks, and the landladies as bunkwives, who could be expected by the University authorities to keep a close eye on the behaviour of "thae students".

The (men's) Students' Union building was the Admirable Crichton's House in North Street, where there was a café and bar, and its dining hall, where roistering Gaudies and heated debates were held, went far back along into Butts Wynd, which in medieval times led to the archery butts. On the upper storeys were a small library and a "swot-room" which overlooked the Cinema House, one of two picture-houses that changed programmes twice weekly. It was thus possible to take in four different films in the six-day cinema week. Tickets were cheap – few of the Scottish students at least had much money. I lived on a grant of around £100 per year, perhaps a little more, and at the end of my first year was so impecunious that I went to my "regent" to seek to borrow some money. Regents were lecturers who had responsibility for the welfare of a group of students.

Dr E.V.K. (Ted) Brill, senior lecturer in German, lived with his family in a university flat at 7 South Street. As I stammered out my request, he eyed me rather suspiciously. "How much do you need?" he asked in his slow voice.

"A pound would be enough." "A pound? Are you sure that's all you need?"

It was. From that my older self has to conclude both that I was not exactly a spendthrift and that I was rather naïve. And I did pay it back.

In May 1958 Ted Brill took a group of us in his little Hillman Husky to Tentsmuir Forest, not to run but for a stroll through the beech glades and along the dunes. It was to be another eight years before I started to explore that forest where my friends and I have run thousands of miles and indeed continue to do so.

Second year student, 1959.

Female students had their own Union, which occupied the building next to the Men's Union. There were regular discussions in the student newspaper Quorum about the possibilities of a merger, but it took a few more years before a vote on the matter was eventually carried and the two became one. The University was very male-dominated and attitudes were still old-fashioned as far as women were concerned. There were few female lecturers, and no female professors. The Principal, T.M. Knox, who had worked at Port Sunlight for Lever Brothers and written much on the philosopher Hegel, was a rather stolid-looking bald round-head of a man. We students mocked his authority by putting words, sung with great gusto at gaudies and graduations, to Rossini's Wilhelm Tell overture: "The Princ's got a head like a ping-pong ball, the Princ's got a head like a ping-pong ball, ping-pong, ping-pong" and so on. The song ended "Ping-pong yiddle-i-po", taken from the Goon Show which enjoyed a large following.

I was a very ignorant student, callow in every way. I was probably not alone. Academically I was starting from a very low knowledge base, and had wasted more than a year when I could have been working. The three subjects I took in first year were French, German and Latin (called Humanity at St Andrews, *latina* "litterae humaniores". The first class in all subjects was called General, the second level Special, and those who passed the Special exams at the end of second year were permitted to enter Junior Honours, followed by Senior Honours. For an ordinary degree, students repeated Special but with an extra subject or two.

The traditional scarlet gown was widely worn, and was in theory compulsory for lectures and in fact for examinations. A tradition of uncertain vintage dictated that bejants and bejantines wore their gowns right up to the neckline; semis and semies could leave one shoulder free, tertians both shoulders, and magistrands could wear their gowns round their waists. This seemed to bejants like me to be both desirable and decadent. All these names for the four years of undergraduate study have now more or less vanished from currency, though "bejant/ines" is making a comeback.

I had done no Latin since passing Higher in 1956, but was obliged to take "Gen. Hum.", because the study of Latin to General Level was compulsory for students wishing to offer Honours French. Ambition almost o'erreached itself, as I failed both French and German in the June exams, passing only in General Humanity. Perhaps that minor success was due to the idiosyncratic lecturers we had in that subject. The professor, Thomas Erskine Wright, had held his chair since 1936, and his lectures were said to have remained unchanged over most of that period. It was claimed that he had his notes marked up with "applause" or "laughter" at the appropriate places. He lectured to us on Virgil's Fourth Georgic, which is largely about bee-keeping. This gave Erskine Wright the opportunity for punning translations like "they sally forth from their residences", a reference to "Sallies" hall of residence where Prince William much later spent his first year. I should add that Erskine Wright pronounced the letter "r" deep in his throat which gave added piquancy to his pronouncements. He was much imitated.

Another lecturer was John Simon, a friendly man who had the job of helping us through one of Cicero's heavily edited speeches, the "Pro Flacco". In 59 BC Cicero had had the job of defending Flaccus, a praetor who was accused of corruption in the province he governed. Mr Simon pronounced the words "Pro Flacco" in an RP accent ("Prowh Flac-cowh"), which was the only amusing thing about it.

Major Terence Bruce Mitford, a giant of a man, with a barrel chest and a booming voice, was a distinguished archaeologist. His task was to guide our fumbling minds through Tacitus's laudatory history of the conquest of part of Britain by the historian's father-in-law, Lucius Agricola. Mitford's technique was to give the Gen Hum students "gobbets", short pieces of text that we were advised to study particularly carefully, as some of them would occur in the exam and we would be expected to write about them. I am sure it was thanks to gobbets that I passed.

Finally, Erskine Wright had the dubious pleasure of taking us also through one of the books of Horace's Odes (Book I), from which I can still quote a few chunks at the touch of a button. Those were the texts I enjoyed the most. It was pure coincidence that Q.Horatius Flaccus, the last part of the name meaning "big or floppy ears", or possibly "fatty", bore the same cognomen as the probably corrupt governor Lucius Valerius Flaccus defended by Marcus Tullius Cicero, whose own cognomen means "chickpea".

The lecturers in General German and in General French were less idiosyncratic and their lectures, with one or two exceptions, less interesting. If that judgement sounds unfair, well, maybe it is, but I suspect it would be shared by quite a few of my contemporaries. It started with the professors: Charles Telford Carr (German) was an expert in Gothic and had been on the staff since before the war. He was a Mancunian, who pronounced "put" as "putt", and was ponderous and dull in his delivery. He did not condescend to teach the General Class, and I did not encounter him until I got into Honours. One of our first year lecturers was Dr Ruth Harvey, a lively teacher who was unfortunately regularly interrupted, to her understandable annoyance, by a claque of foot-stampers at the back of the tiered lecture-room, School II in the quadrangle. She left us during that year to go to a new job in Oxford.

Dr Martin Lindsay spent most of the year giving us an overview of German literature. He leaned heavily on the lectern and on J.G.Robertson's book on the subject, first published in 1933. It would have been possible, had I had a bit more initiative, to have answered all the questions on that aspect of the course by reading Robertson over and over. But I was very lazy, reluctant to learn vocabulary, procrastinating as ever. At the June exams I failed German first time round, though narrowly.

Central parking: Ian Docherty and DFM cross the line, North Street, St Andrews 1959.

In French, Professor R. C. Johnston was another who left the first years mostly to his colleagues. In General French I remember with affection Dr Philip Ouston, Dr R. A. Wilson, Dr D. D. R. Owen and Dr Harry Brumfitt. It is however an indication of my laziness or possibly poor attendance that I can't remember much of what we were taught. Included in the set books list were *La Symphonie Pastorale* by André Gide, and *Le Notaire du Havre* by Georges Duhamel. Dr Ouston took us through the history of the 3ʳᵈ and 4ᵗʰ Republics. In the end I got my reward in the shape of being bottom equal in the exams with a miserable 36%, the other student sharing this ignominy being a man called Norman Lillie, who was a few years older and by coincidence was to be a future neighbour. Norman had had some industrial experience. Experience of any sort was what I lacked.

The results depressed me, but I set to and did enough work to pass the re-sits in September, much to my family's relief. In second year I dropped Humanity and added Logic and Metaphysics.

The Professor was John Nicholson Wright, known as "Johnnie", who had started as another pre-war junior appointee. His stock in trade, while discussing Descartes or Locke and Berkeley or whoever it was, included occasional excursions into his past life, or into monologues about the Master's Garden, for he was at the time the Master of the United College of St Salvator and St Leonard. He had also been a goalkeeper for a professional football team, I forget which. As he soliloquised he would cover his eyes with one hand and utter moaning noises as he wondered where the Master's Garden might be.

In the Metaphysics part of the course we moved from Plato's "Phaedo", in which the "Socrates" character adduces several rather weak arguments for the immortality of the soul, through some of the writings of René Descartes, John Locke and Bishop Berkeley. I was pleased when one of my lecturers, R. N. W. Smith, wrote next to a mark of 13/25 for one of my essays the encouraging words: "I think there is philosophical ability in you, if only it may find a suitable form of expression." Logic I found more interesting, though challenging, and I had to work hard to understand these new concepts.

I had determined to turn over a new leaf. Dr Lindsay set the Special class in German an essay on "Kleist's Women Characters". Making good use of J. G. Robertson's extremely detailed though turgid History of German Literature, I wrote about every single female character in Heinrich von Kleist's oeuvre and scored 45/50. That was probably the high point of the year, but I amassed sufficient credit over the session for my efforts in both French and German to gain automatic entry to the Honours classes for 1960-61, and passed Logic and Metaphysics into the bargain.

In the late 50s there were, as ever, numerous student traditions, some of which persist but in a rather different guise. The "Bejant Skite" in October was a day-long pitched battle between bejants and semis, thought to be rivals. Groups chased each other round the streets. A bunch of semis caught me in Church Street and removed my shoes, and we bejants planned a revenge ambush on the Kinkell Braes in the dark, though it came to nothing.

We still had the long-established walk "Out by Cameron, in by Grange", first commemorated as a private hike by the American "student poet" Robert Fuller Murray in 1892, and later developed into another "tradition":

And I fear we never again shall go,
The cold and weariness scorning,
For a ten mile walk through the frozen snow
At one o'clock in the morning.

Out by Cameron, in by the Grange,
And home as the moon descended …
To you and to me there has come a change,
And the days of our youth are ended.

(Last two verses of "To CCC", from "The Scarlet Gown", my edition 1932, W.C. Henderson, University Press)

In 1958 a couple of haycarts accompanied us hikers, both boys and girls, as we made our way four miles up the Cameron Road (the A916), turned left at John Paul's corner for the downhill mile and a bit to the top of the Grange Road, then over the two miles of switchback before the silhouetted towers of St Andrews and the dark waters of the Northern Ocean swam into sight from above the Grange Inn.

In those days we celebrated Raisin Monday, now an entire weekend if not a week. The origin, as told to us by our seniors, was that in medieval times new students would be looked after by a more experienced student; in gratitude the novice would present the senior man with a pound of raisins – unam libram uvarum siccarum. There were no women students until the very end of the 19th century, but by 1957 bejantines also gave their senior woman a gift in exchange for a receipt, written in Latin on parchment or a paper scroll. Most gifts were still raisins, though grape-related gifts (wine) were creeping in. I still have my receipt, written by Gordon S. Maxwell, who became a distinguished classical archaeologist.

The present day "traditions" of weird receipts in the form of baths, bicycles or other objects, and of foam fights in the Quadrangle of St Salvator's College, were unknown and would certainly have been disapproved of. We were after all creatures of our time – sports jackets, blazers, ties, gowns, duffel coats, skirts and blouses were our wardrobe. The only wines available in the few shops or restaurants that we could afford were Egri Bikaver (Bull's Blood), a heavy red from Hungary, Mateus Rosé, and Blue Nun or another type of

Liebfraumilch. Excessive drinking was confined to the Union Bar or the Cross Keys – few could afford it.

In the summer before "coming up" to university I had envisaged that the student cross-country runners would race through woodlands, although in reality St Andrews lies exposed to all the winds that blow, the two prevailing ones being from the south west (warmer) and from the east or south east (cold). Not for nothing is there a saying "nothing good ever blew out of Crail". Occasionally we get north winds. They tend to be freezing.

The town was still surrounded by open farmland, a lot more of it in 1957 than now, except to the north, where the Links lie next to the North Sea just inland from the West Sands and the Eden estuary. We used to run, and still do, on the Links, for it is defined legally as a public park and place of recreation, and anyone can walk or run over it, although priority should be given to golfers. This is because golfers pay to play the courses and don't expect to have their round interrupted by runners; and also because golf balls are very hard and if they hit your head you may have been on your last run. I have never been struck by a golf ball in more than half a century of running round the Links, though who knows what the morrow may bring?

A former Rector of the University, Air Marshall Sir David Munro, tells in his rather rare memoir *It Passed So Quickly* (1952) of an incident in the 1890s when he,

1959 Edinburgh-Glasgow Relay: Moving up from 16th to 12th on leg 2, Maybury Cross to Broxburn UF Church.

a keen student golfer, hit a high drive over the Black Sheds on the 17ᵗʰ hole of the Old Course which landed on the cap that covering the head of "Old" Tom Morris who was resting behind a low wall near what is now the Old Course Hotel. He was not pleased.

The cross-country club was to provide one of the main strands of my life. Our first training run was on a Wednesday afternoon, the half day allotted to student sport. We assembled in the changing rooms in Butts Wynd, at that time the HQ of the Athletic Union and P.E. Department. The Director, Mr A.S. Strachan (Archie) had his small office half way up the stairs, and the two other staff members had their own offices. Miss Edna Haydock had responsibility for student sportswomen, and the department secretary was a very helpful lady called Mrs Maisie Malcolm, always referred to as Mrs Malcolm, for it was a formal era. The changing rooms for men were on the upper floor, traditionally laid out with a wooden floor, lockers, benches with rows of coathooks, showers and toilets off to the side. The predominant colour was dark-brown painted oak or pine. There was an ancient set of scales on which we regularly stood to check our weight after training. To demonstrate my naivety once more: when the toilet paper had run out, I went one day to Archie to ask if the supply could be renewed. He looked at me and said "That's not exactly my job, you know!". I slunk away, muttering an apology.

About 15 or so runners assembled on that first Wednesday in early October 1957. Most wore club vests, white with two narrow light blue bands and a dark blue St Andrew's cross. Some wore a baggy blue, maroon or bottle-green cotton tracksuit. Most had gymshoes, though one or two had cross-country shoes with spars or studs; it was rare to see running shoes in Henderson's sports shop at the corner of Church Street and Market Street, though the first Adidas and Gola models occasionally made an appearance. Tracksuits, jerseys, vests, shorts and jockstraps, the last widely used as part of a sportsman's equipment, were on display in the window, along with equipment for various other sports and games.

The opening run of the season, a three and a half miler, took us along North Street, down to the harbour and out of town. We vaulted or clambered clumsily over a low dyke and across a stubble field that dipped and rose towards Brownhills on the main Crail Road. Crossing the road we ran diagonally through grassy fields and along farm tracks to Allanhill farm, then turned back towards the Grange and left into a track past Lochend, before veering on to huge stubble fields to take advantage of a long downhill, and at last back via the new town to North Street and a welcome shower. I was exhausted. Three and a half miles? It felt like ten.

Some club runs and all races were recorded at the time in considerable detail in the Club Minute Books, available in the University Library Special Collections Department. The Captain for 1957-8 was a tall, quite heavily built, mature-looking and –sounding second year student called Scott Allan, and the team's stars were tertians: David J. K. Carter, studying English, who came from Dysart, and Ian G. Docherty (History), a native St Andrean. Friendships formed through running tend to last, and I have been in regular contact with all three of these, especially with the latter two as they both live in or not far from St Andrews.

The club's home races were held over longer variations of the 3½ mile course used for the opening run. The final miles across farmland towards Pipeland Farm offered a breathtaking view across the southern slopes. We traversed the fields and entered the town via a track leading past the Polish veteran Walter Maronski's vegetable gardens and into Pipeland Road, right into Watson Avenue, left past Recreation Park, up Dyers' Brae to Abbey Street, which was until 1970 very narrow and contained The Crown pub, across South Street, up South Castle Street and left for the last 300 yards or so of North Street. The route can easily be traced on a map.

The longer courses led out along the Kinkell Braes and, in the case of the 6½ miler, up a very steep hill at the 2 mile stone and then across again towards Allanhill. The 5½ mile course took roughly half an hour for the best athletes (not me, at least at first) and the 6½ miler between 37½ and 42 minutes depending on conditions – it could be very muddy with heavy "plough" in the January/February period when the Scottish Universities Championship was held there every fourth year.

I was very unfit when I started with the club and throughout that first season was on the fringe of the first team of eight runners, but as often as not failed to make the scoring six or sometimes even the team. In my debut race, a North East League Race at Caird Park, home of Dundee Hawkhill Harriers, I was 43rd and dead last. I already thought I was last and pretended to fall over and twist my ankle, but as I lay there for a few moments a bald-headed man came past me. It was no better at my first appearance at Kings Buildings, Edinburgh, when I could not cope with the hilly, stony Braids course, neither on the breathless struggle up nor on the plunge down, and was last for a second time. I got a bit upset at this, and was told by Dave Carter to stop feeling sorry for myself. Quite right!

I did improve a bit, because I was fifth St Andrews runner at the National Cross-Country Union of Scotland Junior championships over the long grass of Hamilton racecourse, Lanarkshire. It was a triumph for St Andrews, who won from Edinburgh University. As only the first four in each team scored, my 41st place did not earn me a mini-shield, but it was easily my best run of the season.

In subsequent years I raced quite a few times over Hamilton Racecourse, where the very first International Cross-Country Championship had been held in 1903. Like others I regret that it is no longer used for cross-country, because of lack of facilities. The showers, if operative, were outside, and I can't recall any changing rooms. We were tough in those days!

On the track I did not shine over the mile or three miles. At the trials in April on the 440 yard grass track where Eric Liddell had sprinted in the 1920s, I managed a 16:42 three miles, 53 seconds behind our star distance man Ian Docherty. Professor Edgar Primrose Dickie, the Honorary President of the Athletics and Cross-Country Clubs, who was spectating as he strolled through the park, described us as "two ships sailing majestically against the wind". Sailing very slowly…

In June 1958 the Athletics Club went on a tour to Manchester, Hull and Durham. In Manchester Ian Docherty acquired a notable scalp by beating Ron Hill over three miles in about 14:45. It would be stretching the meaning of the word to describe my performances as mediocre.

There was in retrospect a clear link between my poor academic performance and the unsatisfactory quality of running achievement. I was taking the first tentative steps towards growing up and rejecting the feeling of inferiority and worthlessness I had developed at school and to some extent at home. Passing my re-sits gave me a boost, and encouraged me to train over the summer "vac", part of which I spent in another pretty awful job as porter and general dogsbody in the Hotel Tantalo in Newquay, Cornwall – my stepmother saw an advertisement in the Edinburgh Evening News, and I wrote and was accepted.

The Tantalo claimed to take its name from a Cornish giant of that name, whose feats bore an astonishingly close resemblance to those of Tantalus in Greek legend – maybe Tantalo was his evil twin. The hotel's managers were a couple who looked as if they were minor characters in *Lucky Jim*, the husband with a small moustache and a cavalry twill trousers, sports jacket and cravat, suede shoes look, and the wife dark-haired and usually in a flowery dress.

My relations with my employers were never very cordial. The uniform consisted of a white jacket, black trousers and black shoes. The pair I wore had slippery soles, which led to great embarrassment when I lost my footing on the carpet while carrying a full tray of coffee, cups etc across the lounge and everything landed on the floor.

I formed a friendship with the chef, who was only a few years older than me, but we fell out over some trivial matter towards the end of my stay, something about alleged interference by me in his sphere of influence (the kitchen) as opposed to sticking to mine (the reception and lounge area). I behaved in a very crass way towards some of the people who worked there, for which I would ask their forgiveness now if I could.

I was shocked at the prices charged by the Tantalo for such items as tea and biscuits brought to a guest's room (3/6!!) and decided to give in my notice. The manager said "We've been very disappointed in you, Donald", and who could blame him? He told me I should never return to the hotel, a condition I have never had difficulty in keeping to.

How was I to get back to Edinburgh? A kind family offered me a lift as far as Birmingham. With that long lift and various others, I managed to get back to Edinburgh, and soon started to train harder in the hope of being farther up the field when we returned to cross-country in the new term.

I stayed in "Regs" until I went abroad for the third term of my third year in 1961. St Regulus was a former hotel at the foot of Queen's Gardens. The warden when I moved in was Mr Donald E.R. Watt, later Dr and then Professor in medieval Scottish history, and the sub-warden Dr A.R. (Roy)

MacGregor. First year students shared rooms, and my room partner was Jack Smart, a black-haired, saturnine and humorous chap, one of several Kirkcaldy High School former pupils. We all got along fine.

In second and third years I had a single room on the B and C upstairs corridors. We assembled in the main dining hall for meals. Some of these were classed as "Formal Meals", when grace was said by the warden and gowns had to be worn.

There was no television in the residence. For recreation we played carpet bowls in the lounge, where there was a piano. In my third year I was "convener" of carpet bowls, which meant organising a knock-out tournament for those who wished to enter. In 1959 Lord Boothby, the rather louche Conservative politician, best-known now perhaps for having conducted a very long affair with the wife of Harold Macmillan, was elected for three years Lord Rector of the University through student suffrage. The four ancient Scottish universities all elected Rectors to represent their interests, the Rector having the duty of chairing the University Court.

Boothby had been at some university lunch, and appeared in St Regulus Hall lounge in a marked post-prandial mood. He watched four of us playing carpet bowls for a few minutes, finally pronouncing in an orotund tone "I've never seen such accurate bowling in my life!" He however declined my offer to join in and made his way somewhat uncertainly to the stairs leading down to the exit.

Regs had a swot-room in the basement. It was very busy in the weeks leading up to exams, but otherwise little used. There was also a library containing a miscellany of books, many donated by ex-residents. One of my great interests as a sixth-former and in my first couple of years at St Andrews was Grand Prix racing, and I bought from Motor Sport magazine a set of illustrated books about the cars that took part in the F1 championships of the early and mid-fifties, including some unsuccessful models, like the Arzani-Volpini or Bugatti GP cars, that had made but fleeting appearances. My interest was by no means technical, though my brother Forbes's was. He used to drive a fantastic souped-up Austin A35 van at hillclimbs such as Rest-and-Be-Thankful in Argyll.

I did however make two journeys to motor races. The first was to the 1958 British Grand Prix at Silverstone. I enjoyed both the practice sessions and the race. It was possible to stand not too far from the pits and watch the action. In the actual race there was less to see, as Peter Collins and Mike Hawthorn stormed to victory in their Lancia-Ferraris.

During the summer vacation of my second year I hitch-hiked to Norfolk, staying in youth hostels as I made my way through England. I could hardly believe my luck as a D-Type Jaguar came to a halt just up the road to the Snetterton circuit, and the driver beckoned me to get in and handed me a crash-helmet. He introduced himself and as we sped off with a throaty roar explained that he was due to race that afternoon in the open sports car event. It was an exciting drive, and I watched as he came 4th in the race, then calmly got ready for his drive home. It was all pretty casual, but heroic in my eyes.

At the beginning of the Easter vacation in 1960 I had to pack up my goods and chattels prior to leaving for my term abroad in Tübingen. As a parting gift I donated the set of Motor Sport volumes to the Regs library, though I now wish I had kept them as souvenirs of a great period of motor racing.

Chapter 4

Working up to a "Blue"

How does anyone make progress at running? By training, of course. For some reason the word "practice" is not much used in Britain, though that is what it is. You are "training" your body – heart and lung system, muscles, skeletal structure, joints, sinews, brain – to respond in a certain way to the effects of exertion. By regular practice you become better, as you do if you are learning to play an instrument or to speak a foreign language. Practice makes perfect. In reality it never will, but a man's reach, or a woman's, should exceed his or her grasp, else what's a heaven for?

All runners have to remember is that improvement is not constant, indeed not guaranteed, and that it comes in fits and starts. Progress has to be looked at over a long term. At 18 I started running on average three times a week, progressed to about four or five days when I was 20, but was still only covering at the most 30 miles a week. I didn't break 4:40 for the mile till I was 20. Too slow to be a good miler, I didn't break 15 minutes for three miles until my third year as a student.

In that summer vacation of 1958 I trained quite hard. I no longer have the details, because in those days I kept my rough training diary on sheets of foolscap that are long since lost, my earliest surviving training notebook being from the last five months of 1965.

The vacation training paid off: in the first North East League race, held in St Andrews in October 1958, I was 3rd in contrast to last in 1957. The club secretary, David Foster, wrote that my "superiority became evident" due to hard training, but my form continued erratic. A delegation went to see the Director of PE at Queen's College, Dundee, Jack Qusklay, to seek help in encouraging more Dundee-based students to take up cross-country. Mr Qusklay agreed to help, but opined that the cross-country club "works its members too hard and burns them out."

"Burning yourself out" and "getting stale" were two of the mantras of 1950s athletes and coaches, but few runners in our team got anywhere near burning themselves out. The mistake we made was to race on too little training. After

Thrashed: UAU team (front) handed out the usual drubbing to Scottish Universities, Durham 1960. Ron Hill in front of DFM – a portent?

a few bad races it was not surprising if people felt stale because they enjoyed neither training nor races. We only slowly learned the answer, which was to train more often and more consistently.

In that 1958-9 season I was inconsistent, but on a slightly higher level. The cross-country club's calendar was made up of four North East League races throughout the season, and of a number of inter-university fixtures. We took part rather half-heartedly in the East District relays and championships. In February we travelled to the British Universities championships, and after our 1958 success looked forward to the next "National" at Hamilton in March. The club members also raced every year in St Andrews for the Taylor Trophy, and the just as alliterative Captain's Cup went to the first bejant home.

Success in student sport depends on continuity, and St Andrews retained a core of good runners for seasons 1958-9 and 1959-60. Thus we were able to beat Aberdeen and Queen's University Belfast in St Andrews in November 1958, when Dave Carter, Ian Docherty, David Foster and I crossed the line together, with Alistair Barrie fifth. We went on to defeat a touring Trinity College Dublin team and arch-rivals Glasgow University Hare and Hounds that same month.

Such good form didn't last, but in January 1959 I ran away with a North East League race over a 6½ mile course at Perth's North Inch. For the first time the team ventured south in late February to Wythenshawe Park, Manchester, for the British Universities Championship. It was a disaster. We travelled in two cars, most of us wearing kilts, and arrived about half an hour before the start after getting lost. The course was three 2½ mile laps of flat heavy mud. Our first counter was Dave Carter in 64th, then Alistair Barrie 89th and me 130th. The team finished 19th out of 23. By the next week we had recovered, and Dave Carter and I came 2nd and 7th in the Junior National at Hamilton, but the team lost to Edinburgh University Hare & Hounds by only two points.

On Friday 13th March 1959 the cross-country club made its first ever tour, subsidised by a £50 grant from the St Andrews Athletic Union, to Belfast and Dublin. Ten of us embarked at Lancefield Quay in Glasgow but the crossing was a rough one. The boat pitched and tossed and rolled so much that Dave Carter, our best runner, was repeatedly sick. We were met off the boat by the Belfast captain John Boyce and taken to the Queen's University Union to

St Andrews University CCC 1959, again National Junior Champions.

recover. This was to be a return match against Queen's Belfast, held over since the match in November. That race in St Andrews, versus Aberdeen as well as Queen's, sticks in my memory because Jo Köchling, the Belfast number one, tried to make me run into a parked car at Allanhill Farm, saying afterwards that it was "all in the game". We beat him then, but Köchling got his revenge now on home soil, winning the race from Barrie and Carter. I was 5th and our team won by 33 points to 49.

We bought Cheap Day Returns for the train to Dublin, these costing less than single tickets. There had been some violent sectarian incidents in the border area and threats of more, but the situation was still relaxed enough for the club secretary to note in the report of the tour that "no-one blew the train up en route". As in Belfast our hosts at Trinity College Dublin gave us rooms in university accommodation. The course for the race the next day took us from the college boathouse through Phoenix Park, round the American Embassy and back through Furry Glen. Dave Carter won from Colin Shillington of Trinity and Ali Barrie and I crossed the line together in third. We took the team race 28 to 53.

A third race had been arranged with Clonliffe Harriers, and two runners from Donore Harriers also started. As good tourists we had visited the Guinness factory on the morning of the race. The smell of stout, and the samples we tried, must have affected us adversely, because we lost by 38 points to 57, our first scorers being Dave Carter and me in 5th and 6th. The winner was Connelly of Donore.

Some of us had been selected for the Scottish Universities team for the annual match the next weekend versus the Universities Athletic Union (i.e. England) in Edinburgh, including me. I was very excited about this honour, and recall Allister Forrest, a more mature member of the team, saying as we set off: "Oh God! I expect we'll hear about nothing else the whole week!" So I kept quiet. Just as well – Alistair Barrie and I disembarked at Holyhead and tried to hitchhike. It took us over 36 hours, so that neither of us was in a fit state to race. The English lads had their customary clean sweep (1st, 2nd, 3rd, 4th, 5th and 6th), and in retrospect I was quite glad to have missed being put to the sword. At the end of the season my "colour" for cross-country was advanced to a "Half-Blue".

Scottish Universities Cross Country championship 1960, North Street.
From left Aberdeen, Edinburgh, Glasgow, St Andrews.

With an even stronger cross-country team in 1959-60 we made our first ever appearance in the News of The World-sponsored Edinburgh-Glasgow road relay. Deciding on the best running order was not easy, and we thought we had got it wrong when our first stage runner, Alistair Barrie, handed over to me just past the Maybury roundabout in 16th place out of the 20 invited teams. I gained four places, and David Jeffery, David Carter, and Terry Willcocks brought us place by place up to 8th. Ian Docherty on the long 7 mile leg from Forestfield Inn to Airdrie overtook one more runner, and Phil Judge kept us in 7th through the finish at Royal Exchange Square in the Glasgow gloaming. We could possibly have won the medals for the "most meritorious" performance but the judges gave them to Teviotdale Harriers who were 6th, though we won them two years later when we were 11th.

In the New Year this form continued. Our team defeated Edinburgh and Aberdeen on 30th January 1960 in very heavy conditions over our tough, wet 6½ mile course, and our hopes of recording an historic victory in the Scottish Universities Championship the next Saturday, February 6th over the same course were high. The four teams lined up outside St Salvator's Tower in North Street, a scene captured in an "iconic" photograph, a copy of which can be seen in MUSA, the university museum, as well as in the book on *St Andrews Street Names* by R.N.Smart and K.C.Fraser (St Andrews University Library 1995). Archie Strachan and Willie Diverty, Glasgow's "manager" and Scottish *Athletics Weekly* correspondent watched as Professor Dickie, dressed in his usual broad-brimmed black hat, black coat and suit, dropped his handkerchief and we were off.

It was quite sunny and much drier underfoot than the week before. The individual and team struggle was intense along the Kinkell Braes, over to the A917 Crail Road, and up the big hill with its "plough". St Andrews were 12 points ahead with 2 miles to go, as we plummeted down from Lochend farm track over the stubble fields with the whole magnificent vista of the city and its towers laid out before us.

Alas for our hopes! The Glasgow middle counters gradually moved up the field. The two best Glasgow runners, Douglas Gifford and Jim Bogan, and I had broken away from the rest quite early on. We stayed together through the streets of the new town and were still together going up Dyers Brae

SUCC 1960 – Winner Doug Gifford leads up to Crail Road after three miles.

into narrow Abbey Street – widened ten years later - and over South Street into South Castle Street. It was only over the last 300 yards that Gifford and Bogan were able to break away from me to take the first two places for Glasgow, with five seconds covering the first three. David Jeffery followed me home in 4th. Glasgow also took the team medals, but there were only 7 points in it. To this day St Andrews has never won the Scottish Universities team championship. Two St AUCCC athletes, Richard Archer (twice) and Owen Greene, have however won the individual title.

On Thursday 18th February we set off, by sleeper this time, for a second go at the British Universities race, at Coombe Dingle, Bristol. The weather on race day was summery, and we were well rested. The Lord Mayor did the honours at the start, and by the finish we were 8th out of the 23 teams, a huge improvement on the previous year. Glasgow and Aberdeen had not entered, and I was the first Scots runner home in 39th. The race was won by three Cambridge runners, Bruce Tulloh, Mike Turner and Alistair Minshall, all a long way ahead of me.

Herrenberg near Stuttgart 1960: a win over 3000m.

I caught a flu-like bug a few days before the Junior National in March and did not score for our squad. The gallant team of Terry Willcocks, (5th), David Jeffery (8th), Phil Judge (15th) and John Brooks (26th) nonetheless won the title for St Andrews for the second time. A week later I ran for Scottish Universities in the annual carve-up by the UAU, this time at Durham. It was again 21 to 63 and I was 14th - a disappointing end to a long season, but the Athletic Union gave me a Blue and I promptly bought a Blues blazer, thus doubling my total of jackets, and a Blues scarf and tie. Autres temps, autres moeurs.

1960: Tübingen track – no shower at the flat.

All members of the Junior Honours Class in French and German had to choose whether to spend the third term in France or Germany. I opted for Tübingen, an ancient University on the river Neckar, not far from Stuttgart. The theological faculty was particularly well known, based in the Tübinger Stift in the centre of town. I am afraid I never visited it.

My only journey abroad had been to Belgium with the school in 1951 when I was not yet 12. Despite my knowledge of Heinrich von Kleist's women characters, I was lacking in confidence or competence in spoken German.

An additional problem was that in Tübingen the people spoke Swabian (Schwäbisch) rather than standard High German (Hochdeutsch). The Swabians had the reputation of being like the Scots, hard-working but thrifty. "Schaffe, schaffe, Häusle baue" (Work, work, build a wee house) was the Swabian motto.

I arrived at Stuttgart main station in early April 1960. I went over to buy a glass of milk at one of the drinks stands, but was confused by the four or five types of milk on offer. Lacking the confidence to seek clarification, I just ordered a Coca-Cola. So much for my seven years of German study!

Tübingen has an attractive town hall on the main square, with a beautifully decorated façade. The cobbled square housed a regular market, and on the northern side was the Hotel zum Goldenen Lamm, where the poet Friedrich Schiller had once stayed. I met up with an English student from Hull, Mike Batty, and we decided to advertise in the Schwäbisches Tageblatt for a flat or room that we could share. A reply came in from a Hermann Raab, who had a room to let in the Haaggasse, a narrow and ancient street behind the town hall. The room was not bad, with a balcony overlooking a garden, but one strange feature was that the shared bathroom had a bathtub full of laundry permanently left to soak. Herr Raab shared the house with his widowed sister Luise Pflumm. Both were in their late sixties or early seventies, and the wrinkled Frau Pflumm had a son called Willi who according to his mother was a kleptomaniac. Fortunately or unfortunately he was regularly in jail and thus not a frequent visitor. While we got on all right with the Raab/Pflumm ménage, it soon became clear where Willi had got his kleptomania from. In May a jar of raspberry jam disappeared from our meagre store of provisions. We said nothing to our landlord, but in June Luise Pflumm brought us a jar of blackcurrant jam, with the words "Hier haben Sie Ihre Konfitüre zurück." (Here's your jam back.)

I did little studying in Tübingen. I registered for several classes but attended about five in total. I had sent three passport-style photos to the university administration, but they had lost them. When I went on my first day to try and register, I was asked to provide some more, but dépaysé as I was, burst into tears! The official dealing with us foreign students advised me sympathetically that I all I had to do was go to the railway station where there was a photo booth. I did so, but the episode shows what a novice at life I was.

I did manage to get signed up for the university athletics club. I spent much more time at the stadium on the western outskirts of Tübingen than at lectures, which I had trouble understanding anyway. As the bathroom in the flat was out of commission, it was just as well I could make regular use of the showers at the stadium. Early on I made friends with another middle-distance runner, Hans Wax from Ehingen on the Donau, near Ulm, who was studying mathematics. His brother Hermann was another talented runner. Hans suggested I join the local club, SV Tübingen 03, and introduced me to Sepp Ehing, the coach. There were quite a few local and club competitions. I was able to run in the Kreismeisterschaften (locality championships) and in a few other races, and recorded times of 2:39.7 for 1000m and 9:09 for 3000m during the season. I once competed in a pentathlon in which I ran 200m in 26.0 seconds and long-jumped a very feeble 4.40m.

We trained in the parkland woods near the Neckar as well as on the track, where I could wear my new Puma white and red spikes. I recall one particular Saturday morning session with Hans of 10x300m which we ran in the rain up and down an avenue of poplars, the "Seufzer-Allee" (Walk of Sighs), so called because girls without a man used to promenade there.

Being in the university athletics team as well in the club was an excellent method, indeed the only realistic one for me, of travelling around Germany. I had little money, and as an athletic team member I was able to visit Göttingen, not far from the Zonengrenze, the border between East and West Germany, as well as Nürnberg, Rothenburg, and various other places. The highlight of the season was the two day German University Championships meeting in Göttingen, where I was to run the 5000m. We travelled by bus and stayed with local families. Although the West German "economic miracle" had been under way for some five years, it hadn't reached everybody. The lady with whom two of us were staying offered us on arrival "einen Schluck Kaffee" (a gulp of coffee). We accepted with pleasure. She appeared a few minutes later with a third of a cup of lukewarm black ground coffee for each of us – literally a gulp. Coffee was a luxury in those days.

I remember little of the meeting or the race. I struggled round in 15:36, in third place, quite a long way behind the winner Lutz Philipp (Freie Universität Berlin) whom I was to compete against in very different circumstances 12 years later. The visit to Nürnberg was memorable because we were competing in the same arena where Hitler had once held mass parades of the Nazi faithful. The complex had been taken over by the US occupying forces after the war, and a cinder track reinstated. I ran 400m there in 54.2, a good time by my standards. In Nürnberg we stayed in the Youth Hostel in the medieval castle. The dormitory windows had superb views over the red roofs of Nürnberg.

Some snapshots of Tübingen in 1960 have remained in my memory, such as the street "Automaten", larger versions of cigarette machines. On inserting coins you could get milk, sausage, sweets and other delicacies. In St Andrews we had milk machines operated on the same principle, but these in Germany offered a wide variety of goods. The local newspaper offices displayed the day's edition in glass-fronted noticeboards. The Schwäbisches Tageblatt offices were near the main bridge over the Neckar, and the bright light attracted hundreds of little black flies which flitted about in the corners of the display cabinets at night. Just round the corner, overlooking the river was the Hölderlin-Turm. The great poet Friedrich Hölderlin had lived in that turret house, looked after by his guardian, a carpenter named Zimmer – "Zimmermann" is German for carpenter - for the latter half of his life after he had had a breakdown at the age of 35. The lovely and bleak poem "Hälfte des Lebens" predicted this:

Mit gelben Birnen hänget
Und voll mit wilden Rosen
Das Land in den See;
Ihr holden Schwäne,
Und trunken mit Küssen
Tünkt ihr das Haupt
Ins heilig-nüchterne Wasser.

Weh mir, wo nehm' ich, wenn
Es Winter ist, die Blumen, und wo
Den Sonnenschein
Und Schatten der Erde?
Die Mauern stehn
Sprachlos und kalt, im Winde
Klirren die Fahnen.

1960 With Hans Wax (l) at start of 1500m
between SV03 and a French Army team.

The poet pictures the summery scene of swans, near a tongue of land overhung by yellow pears and wild roses, "drunk with kisses" as they dip their necks into the "sacred-sober" water of Lake Constance. There is an abrupt and prophetic contrast with the wintry scene representing Hölderlin's later years, for he realises that the tranquil beauty of sunshine and shade will give way to the sterility of rattling chimney "grannies".

The ageing Friedrich had wandered along the banks of the Neckar where we now went running. Sometimes a few of us hired a punt (Stocherkahn, poke-boat) and spent the afternoon lying back trailing our hands in the greenish water under the weeping willows, or steering a safe route under the bridge with the long pole and trying not to fall in.

It was on that bridge that I caused great embarrassment to Hans Wax on one occasion by greeting him with raised right arm. I intended it as a joke, ignorant that using the Hitler-Gruss was a criminal offence. No wonder he grabbed my arm and asked me if I had gone mad. Later that summer he and I went to an afternoon showing of the film "Judgment at Nuremberg", which made me realise my stupidity. Near the end of our stay, while tidying up in our room, Mike Batty and I discovered a broken NSDAP badge in a drawer. We presumed that it had belonged to Hermann Raab. I took it home to Scotland with me, but have since lost it.

As our finances were very limited, I used to calculate in a notebook every few days how much we could permit ourselves to spend daily to avoid having no Deutsche Mark left. The pound was worth about 12 DM at the time – just as well. We could eat Spiegelei und Spinat (fried egg and spinach, plus bread) for a very modest charge at the restaurant beneath our rooms. Our staple diet also included family-size bottles of Coca-Cola, which were very cheap in Tengelmann's supermarket, plus margarine, loaves of soft brown bread and of course jam.

At the end of the semester it was time to go back to Scotland. I had carried out at least some academic work in Tübingen, for all we Honours students had to write a long essay in German on a chosen theme. Mine was "Lessing, Brecht und die Theorie des Theaters". To help me with that I read the entire "Hamburgische Dramaturgie" by Gottfried Ephraim Lessing, one of the 18th century giants of German literature, most of Bertolt Brecht's writings on theatre from the 20th century, as well as modern critics' views of him, and then wrote it all up. Mr Brill eventually awarded me a mark of 74%, so although derivative and peppered with linguistic errors it can't have been too bad. 1960-61 was my fourth year at St Andrews, and all of us in the Senior Honours class had to concentrate on work. Revelations among my lecturers were Tommy Strachan and Roy Owen, who taught us about Middle High German and medieval French epics like the "Nibelungenlied" and "Yvain". They brought life to these and other historic poems and I owe them much.

I found a bunk at 3 Alfred Place, opposite the Volunteer Hall, a drill hall also used as an occasional sports venue or examination hall. Much of my studying was done in the University Library, sited in the quadrangle of St Mary's College. It was a very traditional library: a long hall with shelves all round it going nearly up to the roof. To reach the required book it was often necessary to climb a ladder. Health and Safety precautions were not observed as they no doubt would be today. There was not nearly enough space in the library for all its books. Many were kept in the "Stacks", to which Senior Honours students had access.

From 1710 to 1837 the library had been entitled to a copy of every book printed in Britain under the Copyright Deposit Act, but that privilege was lost in 1837. If it had not been relinquished the library would have had to expand considerably; it was already bursting at the seams.

None of that concerned us. The important thing was to be able to finish off the day's work by about 9.45 pm so that we could head across the street and get into the Criterion Bar – the "Crit" – before the call "Last orders, please" just before 10 pm. "We" in this context refers to a group of fourth year students, runners and others, who tended to go around together.

At weekends, when the library was closed, I sometimes worked in the Union swot-room high up above North Street, where if distracted I could watch the winter clouds and rain scudding across the skies, and be happy that I didn't have to be out in the wind and the wet.

Studying did not stop me from training and competing. Our cross-country team was not quite as strong as in the previous two seasons, and there were inner tensions that arose in the run-up to the Edinburgh-Glasgow relay, when two team members disagreed about the running order. We finished 11th.

In most respects my personal running year was a not-quite-so-good repeat of third year. I again finished 3rd, ahead of team-mate David Jeffery, in the Scottish Universities in Aberdeen, when Callum Laing (Glasgow) won from Aberdeen's John Glennie. In March David Jeffery and I had a nine-mile outing in the National Senior Championship, finishing 19th and 25th respectively, beating Laing, who was 35th, among others.

In May came the Final exams, ten 3 hour papers in a fortnight for those doing Joint Honours. It was as much an endurance test as a scrutiny of how much we knew. Half way through the exams I decided I needed to relax a bit, and ran in an athletics match between the University and Madras Present and Former Pupils. Professor Carr, who lived over the wall from the athletic ground, was one of the spectators. I mumbled to him something about needing to relax, to which his non-committal reply was "Hmpphh." To my surprise I won the 440 yards in 53.7 seconds, a personal best, and also the mile in about 4:26. Then it was back to the books.

It took me a long time to recover from the mental strain of putting down on paper so much material in such a short time. There was also an oral examination to be undergone. By chance I was sitting opposite a man in the train from Edinburgh to St Andrews who turned out to be our oral examiner, Prof. Gillies from Leeds. In the course of casual conversation, in ignorance of his identity, I mentioned that I had been studying Lessing, and had read the Hamburgische

Graduation, St Salvator's Quad 1961.

Dramaturgie. "The whole of it?" he asked, and I like to think that my truthful answer "Yes" persuaded him on the next day to give me the benefit of any doubt that he might have felt.

I awaited publication of the results with trepidation. In those days first-class degrees in Arts subjects were rare, second-class was not sub-divided into II (1) and II(2), and Thirds were also relatively uncommon. I dreaded the thought of getting a Third. For some reason I wrote to Dr Robbie at Stewart's to express these fears, but he wrote back to say that the school would be glad to see me whatever degree I was awarded. That was kind of him.

During the first weeks of the vacation the athletics team went on tour to the North of England. My own running was affected by the strain of the exams I had sat, and I did not run well. We were in Hull when the degree results reached us, and I was mightily relieved to read that I had been awarded a Second. One student in French/German had a First, and two a Third.

My father, brother and stepmother attended the graduation in July at the Younger Hall. For some reason I was unable properly to enjoy the ceremony and the obligatory photography in the Quad afterwards, as my expression in the pictures shows. I was still not at all at ease with myself and the world. I wrote to my father and stepmother to thank them for their support, but I'm not sure just how I expressed myself. I suspect my gratitude had to be inferred. I was a difficult son, a difficult person. But now I was D.F. Macgregor, M.A. Hons, and about to make my first visit to France.

Chapter 5

A Year in the Var

Ted Brill had lectured in Junior Honours on Lessing and Herder, and in the Senior year on Schiller and Goethe. Each student had to deliver a lecture ourselves on some aspect of the quartet, and my topic had been "Das Verhältnis zwischen Goethe und Schiller". Their relationship was purely an intellectual and literary one. At the end of the session, during one of those conversations about possible careers I had mentioned that I might become a teacher. Mr Brill was thought that was a suitable choice, and that I was well cut out for it. Whether that meant I wasn't good enough to be an academic, I don't know, but I decided to apply for a post as assistant d'anglais in France, putting three southern departments as regions of choice. I had never been to France and knew precious little about any of its regions so was excited to receive a letter telling me that I had been assigned to the Lycée de Lorgues, in the Var. I hurried to find Lorgues on the map. In those pre-Internet days information was not so readily available, but I discovered that Lorgues was a village of some 3000 people about 15 kilometres from Draguignan, the administrative capital of the department of the Var, itself named after a river. Draguignan owed its name to a dragon which was said at one time to have roamed around the area.

All the British foreign language assistants had to attend a week's training course in one of Paris's outlying universities, where we were given practical and background information about our role and responsibilities, filled in the many necessary forms, and exchanged addresses with a few of those who would be working not too far away, in case we felt like meeting up for mutual support. The nearest person to me was a student who would be in Hyères on the western Mediterranean, one of the resorts favoured by Queen Victoria when the delights of Balmoral palled.

Around mid-September I got some sandwiches and drinks and loaded my old-fashioned and heavy leather suitcase into an early morning train from the Gare du Midi "direction de Nice". We travelled at varying speeds out of the Paris conurbation, heading south towards Lyon and the Rhone valley. As we approached Montélimar, Orange, Avignon, the scent of thyme, lavender and rosemary began to enter the carriage windows and raise my spirits, as they have done no doubt for millions of travellers and still do for me whenever I am lucky enough to be in the South of France.

It was early evening when we reached Marseille. My instructions from the school authorities were that I should get off at Les Arcs sur Argens, where I would be met. The train rolled on though the darkness, and every time we came to a station I peered out to try to distinguish its name. There were quite a few, all totally unfamiliar, and the signs on the platforms were all dimly lit. I felt as if I were in a different and mysterious world. Eventually "Les Arcs sur Argens" swam into my sight, the train came to a grinding, hissing halt, and I heaved my suitcase and myself on to the platform.

Two young men came towards to me. I wasn't the only passenger to disembark there, but I'm sure I must have stuck out like a snowman in the Sahara with my gabardine raincoat and black suede shoes, National Health spectacles and air of naïve Scottishness. Jean-Claude Martin and Michel Rognin introduced themselves as "surveillants" at the Lycée and took my suitcase to a Renault Frégate – a biggish limousine – in the car park. We drove off through the night along small roads, ending up after about fifteen minutes outside a hotel, the Hotel Moderne et du Parc, in the centre, though I didn't know that at the time, of Lorgues.

My arrival must have been expected, as a number of young people, presumably pupils, were standing around in the street taking in this exotic new arrival. I was led into the hotel, shown my room, a red-tiled comfortable one with a shower, washed my hands and face and went downstairs to the restaurant. The hors d'oeuvre was six snails in a butter sauce. Yes, no mistake, this was France!

M. Delorenzi, the head English teacher, came into the restaurant to welcome me, and offered to drive me round the next day. He told me that the hotel owners were M. and Mme Cauvin, which in the diary I kept was mis-spelled as "Couvain" until I was able to equate the Provençal accent with the written forms. The next morning I had breakfast and went out to explore Lorgues. The village main street was called the Boulevard Clémenceau. From the Lycée at the top a lime tree lined avenue, on whose wide grit-surfaced pavements the village elders played pétanque on the warm evenings, descended gently past the Ecole Maternelle, the Gendarmerie, the Mairie, some shops and a café, an old fountain, and some houses or apartments on the north side. Little winding side streets ran between very old and dark three or four storey houses up and round the back of the village, emerging every few hundred metres into a small sloping "place" with a big tree in the centre next to another fountain. It was charming, and apart from Mobylettes and scooters that buzzed in and out of the shadows like angry wasps, like the representation in Max Frisch's novel *Homo Faber* of Alfa Romeos in Rome as the Greek Furies, the Eumenides or Kindly ones, there was little traffic. The only street that led away uphill out of the village to the north east led to the Mont St.-Férréol, a wooded hill which could be driven

Jean-Pierre Hugon comes up Chemin de la Croix on Mont Saint-Férréol, Lorgues 1962.

up over a series of hairpin bends, or run up, as I soon discovered, via the Chemin de la Croix, a long set of rough stone steps on the left hand side of which stood fourteen stone pillars depicting the stations of the cross.

The other side of the main street led down past more shops, houses and offices, in front of the hotel with its garden restaurant, two other cafés, and a few more houses and shops on the south side. The main street was the through route from Draguignan towards Aups and Salernes up in the hills away past the Lycée, and other roads led to Brignoles to the south-west and to Les Arcs to the south. The roads had numbers but were known as la route de Salernes,

la route de Brignoles and so on. I should say that it took me some time to find out all this information.

About 100 metres east of the hotel was another street leading to the XII century church. It stood in a quiet paved square which was in shadow from early afternoon because of the high buildings behind it. Beyond the church were another two roads. One, the main route to Draguignan, was bordered on both sides by vineyards, and the other was a semi-paved, grassy track that led past fenced-off private gardens through the dry-looking fields and enclosures towards distant

Posing on Vespa – with no licence. Lorgues 1961. wooded hills and valleys.

Where were the best places to run? Although that wasn't the question uppermost in my mind, I started exploring. It was very hot during the day, and the grape harvest was about to start. My first little runs took me along the various roads out of town, to the surprise of the people who saw me. I was the only person who went running, or so it seemed. I soon found that the best time to go out was in the cool of the evening, for there was little traffic, and the sky was usually a velvety blue and as spangled with stars as that painting by van Gogh with the cypress trees.

M. Delorenzi, who lived about 50 metres from the Lycée, gave me a guided tour of the buildings. I met M. Sylvain Cazes, the headmaster, an elderly gentleman with very short pure white hair, M. Jean Chante, the burly "surveillant-général" or S-G who was in charge of discipline and who headed the team of surveillants or "pions' (school pupil slang for "espions", spies).

These three together with the Econome, who kept the books and paid the salaries, were the administrators. There were several S-G-adjoints, deputies to M. Chante, as well, plus teams of cleaners, kitchen personnel, and a Corsican janitor or concierge, M. Mondoloni, who was teased by pupils and not taken too seriously by staff because of his strong Corsican accent and his rather absurd insistence on carrying out any instruction from his superiors to the letter. On one occasion he had been told to keep the entrance door locked every time someone went out, and despite three surveillants-géneraux-adjoints telling him to leave it open so that they could go out and come in again two minutes later, he refused to relinquish the key to them and tugged at the opened door with them all standing on the other side trying to keep it open.

Among the staff I was well down the pecking order, understandably, but was treated politely by most teachers, several of whom mentioned that a Jimmy Clark had been there as an assistant one year before and had done next to no work, as some added almost admiringly ("C'était un gros fainéant" – he did next to nothing). I was given a number of classes for "conversation", and to begin with hadn't a clue how to teach them anything. You learn by doing, or so it is said, but it took me quite a time to achieve very much with some of the pupils. Not a few families spoke Italian as well as French at home, and that was a much more useful language than English, the "langue maternelle" of people like me living in a distant "pays des brumes" (land of mists). They might have preferred American English practice, but the French were in general anti-American at that time, though aspects of US culture, like jazz, dance or cinema (dubbed) were popular enough.

I got on best with the other "pions" who were mostly about my age (21). Some of them were kind enough to help me when I made mistakes in French, or corrected my pronunciation. The diphthong "ui", as spoken by me in the phrase "huit mille huit cent quatre-vingt huit" (888) caused one pion, called Barboni, great hilarity. The pions all called each other by their surname.

But I was called "Don'ald" (stress on the second syllable) thanks to Mr Disney, or "Mac", because it was also an abbreviation for "maquereau" (pimp). Not that I minded. For some reason the pions were rather unfriendly to one of their number, Raymond Castenet, a small chap with a Flaubertian moustache. I felt sorry for him and accepted an invitation to go to the cinema in Draguignan, in his Renault 4cv, to see a film starring Hardy Krüger that was set in the North African desert. I was very thirsty and could hardly wait to get home, resisting Castenet's pleas to be his friend. My friends among the pions turned out to be Michel Rognin and Jean-Claude Martin. The latter came from Orange. His experience of England had been short, for he had crossed the Channel to Dover but had been refused entry as he had hardly any money! At the Toussaint holiday (Hallowe'en and All Saints' week) he invited me to stay at his parents' house in Orange, where I could admire the Roman theatre and the great wall behind it, "la plus grande muraille de mon royaume" as Louis XIV had called it.

In Lorgues I was running most days. I entered a race at Taradeau, a village a few kilometres away. It was billed as "le XXVIIe cross de Taradeau" and was run over 6x1km laps of a hilly circuit. I went into the lead after 3 laps, and held it through lap 6, which should have been the end of the race. As we neared the finish, however, the bell was rung for the last lap, and my nearest opponent gave up. The officials had miscounted. I kept going and won by about 200m, and that evening was carried into the school réfectoire on the shoulders of two of the pions who had driven me there and stood around in the cold to support me. I was representing the Etoile Sportive Lorguaise (ESL) whose athletics section numbered but a few members, the main sports enjoyed by the young people of Lorgues being le foot and le basket. A particularly feeble shot at goal was described as "un shoot de bonne soeur", a nun's shot. The ESL football coach, M. Nouchi, encouraged me to come along to one of their training sessions, but very quickly discovered that my running prowess did not transfer to soccer. I was too slow off the mark and too reluctant to challenge for the ball. I had told him that before, but he wanted to see for himself before shaking his head and wishing me further success at cross-country.

The PE staff in the Lycée included M. Saint-André, a grizzled veteran who was a real father figure to the pupils, and M. Salvarelli, who fancied himself as a rather superannuated swashbuckling beau garçon. He had shiny black hair and an idiosyncratic method of operating a stopwatch. He held the watch high up in his right hand, and as the runner approached the line he brought it down- swoosh!- but pressed the stop button at the top of the arc so that the time recorded was invariably a couple of tenths fast. "Chronométrage maison" (homemade timing) M. Saint-André muttered once in an aside to me. At the school dances M. Salvarelli would do a Berlusconi and sing for the crowd. It was hard to part him from the mike.

I had offered my services to go for easy runs with some of the pupils during the games lessons. One of the most promising runners was a 16 year old lad called Jean-Pierre Hugon. He was also good at football, but we started to train regularly and after a few months he told me that in the football games the other players' "tongues were hanging out" but he was still as fresh as a daisy.

Pupils at the Lycée were mostly day-pupils, but some were boarders who went home at weekends – unless they had behaved badly, in which case they might

Lycée de Lorgues 1962. The 2CV belongs to Surveillant-General Jean Chante.

be "consignés" and have to stay in school. That was very tedious for them, as there was little to do at the weekend other than the extra homework that was doled out. Parents sometimes protested at the "consigne", but M. Chante or one of his deputies, Gaston Puppo, André Deleidi or André Rouvier, was usually polite but inflexible. M. Deleidi always reminded me of one of the two identical policemen in the Tintin books (Thompson and Thomson in the English versions).

After two months or so I was making good progress in speaking and understanding French, helped by the fact that with one exception I was the only native English speaker in Lorgues. The exception was a Mme Digonnet, the British-born mother of one of the pions. She had last been in the UK in 1935 and spoke a version of English that was both charming and rather

Cross de l'Humanité 1962: after a night in the train.

weird, as if she had arrived in a time machine. Outside my hours in class, hardly anyone spoke to me in English apart from a tall Norwegian called Thoresen, who was associated with the shipping line. He was an habitué of the hotel café, "chez Lili" as it was sometimes called because that was the name of the barmaid-cum-waitress.

It was only about 400m from the school at the top of the village to the café in the middle, and for the pions and me it was the social hub. "Le Baby" (table football) and "le flipper" (pinball machine) were extremely popular during the daytime, though regarded by the evening regulars as too noisy. Over the school year I became reasonably proficient at Babyfoot, which needs a lot of skill.

After a week or two I had moved out of the hotel, which was very comfortable, to a flat across the road owned by a Mme Avon. It turned out that I could have stayed in the hotel, which was not expensive, but the question of payment was wreathed in mystery and I was concerned that I would land myself with a big bill. In fact no bill ever materialised for my initial stay, and so I imagine the school paid for it. The flat was fine, but as winter approached it was rather cold and the heating not very efficient.

I stayed in Lorgues over Christmas and New Year and celebrated "le réveillon" with my friends, going from café to café, emerging bleary-eyed from the last one to close at 4 am. One family in particular, the Goberts, had "adopted" me. Three of their children, Florence, Eric and Franck, attended the Lycée and were all in my classes. The family lived in a big architect – designed house about 5km outside Lorgues along that track that led towards the wooded hills. The house sat in an idyllic position overlooking the valley and the woods beyond, as if in one of the nicer fairytales of the Brothers Grimm. M. Gobert was a Paris-based manufacturer and part-time author, a genial gnome-like figure. His wife had a really beautiful smile which all the children had inherited. Sometimes I would jog out to the Goberts' alongside one or two of them on their bike or Mobylette. It was permissible to ride one of these low-powered motorised bicycles, without requiring a crash helmet, from the age of 14.

After the Cross de Taradeau I had had quite a lot of publicity in the local pages of Nice-Matin and Le Provençal, and competed in a few other short races, all of which I was able to win, in the Var and Bouches-du-Rhône departments as far afield as Marseille, three hours away by coach. The standard at that time and in that region was not terribly high. In Lorgues Jean-Pierre Hugon and I were the only regular runners, and I became "connu comme le loup blanc" (as well-known as the white wolf), in the words of the pion Barboni.

I continued to train over the winter. It was much colder than I had expected. In January we even had heavy snowfalls. Somehow I caught a severe cold, and went to bed in my not very warm flat for almost 24 hours. Struggling out of bed in the late morning I walked over to the café and ordered "un grog" - coffee with rum. Before I could finish it I fainted over the table, and woke up to find myself in the school "infirmerie". The nurse, Mme Merle, the mother of yet another pion, told me I had "une mauvaise grippe" (a bad case of 'flu) and had to stay in bed until I was better. "Pas courir! Pas courir!" she warned me, wagging her finger. There was however no risk at all of my running at that moment, for I was as weak as a kitten.

Meanwhile in Draguignan a veteran sports organiser and Communist, M. Emmanuel Micheneau, had contacted me and asked if I would like to join a team of runners of various ages in an expedition to represent his club "La Dracénoise" at the famous annual meeting in the north of Paris at La

Courneuve, the Cross de l'Humanité. This was number XXV in the series. Of course I said yes.

The bout of 'flu forced me to rest a good fortnight, but I was able to start to start easy running again in very late February, after a long weekend spent with three friends in Italy. We went via St Tropez, at that time of year not unlike an East Neuk fishing village, then drove through Monte Carlo and over the border at Ventimiglia, overnighting in the small and unremarkable town of Albenga. All I can recall of the weekend is that on the way back on the French side of the border I had the stringiest steak and most wooden chips I have ever eaten. It was my own fault, as there were superior steak and chips offered for 500 francs and 750 francs. Parsimoniously I had chosen the cheapest at 250 francs.

During the period of convalescence friends had lent me a record-player and some 33 and 45 rpm records, including two with songs by Georges Brassens, the great French chansonnier, then in mid-career. I had never heard of him and could make little of the texts of the songs. However I like them so much that I played them over and over, asking Jean-Claude Martin for help with the allusions and references when I got stuck. Months later I found Brassens texts in the series Poètes d'Aujourd'hui (Poets of Today), but it was satisfying to have found out so much (almost) by myself. Today I have all Brassens's CDs and the texts of all his songs, which I cannot recommend unstintingly enough to French speakers.

Our Draguignan group travelled overnight on the 7th/8th of April "sitting up" in the train to the Gare de Lyon, then on by Métro to La Courneuve, a run-down, left-wing voting part of the Paris conurbation. By 10 am I had had breakfast and walked around a bit in the chilly wind, feeling and looking as if I hadn't slept very well, which was certainly true. There was a day-long programme of races for both sexes and most age-groups, from "minimes" up to international class runners, most of the latter from the Soviet bloc. My teammate Michel Allongue and I, as well as a third Dracénois called Guidali, were entered for the Séniors-Juniors Populaires 4km event. It had attracted entries from all over France and I was a bit concerned lest it were too short. The men's IAAF event later in the afternoon, won by Ivanov (USSR) from Kolov (USSR) and Jerzy Chromik (Poland) was over 8km. The women's IAAF race was 2 km, and was won by Tamara Botkmtseva from her USSR teammates Karoblema and Lyssenko, who had become the 1960 Olympic

Cross 1962: on the podium.

800m champion in Rome under her married name Ludmilla Schevtsova but had since divorced.

Our event was earlier, at 2 pm. We lined up across the field and raced off. To my surprise and pleasure Michel and I very soon found ourselves in a three-man spearhead, going away from the rest. By half distance we had a clear lead and I extended it to about 100m by the finish, covering the 4km in 12:55 min, 15 seconds ahead of Michel who took the junior award. In retrospect it was an astonishing result: athletes from a remote village club had taken the first two places in a field of well over 100 and I had run well on very little recent training. I'm afraid I don't know how our third man Guidali ran, and can find no mention of him in the reports.

After the race I was surrounded by reporters, offered free "Viandox" (a sort of French Bovril), and received a bouquet on the podium. Later that afternoon we all attended a prize-giving in the town hall at which I was permitted to shake hands with Maurice Thorez, the then secretary of the

Official, DFM, Michel Allongue, Emmanuel Micheneau.

PCF (Parti Communiste Français). He asked me if I was Corsican, thinking that my name was Macgrégori. This was a not uncommon mistake in the Midi, where many Corsicans lived, but this was Paris. I was intrigued to hear that while Emmanuel Micheneau, our venerable team manager and lifelong Communist, addressed everyone he met as "tu", Thorez was more conventional and used the more formal "vous", as in "Vous êtes Corse?" "Non, monsieur, je suis Ecossais."

The local press lauded our performances when we returned south, and to crown all the organising newspaper "L'Humanité" printed caricatures of all the event winners, including a lantern-jawed version of me, in its Monday edition. That was a first!

Back at school, I had, I regret to say, adopted a lazy practice pioneered by my predecessor Jimmy Clark. This involved suggesting to some members of the senior classes that the next day's conversation class was not that important and their attendance was up to them. As a result only a few turned up and I used this as an excuse to cancel the class. Word must have got round, because

M. Cazes announced to me one day that he would be coming the next day to see how I was getting on with a senior class. Obviously I was at pains to ensure a full attendance and asked the pupils to be particularly cooperative. They obliged, and at the end of the lesson M. Cazes's judgment was: "Je suis content de vous." The wool had successfully been pulled over his eyes, and from then on he looked upon me with a benevolent eye.

During that year in Provence I had on occasions felt lonely and depressed, but never for long. The only contact I had with home was the occasional letter or copy of The Observer that mysteriously found its way irregularly to the local newsagent's, probably having been ordered by some previous British resident or local Anglophone. After the first month I recall waking up one morning wondering if I could handle speaking French all day again. However I overcame that with more practice and eventually returned to Scotland with a Provençal accent that I didn't lose for a long time – it sounded very authentic. One of the characteristics of the village dialect was and is that it includes a lot of profanities, such as " con", "putain" or even "putain de Sainte Vierge" which are not used in polite French society. These and other words ending in –ain, -an, -en, -in, -on, and –un are pronounced as if they were spelled with an extra g, thus sounding like "putaing", "cong" and so on. In a way they reminded me of phrases like "Ya hoor!" that my fellow-students who had been brought up in Kirkcaldy scattered liberally throughout their conversation.

At the end of the school year the parents of Jean-Pierre Hugon invited me to spend a few days at their house in La Seyne, a small town close to the Mediterranean not far from Toulon. M. Hugon was a lorry-driver, and the family lived very simply in a small house near a pine wood. There were a huge number of ants living in and around the house, and it was impossible to keep them out of the bread bin. After a while we gave up trying to knock the last ants out of our tartines and just ingested some extra formic acid-flavoured protein, much as 18th century sailors probably did with weevils in the ship's biscuit.

M. Hugon was very politically aware, and gave me running commentaries on issues of the day. I did not understand French politics in depth, though I was aware of the situation in Algeria, where there had for some time been an armed struggle between the Arab FLN (Front National de Libération) who sought independence from the colonial power, France (la métropole), and the "pieds-noirs" (French people of European origin born in North Africa, thus "black feet") whose armed organisation was the OAS ("Organisation de l'Armée Secrète"). It consisted of "pieds noirs" and some Army officers in Algeria and in metropolitan France. Their slogan was "Algérie Française". Both sides made use of explosives and the transitive verb "plastiquer" entered the language, meaning to blow something up with plastic explosive.

General Charles de Gaulle had been inaugurated as President on 8th Jan 1959, to a considerable extent on a promise to solve the Algerian crisis. In 1961-2 he embarked on a grand tour of France delivering speeches that all included the phrase "Françaises, Français ! Je vous ai compris!" and ending with "Vive la République! Vive la France!" and the singing of "La Marseillaise", led by the president. I had gone to hear him at Draguignan in November 1961, when he stood bare-headed in heavy rain, visible from all sides because of his great height, disdaining an umbrella. His speeches promised whatever the audience wanted to believe, and in the end he negotiated independence with the Algerian nationalists of the FLN. The last resistants of the OAS were arrested and put on trial.

We had one Arab pion at the Lycée called Adda Brahim, who was popular with pupils and the other pions. He was a good footballer and "baby" player. He once quite correctly told me when I ventured a comment on the Algerian situation that "tu n'y comprends absolument rien" (you don't understand a damn thing about it). It must be said that in the villages of the Var, then as now, there was a marked hostility to Arab residents. The southern fringes of France, to which many Arab migrants first come, are home to many of those who vote for extreme right-wing parties in French elections. As a 21 year old I was not really aware of any of that.

In July I did not return to Scotland straight away but spent a month sharing a flat in the old part of Avignon with David Jeffery, my colleague in the St Andrews University cross-country team, who had been spending his term abroad at the university of Aix-en-Provence. It was an enjoyable month, though our training was interrupted for a week or so when a car driver emerged from a side road in front of David's Vespa, causing him to brake hard and skid. We both fell off on to the gravel, which was sore but not serious except for its effect on our ability to run without pain for a few days.

In mid-August I returned to Edinburgh, very suntanned in comparison to my brother Forbes. He was now 17 and had recently passed his driving test, the day after he was eligible to sit it. He was a natural, unlike me, who didn't pass till several years later at the third attempt. During my first test I was asked by the examiner to do a hill start in heavy rain. I tried to start the car until the examiner said calmly "I think you'll find the engine's running, Mr Macgregor." Failed.

Chapter 6

Fankled

While in France I had applied to Queen's College Dundee to do a Diploma in Education (Dip. Ed.) and to Dundee College of Education to start the course for certification as a secondary teacher. By matriculating at Queen's, which had not yet cut itself adrift from St Andrews, I was eligible to run for the university cross-country and athletic teams. I had decided to remain based in St Andrews as I did not know Dundee at all well, and it would be possible to catch the 8.13 am train from St Andrews Station across the Tay every morning in time for lectures.

In the last weeks of the vacation I went over to Dundee hoping to speak to Professor J.W.L. Adams, known to his intimates, among whom I did not of course number myself, as Leitch Adams. He was the Bell Professor of Education. I'm not sure what I intended to ask him, but in any case he said quite politely, peering over his rimless half-moon glasses like Wise Owl in the Little Grey Rabbit stories of Alison Uttley, that he was extremely busy and that he would see me at the start of term.

The university classes were to be held in the Tower Building, not long completed, in contrast to the College of Education, no longer called Training College, a red sandstone edifice in the adjacent Park Place. I wasn't sure how the two courses would mesh with one another, and soon discovered that they were very different in both quality, ambience, and staff personnel.

The students on both courses were all graduates, most of them recent with the exception of one chap who had a lot of teaching experience already. He was all too willing to impart this in any question sessions or tutorials, so that he rapidly acquired the nickname "Gabby" among the cynical greenhorns. The Dip. Ed. Course included lectures on the history and theory of education, as well as on basic aspects of psychology and statistics thought relevant to our careers.

Professor Adams told us at his first lecture that he was contractually obliged as Bell Professor to mention its founding benefactor Dr Andrew Bell, whose "Madras method" had been developed in India and later widely adopted in the United Kingdom for several decades of the mid-19th century. The principle was to teach the older pupils who then taught the younger ones in a drip-down process, rather like the Thatcherite doctrines of trickle-down wealth creation of the 1980s.

Bell, a native St Andrean, had taken holy orders and worked in Madras, now Chennai, in India, where somehow he had amassed a fortune, most of which he devoted to educational causes. These included the foundation of the Madras College in St Andrews (opened 1833) and the Madras Academy (later Bell-Baxter High School) in Cupar, as well as a primary school (now closed) in Leith. Despite this generosity, he quarrelled constantly with the trustees and I have the distinct impression that in his later years at least he was a curmudgeonly old fellow. In the 1990s I translated an article about an encounter he had with the Swiss educationist Pestalozzi. The meeting was described by a young German who had worked for both men. "Education" is derived from the Latin verb "educere", meaning to "draw out" what is in the student rather than to stuff him or her with information. In the German's account Bell comes over as a classroom tyrant, getting angry with his charges when they failed to respond correctly and constantly moving them up and down the rows depending on their answers. Pestalozzi on the other hand drew out the information from his pupils in a much more productive and kindly way.

The professor summarised Bell's achievement briefly and said: "Well, I've mentioned him. Let's move on."

We were asked as a prelude to the course to write an account of our own education to date. It was notable that some of the science graduates found writing this sort of discursive essay more difficult than most of the arts graduates. In the course of the term we moved from Isocrates through Rousseau and on to the modern theorists of the nature/nurture argument.

There was a second lecturer on educational topics, Mr Henry McFarland, but all of what he put before us I have forgotten, except his occasional very loud braying laugh that he racked up from the back of his throat and was almost painful to listen to. The psychology tutor, Dr Terence Lee told us about the functions of eye, ear and brain and introduced us to distribution, graphs and other statistical knowledge. In this field it was the arts graduates who were at a disadvantage.

In the College across the road things were different. My first encounter was with the college doctor, who gave us each a physical examination. She was checking my chest with her stethoscope but it was tickly and I started to giggle. The doctor said this was a sign of immaturity. She was probably right, but I must in that case still be immature as I still giggle if tickled. Not that it happens very often.

The half-dozen modern language graduates were assigned to a tutor, Mr James Buchanan. How to describe him? He appeared a profoundly conventional man. This was 1962, but he still wore separate collars attached to his shirt by a collar stud. Outside the college, he invariably wore a stiff trilby-style hat and an overcoat over his dark suit. He liked to demonstrate his mastery of Dundonian French by the use of the imperfect subjunctive, a practice by then rare in its country of origin except in a literary context. I was once quite correctly rebuked by him for getting an imperfect subjunctive form wrong; but for him to explain my error by saying "I'm surprised at you making such a mistake, with your long residence" was wide of the mark. During the first term we had a visit from a group of French educationalists, and it was pure delight to hear Mr Buchanan struggling to insert as many imperfect subjunctives as he could into the conversation.

Teaching practice formed a large part of our course. For some weeks we went into schools twice a week, followed by a continuous period of a month or more. I was assigned in the first term to Morgan Academy in Dundee. "The Morgan" at this time was still a senior secondary school with a selective intake. It was a rather traditional place, as were most such schools: teachers wore gowns, pupils adhered strictly to the uniform dress code, and most of them were well-behaved. They risked lines, detention or even the belt if they were not. I remember next to nothing of what classes I was assigned to teach, but recall that in the rather poky and dark staffroom I was received in a generally friendly way and that I was able to join in the table-tennis games that were played at lunchtime. Mr Buchanan appeared on one occasion to hear me give a "Crit" lesson which I had prepared with some care, and that he gave the class a fright.

This was the dawn of technical advances in language teaching as we moved from "chalk and talk" to reel-to-reel tape recorders, but Mr Buchanan was not always comfortable with the latter, confessing on one occasion that "the tape's got all fankled". One of his tried and tested methods of teaching verbs was the "Rub-off Technique": the teacher wrote the persons of the verb conjugation on the blackboard – "je vais, tu vas" etc - then had the class recite them. That was Step One. Steps Two, Three, Four, up to Thirteen or Fourteen involved rubbing out one form in turn and repeating the chorus of repetition. Theoretically it would be possible for the class finally to be staring at an empty board and reciting the entire conjugation. Magic!

Slide projectors and screens were occasionally used, and then as now required a thick book to prop up the front of the projector as without one the image was always too low for the screen. Even in the PowerPoint age a thick book should perhaps be sold with projecting devices as standard.

In term two, from January to March, Lawside Academy was my destination on teaching practice days. Lawside was a Roman Catholic senior secondary, and at the period I attended to do my practice it had a number of "temporary" huts out in what had once been the playground. The individual classrooms had internal windows to the corridor at head height. One chilly, foggy morning in February 1962 the pupils I was teaching were suddenly distracted to see a grim, unsmiling, bespectacled face under a dark grey trilby bobbing along from one window to the next. "Ma Goad!" one pupil exclaimed, as the apparition moved along and Mr Buchanan's prominent Adam's apple emerged from and retreated behind his stiff collar. The door of the classroom opened and the ghost of Christmas past came in. "Good morning, boys and girls", it said in sepulchral tones. It was time for my second "Crit".

What about running? David Jeffery was now captain of the St Andrews cross-country team, although he was not as active as he had been since it was his Senior Honours year. I had nothing inhibiting me, however, and started the season promisingly ith a second place in the first NE League Race at Caird Park on 13th October behind Hawkhill's flame-haired Ron Coleman, with our team also second. In the following weeks I was third on the first leg of the Kingsway Relays, still run on the coned-off dual carriageway, and led us to a mid-week 26-62 victory over Durham Colleges at St Andrews. A new recruit to St AUCCC was Michael J. R. Tolkien, a raven-haired grandson of J.R.R.. Mike was 6th that day but competed irregularly thereafter.

Fergus Murray and Martin Craven (Edinburgh University) beat me in another home match, and on 10th November at Garscaddden, Glasgow, Allan

Faulds (GU) was the winner, but a relative triumph came in the Edinburgh-Glasgow Relay on the 17th when 11th place was sufficient to get us the Most Meritorious Performance medals that we had missed out on in 1959. In 1962 the team had finished only 19th, and Ron Bacchus, the News of the World representative, said at the presentation that St Andrews had been lucky to be invited again.

A mixture of narrow defeats and victories followed in that first term, including a win over Glasgow who had three of their best runners Callum Laing, Jim Bogan and Doug Gifford absent.

I had been training occasionally with Fergus Murray, still only 19 and two years away from Olympic selection. Fergus's family lived in Angus in the hills behind Dundee, and during my teaching practice we sometimes met at Caird Park after school and ran from there. That ceased after one failure on my part. It was a wet, cold November evening and I couldn't face making my way across town to the Hawkhill changing rooms. I had no way of alerting Fergus, and just went home to St Andrews. That was a terrible betrayal in the runners' unwritten code, and Fergus was so furious at being left waiting that he refused to train with me for about a year. I deserved it.

In the second term I ran indifferently, coming 4th in a joint League and Inter-university race at the end of January 1963. There ensued poor runs versus Edinburgh and Glasgow, where I had a bad knee and was 23rd, and a shocking performance in an ill-advised trip to the snow-bound British Universities Championships at Brentwood, Essex. Our result was almost as bad as in Manchester in my first year. David Jeffery was 71st and I was 86th. The first five finishers were Tim Johnston (Cambridge), John Farrington (London), Mike Turner (Cambridge), Ron Hill (Manchester) and John Whetton (Nottingham) – a good list for crystal ball gazers as they all became prominent internationalist runners.

My last open cross-country races for St Andrews were the National at Hamilton, where David Jeffery and I ran into 27th and 31st places in the Senior 9 miles, and the fourth League Race where I was 3rd and the team won the North-East League. Then came the Taylor Trophy race in which I beat Bob McKean, older brother of future four-times Scottish champion Andy, into second place. Bob, a bejant, won the Captain's Cup.

I had been elected track and field captain, and started the season in late April with a double-header in the space of a week. On the Wednesday evening at Craiglockhart's grass track against Edinburgh University in the mile, Fergus set a slow pace in the first two laps, and I was able to run away from him over the last two for a surprise win in 4:25.3. On the Saturday was again successful in the mile over another grass track at King's College, Aberdeen, this time outsprinting Mel Edwards in 4:19.3. Things were looking good for my chances at the Scottish Universities Championships at Glasgow in late May, but I dissipated my emotional energy in a hopeless pursuit of a female member of the team – a not infrequent cause of periodic losses of running form over the years – and ran equally hopelessly at a windswept Westerlands at the championships.

I had had more success in the employment and academic spheres. My teaching practice was to be in St Andrews, at Madras College. Those months were to determine the course of most of my professional life.

Madras College in the spring of 1963 was like paradise compared to Morgan and Lawside. Partly it was the season, but also the atmosphere of figurative as well as literal lightness within the school, or so it appeared to me. Also I had a connection, for the Rector was Dr John Thompson, my history teacher at Stewart's until he left to take up the Madras job in 1955. Now I was able to get to know him rather better.

The original Madras College had been designed by its architect, William Burn, as a three-piece unit and opened in 1833. The school building with its attractive frontage is set well back from the main street (South Street), on land that was once occupied by a Dominican church, of which only a fragment (Blackfriars' Chapel ruin) remains. The classrooms and offices are placed round a square-pillared and flagstoned quadrangle, and large houses for the original Rector and second master stand near the street on the eastern and western sides. By 1963 the Rector and his family still occupied the original house and the school janitor lived in part of the western building, the other rooms being used for music tuition.

The principal teacher of modern languages was Ian M. Hendry, who impressed me from the moment I met him, and who was unquestionably the person who had the greatest influence on my development as a teacher. Originally from Forres, he had served in the jungles of the Far East and the sands of North

Africa in the war, and had qualified at Aberdeen University along with his wife Betty. He had been recruited by Dr Thompson in 1958-9 as head of department from his previous post in the south west of Scotland. Madras had until John Thompson's arrival been known as "the elephants' graveyard" because its staff rarely moved on. Under the Thompson regime dynamic young staff were appointed and the school had begun a renaissance. One of "Doc Thom's" key changes had been to make German the first modern foreign language instead of French. This had apparently not gone down well with all colleagues. After all it was just over a decade since the end of the second world war. To anchor German firmly in the school's life, Dr Thompson and Ian Hendry had with help from colleagues in Germany established in 1956-7 a school to school, home to home exchange with a famous and ancient Gymnasium in Schleswig-Holstein, the Kieler Gelehrtenschule, founded in 1320.

Mr Hendry exercised both charm and control in his teaching. For the first few weeks of my practice visits I was able to "compare and contrast", to use an exam question-setter's cliché, the methods and attitudes of all the French- and German-teaching staff. Spanish and Russian were also taught, there being a vogue for the latter in the 1950s and 60s.

There were four modern language teaching rooms at the time, all along a first floor corridor of a block built in 1955. The biggest and most westerly room, numbered 19, was that used mostly by Mr Hendry, and had a cupboard at the back where he and a couple of close colleagues, the head of chemistry Sandy Jeffrey and the head of history Dr Harry Gordon, had their morning interval coffee, thus forming a breakaway group, one of several throughout the school. The majority drank their coffee in either the male or female staffroom downstairs. The staffrooms were strictly segregated. If a male teacher wished to visit the female staffroom he had to knock first. Some teachers had a chair reserved only for them. Even an innocent breach of that convention would be greeted by a display of huffing and puffing by the usual incumbent. There was a regular train passenger on the 8.13 from St Andrews to Dundee who had the same attitude to the corner seat he usually managed to occupy.

The most experienced teacher in the department was Miss Margaret Crosthwaite, who had spent all her career at Madras and taught only French. The atmosphere in her classroom, Room 18, could fairly be described as somnolent. The ambiance next door in 17, the realm of Alexander Mackenzie, a black-haired, small, fierce Gaelic speaker from Inverness, who suffered from stress-related psoriasis, was just the opposite. Known to the pupils as "Wee Mac", he taught both German and French with a devastating and sometimes frightening intensity.

Then came an all-purpose room, 16, used mainly by Mrs Betty Hendry (French), who influenced her pupils by her soft, pleasant but insistent approach, as well as the knowledge that the pupils in the event of bad behaviour would have her husband to reckon with. In the final room in the corridor, 15, Douglas Johnson, in a previous existence one of the designers of the Wellington bomber, taught Russian. I had little to do with him as a student; he was a quiet unobtrusive gentleman, one of the few who went about the school without a gown.

At the east side of the front of the school were huts, and in one of these James C. Halliday taught, an affable man with a bushy moustache, but just a little like the comedians Terry-Thomas or "Professor" Jimmy Edwards in appearance and demeanour. One of the first things I noticed was that he referred to homework as "homey" and to an "ink exercise" (homework to be done more formally, for correction and assessment) as an "inky". I found this a bit too couthy. Through no fault of his own, he had not built up any record of residence abroad in any French or German speaking country. Mr Hendry confided in me that Mr Halliday had been in Italy with the Catering Corps and thus felt himself qualified to teach junior classes Latin. The impression was generally given that Mr Halliday was a little bit suspect on the language side, rather like the cricketer R.H.E. Chisholm at Stewart's. I watched him for instance hold up a ruler (das Lineal) and say to the beginners' class: "Das ist eine Regel" (a rule as in sport). As I was suspect at the time for the occasional wrong adjective ending in German and for the previously mentioned mistakes in the French imperfect subjunctive, I should not however be too critical.

The term at Madras passed very quickly. I had my final crit lesson from Mr Buchanan, who was good enough to recommend me for what the College of Education called a "They came nearest", a plural version of what was more traditionally styled "proxime accessit", and I was awarded my certificate in secondary education. I also passed the Diploma in Education exams, roughly the same level as Special Class exams at university. Best of all, there was a vacancy at Madras, and I secured it. That was good luck indeed. I arranged with Mr Hendry to come in a few days before the end of term to discuss arrangements, and went on my way rejoicing. My parents were delighted to hear that I had a job at one of Fife's best schools.

When the day arrived to visit, Mr Hendry had forgotten I was coming. His friend Dr Harry Gordon had died the day before, and the whole school was in shock at the loss of a popular colleague. Ian Hendry could have asked me to come back another day, but he didn't. Instead he said: "Ach! Did I ask you to come in today? Ah well, I suppose life goes on. You'd better come up to Room 19 and we'll have a chat." And so we did.

Running continued through the summer. I was invited to join a Glasgow University athletics tour of the Black Forest. Manchester University were also touring, and we had several contests during which I lost to Ron Hill, John Whetton and others. The best performances were second to John Whetton in a 1500m in 4:06.6 in Freiburg im Breisgau, and second again to Horst Steffny in a 3000m in Troisdorf, near Bonn, in 8:33.8, my best to that date. I joined in some training runs in the forest around Freiburg, and distinctly recall Ron Hill saying I would "get my nice leather shoes wet": he was running in canvas gymshoes. He liked to emphasize his working-class origins and the Alf Tupper, Tough of the Track image as "plain Ron Hill from Accrington" instead of Dr Ron Hill, B.Sc. Ph.D, industrial textile chemist. The Germans, with their traditional love of titles, liked and still like to refer to him in results of races as "Dr. Ron Hill". Ron accused me for some reason of being a Tory voter, not a sin I have ever committed.

My role on the tour included that of interpreter. I made particular use of my language skills before and after a session of interval training conducted by Woldemar Gerschler, who before the War had become famous as the coach of German world record holder Rudolf Harbig (an anti-Nazi who was sent to the Eastern Front and died there). Gerschler enjoyed fame in British athletic circles as Gordon Pirie's coach and adviser. Pirie was renowned as one of the hardest trainers in the world, along with such legends as of Emil Zatopek, Vladimir Kuts and Pyotr Bolotnikov. Pirie ran a big mileage, much of it in the form of large numbers of interval repetitions over 200m or 400m. When he was in Freiburg he ran these on forest trails, his heart rate and recovery rate being monitored by Gerschler and sometimes by Gerschler's scientific collaborator Prof. Dr. Herbert Reindell.

I did not know in 1963 just how effusively grateful Gerschler had been in late 1930s articles in "Der Leichtathlet" praising the glorious achievements of National Socialism, or I might not have been so impressed by the later version of him. I translated his brief introduction to the Gerschler/Reindell training ideas, then we took part in a sample session, I think 12x200m with 200m recovery jog. Later that afternoon we attended a longer talk by Gerschler, which I also translated, I hope more or less accurately.

Much later some of the Freiburg sports scientists were said to be implicated in a drugs scandal. It apparently began in 1952 when Dr. Reindell, working with Gerschler at Freiburg, decided to use drugs. Gerschler coached a mediocre middle distance runner from Luxemburg named Joseph Barthel. At the time, Barthel was ranked 41st in the world. Oscar Wegener, a colleague of Professor Reindell, recently said that when Barthel won the Gold medal in the 1952 Helsinki Olympics it was partly due to being doped with Pervitin, a substance given to world war to German soldiers to make them feel temporarily invincible.

The story about Josy Barthel is to be found in the dissertation by Wegener, "Die Wirkung von Dopingmitteln auf den Kreislauf und die körperliche Leistung" [The Effect of Doping substances on Circulation and Physical Performance], Diss. Universität Freiburg 1954. Wegener's academic supervisor was Reindell, who became German Olympic team doctor after Dr Martin Brustmann (Otto Peltzer's doctor – see Chapter 12) had had to resign following a drugs scandal at the German rowing championships on 29th June 1952. At that time to general surprise the Köln Eight, who had been provided with "red pills" by Brustmann, had won and the favoured team Rüsselsheim lost by taking "the wrong pills".

Tim Johnston, who was eighth in the 1968 Olympic marathon in Mexico, tells me that when he was 19 he had a test with "Reindell and his mates" at Freiburg. He was pronounced "sehr leistungsfähig" (very capable of a good performance) but relatively weak in the legs, and recommended to write off to Hoffmann Laroche in Switzerland for a product called Oranabol, to beef up his skinny calves. Such things were not illegal at the time, but, through inertia, plus not wanting to be beholden to anyone, he never got round to it.

The sports historian Volker Kluge in Brandenburg has given me more information about Pervitin. It is a methamphetamine and was developed in 1938 at the Temmler-Werken in Marburg. (In the USA there was a similar product.) Until 1941 you could buy Pervitin over the counter in Germany, but then it was banned under the "Opium Law". During the war these drugs were popularly known as "Stuka–Tabletten" or "Hermann-Göring-Pillen", and of course they were used in sport. After the war, for instance the mountaineer Hermann Buhl used them when he climbed Nanga Parbat in 1953. About the same time the amphetamine Benzedrine was also developed.

Volker does not know when the close co-operation between Woldemar Gerschler and Prof. Dr. Herbert Reindell began. From 1949 till 1971 Gerschler was head of the Institut für Leibesübungen [Physical Exercise Institute] in Freiburg. Gordon Pirie came to him for coaching advice in November 1953.

None of this is to cast aspersions on Pirie, who was a very intense trainer, but to point out that drug usage is endemic in sport and has been for a very long time, probably since the Greeks started offering rewards to returning Olympic victors. In April 2010 there was a press report that Olympic and world 400 metres champion LaShawn Merritt (USA) had failed three doping tests for a banned substance and accepted a provisional suspension, caused by his use of "an over-the-counter male enhancement product" according to his attorney.

On return to Scotland I enjoyed a period of leisure, training desultorily, occasionally golfing badly with my brother and father at Carrick Knowe near Pinkhill in Edinburgh and on the nine-hole course at Anstruther, where my stepmother and her sisters had bought the Old Manse, Anstruther Wester. Forbes and I amused ourselves paddling around at the mouth of the Dreel Burn in a flat-bottomed canvas boat our father had constructed. I was looking forward to starting my teaching career.

On 21st August 1963 my father and stepmother drove me up to St Andrews in their car, a two-tone MG Magnette, and dropped me off outside the school building in South Street to start my first real job. I was dressed that day in a dark blue suit with fashionably narrow lapels and slim cut trousers, a dark blue striped shirt and, I think, a narrow dark blue tie. I strode into the quad trying to look confident, and turned left towards the school office to present myself to Miss Nicol, the prim, ex-WREN school secretary as "a new, weill-harnit dominie", to quote my father's friend Robert Garioch the poet. "Weill-harnit" means with a full head of hair. Very many years were destined to go by before I left that building, at least as a member of staff, for the last time.

Chapter 7

Let Them Eat Bun

Madras College in 1963 was a six-year Senior Secondary School. Every August there was a three-class intake of just under 100 pupils from the local primaries. These included Madras Primary, Langlands, Leuchars, Strathkinness, Boarhills, Dunino, and Kingbarns. The parents and children of Tayport, Newport and Wormit could choose between Bell-Baxter in Cupar and Madras, these two big schools being roughly equidistant from the Tay bridgehead area. At Madras, two of the three entrant classes studied German and one French. Entry to a senior secondary depended on the results of the "qualy" or qualification examination, sat by Primary 7 children. Those from St Andrews who did not gain entry to Madras went to the Burgh School in Abbey Walk, or to Tayport Junior Secondary. It was a socially divisive but, at least for the senior secondary pupils, an impressive system from the point of view of academic achievement.

On the whole the atmosphere in the South Street complex was relaxed and happy. In my opinion, which I am sure would be generally shared by those who knew him, Dr John Thompson was "a big man" in every sense, to use an expression he was fond of employing as a description of others. Thus, when the Stewart's headmaster Dr Robbie died in my first year of teaching, Dr Thompson came into my classroom to tell me the news. "A big man, big man", he said. "Killed by the FP Club." What I assumed he meant was that pressure from the Former Pupils' Club in connection with the organisation of the school had put stresses on Dr Robbie that had finally proved too much for his health. Dr Robbie is buried in the Dean Cemetery off Belford Road in Edinburgh. On a visit there a few years ago I took a photograph of the gravestone, more as a memento mori than anything else.

John Thompson was much loved by pupils and staff. In those days it was customary for the pupils to stand up when the Rector came into a room. One of JT's endearing habits was on entering the classroom to make a calming gesture with outstretched palms for the children to sit down again, as if he were really just hoping to sneak in unobserved to see how things were going.

Hamilton Racecourse 1963. (Glasgow Herald).

My very first class on that first morning on 21ˢᵗ August 1963 was a beginners' French group consisting of about half a dozen talented German pupils who were starting a second modern foreign language. Dr Thompson came to visit the next week. I was teaching the class names for things in the room, without using more than a minimum of English, the so-called Direct Method. I asked the Rector therefore not to pose questions to the pupils, but just to point at the ceiling, floor and so on. He did that, and I can see him now, standing with an interrogative look on his face and pointing at le plafond or le plancher.

From that first year I have retained a much clearer recollection of some of the members of my classes than from later when the memories merge and mingle. I was the register teacher of a first year French class, called IP. Dr Thompson was under the illusion that if all classes had random letters of the alphabet assigned to them rather than being called IA, IB and IC the pupils would not realise that any "setting" or "streaming" was in operation. Of course all the pupils had penetrated this subterfuge within a day or two.

The members of the S4 German class I was assigned were preparing to sit the SCE "Ordinary Grade" examination. It consisted of a Reading passage with questions in English, a "Language Practice" with questions in German and some grammatical exercises such as providing verb forms, giving the "opposite" of an adjective, or defining things in German. Some of these questions were of mind-numbing obviousness, for example "Was ist 'ein vierzehnjähriges Mädchen'?" [What is 'a 14 year-old girl'?]. The answer expected was "Es ist ein Mädchen, das vierzehn Jahre alt ist."[It is a girl who is 14 years old.] Answer in a complete sentence, please.

Then there was an Aural Comprehension, a text read aloud twice by the teacher, again with questions in English which the pupils saw but not the teacher who was reading. The teacher had only a limited time to read the text but, even so, there was scope for a teacher with even minimal dramatic ability to lay emphasis on what he or she imagined to be the crucial phrases. Some colleagues had more of an accent of their native Scottish region than of the foreign country, and that was of course to the pupils' advantage as it sounded more familiar. The part of the exam that was invariably worst done was the so-called Essay, where candidates had much less guidance and often ignored their teacher's injunction to "write what you know" and not give rein to their imagination. Originality of thought tended to result at that level in a high number of grammatical errors.

Madras College cross country team 1965-66.

I found the S4 class, which contained about thirty 15 year-olds, not quite so easy to control as the younger ones, but the stirrings of rebellion never got out of hand. Coincidentally one of those in that class, Jim Bennett, was later to become a Depute Rector of the school.

Revolution in Scottish education was in the air. The decision had been taken by Fife County Council Education Committee that Madras College and the

Burgh School were to amalgamate. A modern building was to be erected on the higher ground to the south of Langlands Primary. Construction had not yet started, but in the meantime contacts between the two schools had been tentatively instigated. It was perhaps understandable that the move to join up was not welcomed by many of the Burgh staff, who like the citizens of the GDR after 1990 regarded the whole thing as a takeover and the Madras Principal Teachers, when they made exploratory visits, as "Wessi"-like interlopers. Vestiges of ill-feeling, and more than just vestiges sometimes, persisted for many years, long after the new building was occupied.

Happily for the Modern Languages department, no foreign language had ever been taught in the Burgh School. That was going to change under the new system, and as the new recruit I was sent "down the road" once a day to introduce the first year Burgh pupils to la langue des Français. Because there was no feeling of being taken over, I was received in a friendly way, though occasionally condescended to by a few of the staffroom veterans as a beginner in the profession.

This pioneering class was held in one of the huts adjoining the Victorian main building. The class teacher was a lady of a certain age called Miss Wilhelmina Brace, with whom I got on well, as indeed I did with the class, most of whom were eager to learn some French. Again, I retain even today some contact with one or two of those first pupils, though of course many subsequently left St Andrews.

Teachers are all idiosyncratic in the eyes of their pupils. We all perceive that at school, and as a young teacher I was aware of it at Lorgues and at Madras as well. It would be tedious to anyone reading this if I were to go through all my former colleagues recounting anecdotes and personal observations about them, and yet to attempt a fair picture of life in Madras in the last years of its existence as a six-year senior secondary without writing something about them would be wrong too.

At South Street the staffroom was the centre of what social activity there was during the school week. The custom was for the mail to be laid out on a central table. The principal classics teacher, the elderly, bald-headed Mr Charles Anderson, was in the habit of going round reading the names of the mail's recipients under his breath. My former "senior man" at university, Gordon Maxwell, was a colleague of Mr Anderson and one morning turned all the envelopes upside down so that "Charlie" had to crane his neck to read the addresses.

In my second year of teaching, some of us younger members started to play a "Madras version" of table-tennis on that staffroom table. The uniqueness of our version was that we played with books as bats and a pencil as a net. We developed quite a lot of skill at this curious game, and soon started to play for money. The stakes rose over several months from 6d to a shilling, then two shillings and half a crown, eventually peaking at £1 – the equivalent of about £10 today. It couldn't last. It wasn't quite like the tulip bubble of 17th century Holland, but not unlike it either. Book table-tennis petered out.

Mr Sandy McLees, a tall gaunt gown-clad figure who was head of English and also Depute Rector, occupied an armchair diagonally opposite the staffroom entrance. If a pupil should be so rash as to enter without permission, the long McLees forefinger would point at the intruder as its owner said menacingly: "Out!" On one occasion I had just uttered the solecism "less books" when from the corner I was transfixed by Mr McLees's rather sepulchral voice: "Fewer!" Ever since then I have had to hold myself back from correcting everybody who says "less" with a plural noun.

My friend Donald Mackenzie, another English teacher, book table-tennis pioneer and the source of some of my updated information about the seamier side of Corstorphine in the 1950s, told me that one of Mr McLees's holiday pursuits was to visit French cathedrals, where he would gaze up towards the high vaulted ceilings and say to himself: "If only it were true!"

I move appositely to the Religious Instruction teacher, a Welshman, Will Vaughan, a kind and friendly man who wore black boots, which he knocked against one another as he sat in the staffroom engrossed in discussion, interjecting "Tsss!" every so often when a telling point was made. Miss Margaret Affleck was the chief music teacher, a dynamic and enthusiastic organiser of concerts who lived in Ladybank. Her assistants included Bob Taylor, a fine bass singer who performed regularly on the BBC as well as for Ian Hendry during the biennial visits of the school's German partner pupils from Kiel. He would recount jokes and anecdotes from behind the back of his hand, looking around to see if anyone was watching.

A third music teacher was John Fletcher, a Barbadian who was one of the very few black teachers in Fife at the time. He was a delightful man and a very talented musician who some years later returned to Barbados to take up a senior position on their version of the "B.B.C." He was unique in quite obviously not giving two hoots what people thought of him, and made outrageous comments to his senior classes. With a huge grin and his normal strong Caribbean accent he reportedly said to one fifth year class when he had overheard a pupil using a naughty word: "Ah doan like buggahs that sweah". Nobody complained.

The "Lady Superintendent", Miss Hester M. Rain, had a hard job to ensure that the girls in the school dressed and behaved according to her notions of decorum. Miss Rain was able to assume an air of outraged propriety when confronted by a supposedly delinquent pupil. She was a very good mathematics teacher and did a lot of good, like us all a victim of the Zeitgeist.

The era of the Beatles had just begun, and with it a profound shift in fashion and public standards of appearance, behaviour and "morality" as well as music. Schools, as ever, found it hard to keep up with the reality outside, and Miss Rain was fighting a long but losing war against shorter skirts. These were one of the symbols of the new age, along with trousers for women, a battle some of the younger female teachers also had to fight against the grim-faced and tweed-skirted forces of reaction.

Traditionalists had inveighed when I was a schoolboy against crew cuts, and now long hair was the target, although in retrospect the Beatles' "mop" haircuts of the mid-1960s were pretty tame. As one of the youngest teachers, only a few years older than the senior pupils, I was of course on their side against authority – especially if those senior pupils were pretty girls. How unprofessional. I remember one Sunday assembling with four other runners behind the medieval St Athernase Church in the village of Leuchars, ready to head off round Tentsmuir Forest on a 15 mile run, when a girl pupil in her late teens wearing a very short skirt came round the corner. "Jings, Don", said one of my companions, an earthy fellow from Markinch. "How can you teach thon?"

First Kiel Exchange Group with Dr John Thompson on St Rule's Tower, St Andrews, 1957.

In my second year at Madras I was given a form class called IH, who were to learn German. Ian Hendry had introduced a Swedish course book written by Eie Ericsson and Christian Eisenberg, the first volume being called "Wir Fangen An" [We're beginning]. The book had a colour gender code, blue for masculine nouns, red for feminine and green for neuter, which was a great help for learners, unless they were colour blind, I suppose. It featured various characters like Frau Süß, a chubby optimist and Herr Sauer, a skinny pessimist, as well as a number of schoolchildren of an appropriate age, and a "comical" character called August who featured in jokey conversations like "Why do you have a scar on your forehead, August?" – "I bit myself!"

The only snag, apart from the jokes, was that the book had vocabulary lists in German and Swedish, and no practice exercises. To remedy these gaps, we reproduced the texts in colour on the school's "Banda" reprographic machine, and made up our own vocabulary lists and exercises. I distributed all this to IH, who enjoyed the experiment and benefited from it. Unbeknown to me, Ian Hendry was in negotiation with W&R Chambers, the well-known Edinburgh publisher, and a year or two later the first volume of "Moderner Deutschkurs", i.e. Wir Fangen An, was produced following a longish period of gestation and experiment. It had an accompanying exercise booklet or "Übungsheft", as did the subsequent three volumes, edited by my colleague Alexander Mackenzie ("Wee Mac") and me, Ian Hendry having by then departed to take over the Rectorship of Dunoon Grammar School. I may say that Ian and I did the lion's share of the preparation and proof-reading, as "Alick" was nearly always late for our 8 am pre-school meetings to discuss progress. He nonetheless shared the 2.5% share of the profits – not that I grudged it to him - while the original authors Ericsson and Eisenberg pocketed 10% between them for doing nothing. To the originators the spoils.

IH was a lovely class to teach, and I am still in regular touch with some of its members, one of whom, Anne Rudder, née Gulbrandsen, is a German teacher in Toowoomba, Queensland, Australia. I met her on a visit "down under" in 2010. Once a week the last 40-minute period of the day was used as an extra class, when we teachers could do with our charges anything educational that occurred to us. I suggested to the children that I read *The Hobbit* by J.R.R. Tolkien aloud to them, and rather surprisingly they agreed. Their enthusiasm and attentiveness were astonishing, and I read the entire book to them in Room 15 in weekly instalments over the session, sometimes fitting in five minutes here and there at the end of a normal period as well. I cannot conceive of a modern class being so tolerant or indeed interested.

A feature of the school was the daily visit of the MacArthur's "bun van" to the South Street staff car park at 11 o'clock. Various items of Scottish patisserie from iced buns, "flies' cemeteries" (fruit slice) to chocolate doughnuts were on sale. Any teacher who had a non-teaching period was free to queue up early before the pupils were released, and thus got a wider choice of goods. It was a small or even a medium-sized tragedy when Fisher & Donaldson bought MacArthur's bakery and soon thereafter stopped the daily "bun van". Mais où sont les brioches d'antan? as François Villon might have asked – where are the buns of yesteryear? Incidentally Marie-Antoinette did not say "Let them eat cake!", if indeed she said anything along these lines at all, but "Qu'ils mangent de la brioche!" – Let them eat bun!

Those first three years I spent at Madras were among the happiest of my entire career, though I was very full of myself and no doubt unwittingly committed many breaches of convention or decorum that offended some of my seniors. I got on very well with my head of department Ian Hendry and his wife, and quite often was asked to babysit for their two sons Ian and Peter at their home, "Lade Braes Hollow" just off the Lade Braes Walk. At the end of the evening Ian and I used to walk the golden labrador Dan. It was at the end of one of these early strolls in the November moonlight that we returned to Lade Braes Hollow to be greeted by Betty Hendry with the words: "Kennedy's been shot!" And so, like everyone else, I can recall exactly what I was doing when that momentous and sad news reached me.

A regular visitor to the Hendry household was a fellow Northerner – the Hendrys both came from the Forres area – called George Gray, a University librarian. Mr Gray had a rather snippy voice which I took great delight in imitating. He had dogmatic opinions and expressed them forcefully. For example after some altercation he said of my colleague Alex Mackenzie (born 1934): "Young Mackenzie was intolerably rude!". Many of his anecdotes involved "my Hungarian friend": "My Hungarian friend told me – and if he told me that it was certainly true! – that Jan Kadar [the Hungarian Prime Minister during the 1956 uprising] was arrested and taken to Moscow, and Khrushchev shook him! shook him like a dog!…Jan Kadar was a very honest man. My Hungarian friend…"

Another example of Mr Gray's approach: I had bought a fashionably short raincoat, and George Gray commented on it unfavourably: "You'll catch your death of cold, I shouldn't wonder! I got my coat, a warm, heavy overcoat of a decent length, from Mr Andrew, Mr Andrew the tailor in Bell Street, a very honest man…"

One last example: I met Mr Gray in the town library one Saturday morning. He accosted me by saying he had heard I had been ill. "No, I'm fine. It's my colleague Alex Mackenzie who's been ill."

"Well, I'm sorry to hear that. (Then, changing the subject abruptly) Have you heard of a book called 'The Witness House' by Countess Kalnoky?" – "No." "Well, it's set in Nürnberg, during the trials of the Nazis in 1946. It's a fascinating book! She recounts how a big limousine drew up outside the witness house, and do you know who got out? No less a personage than Julius Leber…the Jew-baiter, the Jew-baiter got out…. Oh yes, I know all these streets, I know Nürnberg like the back of my hand… you should read it... there's a copy in the County Library, in fact I put it there myself…" I said I would look for it, and Mr Gray finally took his leave of me with the words: "Well! I hope you'll be better soon!" After writing this I found a copy of The Witness House on amazon.co.uk and in fact it's a very interesting read – so much for my mockery!

I could go on a long time, and probably did, as the Hendrys quite enjoyed listening to George Gray being taken off. I used to note down the conversations later the same evening.

In 1966 the new Kilrymont Road building was finally complete. It was officially opened in the following year by my former professor J.W.L. Adams from Dundee. The entire staff of Madras had been addressed a year or so before in the South Street Library by Cllr J. Devlin, Fife County Council's chairman of education, who told us about the county's plans for "comprehensivisation" of our schools. We listened to him in suspicious silence. As has historically always been the case, and probably always will be, the far-seeingness of the plans was not matched by the generosity of financial provision nor by the length of time allowed for implementation, though in the case of the new Madras structure the education authority did rather better than government authorities when introducing other later reforms such as the Raising of the School Leaving Age [RoSLA] to 16, the introduction of Standard Grades [the Dreadful Duo of Munn and Dunning] and later examination reforms like the optimistically named Higher Still or Curriculum for Excellence. At least at Kilrymont we had a new building which was in most respects well equipped, even though it had been designed originally as a replacement Junior Secondary and had a shelf-life of around 25 years, now exceeded by almost twenty.

Architecturally unusual, it had a wing-shaped roof a bit like a Vulcan bomber, huge areas of glass, especially facing south so that occupants would frazzle in the heat of the spring and summer. It had a separate swimming pool and Games Hall complex, and plenty of flat roofed areas to store up leakage problems for the future. Mr Alexander Inglis, the Headmaster of the Burgh School, was to preside over this wonderful school as Depute Rector overall to Dr Thompson, who decided to restrict his role and not interfere in the day-to-day running of the place. It is hard to know if that was a correct decision or not.

A structure of Principal and Depute Principal Teachers was to be set up. In most cases the South Street Principal was appointed to the new job, and the Burgh School head of department became the new Depute. It had been decided that all first and second year pupils would go to Kilrymont Road and that the so-called "high-fliers" in class III would move to South Street, thus continuing the "snobs vs yobs" hostility that had existed previously.

I was encouraged by Ian Hendry to apply for the vacant post as Depute, which I did, though with some reluctance as I did not really want to spend all my time teaching classes I and II and the less interested class III pupils in the junior building. In the autumn of 1966 I travelled for the first time to the education offices at Wemyssfield, Kirkcaldy, had my interview, and sat with the other applicants in the waiting room. I recall nothing of the interview except that I was nervous. I got through it, went out again to the silent waiting area, and in due course the council officer came out and pronounced in stentorian tones the name of the selected candidate that signalled as much at Wemyssfield as "Habemus Papam!" in the Vatican: "Mr Macgregor!" I followed him into the committee room again in some confusion and was offered the post. Mr Inglis (known to staff and pupils when he wasn't listening as Auld Eck) suggested he give me a lift back to St Andrews in his Rover. We stopped off on the way at a cash-and-carry, where he had provisions to buy. Full of the excitement of success, I bought six tins of pears.

The Burgh School had transferred lock, stock and barrel to the exciting new premises, which were on several levels. The pupils' entrance from the bus parking zone led to a cloakroom area, mobbed and noisy at the beginning and end of the day, fetid, mobbed and noisy when it was inclement outside and the 1000 or so children were allowed to stay indoors at the morning and lunch intervals. To begin with, until the time some years later of "industrial" unrest, staff had an interval rota during which the people on duty patrolled the extensive playground and the toilets or kept a lid on trouble if the children were rampaging indoors. Some teachers held regular lunchtime clubs that kept a minority out of mischief.

On a lower vestibule entrance hall were the prefects' rooms, an office and beyond that the school Assembly Hall, ornamented with sculptures created by the Art Department, and then two connected dining halls off the middle of a corridor that led left to a series of Technical rooms and, off to the right, to the Music rooms.

The traditional teaching classrooms were on the three upper floors, access being gained by stairs at either end. The rule for using these was summed up in the acronym DRUL (Down Right, Up Left). Teachers stood at various crucial points in the staircases ensuring that the DRUL rule was obeyed, especially at the start of breaks or at the end of the day, when the hordes did not stand on ceremony in their desire to be first on their bus or to get out into God's fresh air before they expired from lack of oxygen.

My modern language colleagues and I were quartered on the top floor, below the flat roof, to which there was very limited access via a narrow stairway for art and janitorial staff. Rooms 309, 307, 305, 301, 316 and the Language Laboratory (318) were the corner of the vineyard in which we laboured – a metaphor of which, in a more general sense, Ian Hendry was very fond.

The 20-booth language lab, sister to that newly installed in South Street, was the department's pride and joy. The Depute Principal Teacher of English, Mr J. D. Wallace, tried to persuade me to allow some English classes to use it, but Ian Hendry gave me strict orders not to let him. Wallace was angered by this and told me it was "not in the spirit of this school", meaning the Burgh even though we were no longer there. David Wallace's room was directly under the Lab and I could hear him intoning to his rapt charges such instructions as "Turn to page 46 and do exercises A to H", before departing for some meeting in Glenrothes and leaving a long-suffering colleague from Tayport, Miss Smart, to cover the class.

Mr Wallace edited the school newspaper, which at the Burgh had been called the "Abbey Times" and continued under that name at Kilrymont. It appeared weekly, priced competitively at 2d, its sale advertised on small posters pinned to notice boards in the cloakroom area. My good friend Duncan Monteith, Depute Principal Teacher of Geography, and I saw early one morning that someone had written on one of these posters "WALLACE IS A CHIMP". This caused us great hilarity and ever afterwards we, though only we, referred to poor Mr Wallace as "the Chimp". No wonder that medical officer at the College of Education said I was immature. When I much later discovered a childlike interest in Rupert Bear and found out that the village headmaster in Nutwood was in fact not only a chimp, but Dr Chimp, that was manna from heaven indeed. How did a PhD, let alone a primate, come to be the head of a village school? Some things have no rational explanation.

Tim Grove had also endured the Buchanan regime at the College of Education and exchanged glances of suffused mirth with me when Mr B had got his tape recorder "all fankled". Tim had joined the Madras staff, initially at "the Burgh" in January 1965 after a short period teaching in the South of England and at Harris Academy in Dundee, and proved a very popular and effective colleague, as of course were a number of others. However I do not intend to discuss all my modern language stable-mates of that period or later, lest I wittingly, or worse unwittingly give offence. Not that such consideration has inhibited me in other cases, perhaps because it is one thing to comment on the peculiarities of people who are much older, senior or experienced, or no longer with us, but quite another to embarrass colleagues with whose work you have been involved or co-responsible for.

Ian Hendry was quite happy to leave the Kilrymont end of the operation to my colleagues and me, but I hankered after more stimulating work, and in 1969-70 was given a share of the Sixth Year French class, with whom I undertook the study of a Certificate of Sixth Year Studies (CSYS) topic on "Napoleon". The class was small and made up of former members of IH and the parallel class IM from 1964-5.

The previous summer I had driven, in a sort of exploratory preparation, my little white Renault 4TL down to Provence and the Côte d'Azur, where I visited the village of Lorgues again and the Gobert family, driving back up the mountainous "Route Napoléon" through the Alpes Maritimes, the same route from Golfe-Juan to Grenoble taken from 1-6 March 1815 on horseback by the Corsican ex-Emperor and his ever-growing band of soldiers and supporters after his escape from exile on Elba. His period of renewed power lasted 100 days until the defeat at Waterloo in June 1815. My journey was interesting but less momentous.

As well as travelling the Route Napoléon I had read up on Bonaparte. I had asked Dr Thompson what he thought the sixth year pupils would be likely to know already about the topic. He paused before replying, rubbed his bald pate and said in his fatherly way: "I should assume *tabula rasa*", ie a blank slate, which proved good advice.

Apart from teaching, I got involved in various other school activities, such as coaching the cross-country team. One of the runners from 1965-66, Ken Morris, lives in St Andrews after a career in the RAF, and he and his 9 year old son ran in the annual Boxing Day handicap in 2009, the latter winning the one lap event. Another, James "Curly" Reay, is a head teacher in Blackwater, South Australia and wrote a couple of years ago to say how he had enjoyed training and racing with our group in the Sixties, even though I remember him tripping on a country road and hurting his knees quite badly on the rough surface. Somehow we helped him struggle back to the showers and get cleaned up.

For a short period I was also the EIS [Educational Institute of Scotland] rep at South Street, at a time when most teachers did not really regard the Institute as a union, many feeling themselves too "professional" to take any form of effective action to improve pay and conditions. That was to change for good in the 1970s. The job of EIS rep was thus a sinecure, and I relinquished it after a year or so.

Every October schools had a week's break, a replacement for the "tattie holiday" that modern machinery in the potato fields was rapidly rendering unnecessary. Some adventurous teachers led expeditions to the Cairngorms, and I joined them, though my experience of hill-walking was negligible and my love of sleeping in a tent slight. Led by Donald Mackenzie ("Big Mac"), the long-serving head of PE Tom Croll and his wife and colleague Lena, as well as Mike Gill, a rather flamboyant and dashing Art teacher –

and that is not a euphemism but just refers to his ties, handkerchiefs and expensive tastes – and with me tagging along, we headed north in the school minibuses to Aviemore, Coylumbridge and points east, camping in a sloping field near Loch Morlich. I recall getting into a very bad temper one morning at breakfast when the toast was burnt. Donald Mackenzie laughed himself to tears at my tantrum, which was as quickly extinguished as it had flared up.

Every day we would climb up one of the hills – Braeriach, Cairn Gorm, Ben MacDhui, Cairn Toul come to mind – and sing our way along the last miles in the gloaming after a long day. On reaching the peak we usually saw very little because of the mist and rain, but that didn't matter. The cook back at base was usually Tom Croll, as he had problems with his feet after so many years teaching PE and couldn't march so far. We were soon tucking in to potatoes, soup, sausages or whatever else was on the menu, washing it down with mugs of tea and for the staff a bottle or two of beer. The first camping expedition I was on coincided with the General Election when Harold Wilson's incantation of the white heat of technology finally expelled Sir Alec Douglas-Home's government from office after what Labour called "thirteen years of Tory misrule". We sat up all night listening to the results on the radio, getting very excited as it became clear that change was on the way. I was a red-hot socialist in those days. The Madras head of mathematics, Lindsay Hodge, used to shake his head and say: "Aye, socialist at twenty, conservative at forty…" but that was never likely. Lindsay was a Liberal.

Before I started teaching I had envisaged that there would be a busy social life among the colleagues, with dinner parties, stimulating intellectual conversation, and so forth. The reality was that teachers were too busy to indulge in much of that sort of thing. However I made friends quickly with several colleagues and spent a lot of time with them. On most Friday evenings there was an auction at Ladybank, near Cupar, and my colleague Duncan Monteith lived there with his wife Linda and their family of four. I was regularly invited for a meal, after which Duncan and I would go along to hear the auctioneer in action. He spoke very very fast in comparison to his equivalent in the MacGregor's auction rooms in St Andrews.

Lena and Tom Croll lived at 6 Southfield, just off Kinnessburn Road, and kept open house of an evening. One of the most senior (in age) maths teachers, John [known as Johnnie] Mason, often came along with a box of cakes from Fisher and Donaldson, and Mike Gill, Donald Mackenzie, Ann McGhie (later Bridges) and I were also frequently there for a cup of coffee and a long chat in front of the fire. Sometimes one of the Croll daughters, Christine or Janette, would look in. It was a home from home that I much appreciated.

St Andrews was not a very politicised place, even among the students. In the 1920s the author Andrew Lang had evacuated his house in Queen's Gardens, fearing that striking coal miners would invade from Central and West Fife and attack, rob and murder him and his family. The general political mood of the decades since then had continued traditional and conservative. In 1968 the European continent was aflame with uprisings of one sort or another: in Kiel, Schleswig-Holstein, our partner school was barricaded by pupils to stop staff getting in, and there were general strikes in France; the "velvet revolution" took place in Czechoslovakia and was harshly suppressed after a false dawn. In Madras College, South Street, St Andrews some rebellious and iconoclastic senior pupils protesting against the established order climbed out of the music room window on a Friday afternoon and escaped into town.

There was a Friday evening demonstration when Enoch Powell came to speak to the University Conservative association at the Town Hall in 1968, soon after his "I see the Tiber run with blood" speech, and quite a few of us teachers joined the small crowd in Queen's Gardens to boo him as he got out of his car and went into the Town Hall, ignoring us completely. I'm not sure if that demonstration was even as effective as the escape from the music room – at least the pupil fugitives went for a coffee, but we just went home.

Mike Gill the art teacher got a new job as head of department in George Watson's College in Edinburgh. His own principal teacher in Madras was Magnus Dawson, a member of the Close Brethren sect, who because of his exclusive beliefs was unable to sit when non-believers were sitting, or stand when they were standing. He was a gifted engraver and a small quiet man, whose department had inherited Room 19 from Ian Hendry when a new extension was built on to the back of the South Street school in 1967-9. Mike Gill owned a charming though not completely modernised cottage in the village of Boarhills, some four miles east of St Andrews. I often visited him there, enjoying particularly the large living room with a beamed ceiling and an open fire blazing in a huge stone fireplace. A large watercolour of Aberdeen Harbour, done by Mike when he was at Art College, hung over the hearth. The toilet and bathroom were however incomplete, so that on cold days it was no pleasure to expose yourself to the icy blast.

Mike agreed that I could rent "Byways" from him on an annual basis, and I did that for more than two years. One of the conditions was that I should keep the large back garden in order or employ a neighbour to do so. I signally failed in both of these alternatives, so that Mike had to give me a severe telling-off at the end of the first summer in residence. I employed the neighbour thereafter.

I had attempted my driving test once, a year or two before, in St Andrews, and failed it. The instructor, the eternally patient Mr Bobby Campbell, was not at all to blame, as I was a very nervous pupil. When I was timidly approaching the West Port, a narrow medieval gateway, in the driving school's Austin A40, Mr Campbell used to encourage me with the words "Ye'd get the Queen Mary through there, Mr Macgregor." In the end it took me three attempts to secure the pink slip of success. I did not buy a car straight away, but continued to ride my red and white 50cc Honda motorbike, and even replaced it with a 90cc grey version. The 50cc bike occasioned my first traffic offence. I was giving a lift on the pillion seat to a French girl called Monique Cojean, the sister of our Breton assistant Michel, but was riding so slowly (because the bike was overloaded) that the police drew me over. After a few questions they found out that I had no M.O.T. certificate for the Honda, which I had very recently bought. I pled guilty as charged and was admonished.

I was not a born motorcyclist, and the 90cc bike was fast enough to be close to my frontier of fear. Riding these machines could be very cold if your journey exceeded about 20 minutes. I had discovered this in 1958, in fact, when I travelled pillion to Edinburgh on the Vespa of a fellow-runner called Graham Pearson. I was foolishly wearing a blazer and open-necked shirt, and when we eventually got to Craiglockhart to race against Edinburgh University, it was all I could do to get warmed up at all.

In 1969 I did buy a car, a dark blue Renault 4, about 5 years old. I swapped it two years later for a new white 4TL, and soon afterwards saw the old blue one in the West Port garage forecourt with its front wheels off and radiator stove in. The new owner had been involved in a head-on crash, which happily did not result in any fatalities. The national accident statistics at that time were far worse than today's. Compulsory seat belts had not long been introduced, and drink-driving was not yet regarded as seriously as it is now.

As time went on I became disenchanted with teaching at Kilrymont Road. The whole building was unpleasant, the work unexciting and on the whole unchallenging, and the staffroom dreary – or so I thought. Not all would have agreed with me. Teachers in Madras College were either South Street people or Kilrymont people, and I was unquestionably a South Street person. I decided to look for a way out. The virus of wanderlust had invaded my system.

Chapter 8

Barefoot in the Park

When I left university I decided to join Edinburgh Southern Harriers, but deferred signing up until after my season in the Var. For a short while after leaving school I had been a member of Octavians AC, a newly formed club that drew its membership from former pupils of eight Edinburgh schools. I only competed for them in the holidays for a couple of years in the late 1950s, usually, and without notable success, at 880 yards and the mile. In 1961, between graduation and departure for Germany I had tried a longer race, the Musselburgh 13½ mile road race, for which I prepared by cycling round the course – once! In my almost total ignorance of Scottish athletics, I did not realise just what a high quality field lined up that July evening. It included Joe McGhee (Shettleston Harriers), one of Scotland's sporting heroes since winning the 1954 Empire Games marathon in the heat of Vancouver. Joe had beaten Jim Peters, the English favourite who had gone too fast for the conditions and had collapsed in the stadium, rather like Dorando Pietri at the 1908 Olympics at the White City. McGhee felt ever after that he had never been given full credit for his victory. Fleet Street had embroidered the simple fact of his triumph with all sorts of nonsense intended to suggest that he was a second-rater who had been lucky. The journalists claimed for instance that he had been sitting by the roadside, ready to retire, or alternatively waiting for an ambulance, when he was brought the news of Peters's collapse, at which he got to his feet and struggled on. Peters, who had taken the world best down to 2hrs 17 mins 39 secs, was undoubtedly a superior marathon runner but on the day McGhee ran a more sensible race. If the distance had been 26 miles 85 yards rather than 385, Peters would have won. But it wasn't.

Also there was Andy Brown, the tough Motherwell YMCA Harrier, who had been the 1958 Scottish cross-country champion and was later in the summer to become Scottish native record holder for 3 miles. Norrie Ross (ESH) and Davie Simpson (Motherwell YMCA) were the other leading runners. By a miracle I got round in 5th place, to the excitement of my Octavian team-mates. Andy Brown was the man in form and led Ross and McGhee home, while Simpson was not far ahead of me.

Southern had the basis of a good team, and while I was of reasonable standard my presence didn't make a big difference. Over the season of 1963-4 the results were respectable but nothing more. In early April we travelled south to take part for the first time in the News of the World's flagship event, the twelve-stage London to Brighton relay. For some reason I travelled down a day early, and embarrassed myself by phoning up the organisers to ask if it would be all right to stay in the hotel near Hyde Park where our team would be putting up on the night before the race. I'm not sure what response I expected, but what I was told was that of course it would be fine as long as I paid for the extra night myself.

The race itself revealed what we should have expected, and perhaps did: we could put out a quite strong eight man team, but we did not have an extra four good runners. I had been worried before the race about an infected bruise on my right knee, incurred when I had very painfully tripped and fallen as I manoeuvred through a double gate near the finish of the Fernieside Relays in Edinburgh a few weeks before. Our manager had put me on the last leg into Brighton. I took over the baton in 20th place but managed to overhaul one team just before the last turning on to the promenade.

1964-5 was my second cross-country season with Edinburgh Southern Harriers. Form was inconsistent, and in hindsight it is clear that was because of the low mileage I was doing. The training diary for 1964 has been lost, but I note from the 1965 diary that in the first eight weeks of that year I ran only 357 miles, about 45 miles per week. Quite a lot of it must have been fast running, for there is no other way to explain how I was able to challenge seriously for a place in the Scottish cross-country team for the "International" at Ostend, Belgium.

The Scottish Championships were held as usual at Hamilton Park Racecourse. It was a sunny but very cold day in February. The team for the ICCU championship would be selected the day after the race, and the evening before I had gone through the top runners mentally ticking them off one by one to convince myself I had a chance: "I can beat him, I can maybe beat him…" Despite the cold I decided to copy Fergus Murray's example and run in bare feet, believing that over the long grass it would give me, with my short stride, an advantage. After the first couple of miles I was up with the leaders. Lachie Stewart gave me a rather surprised look as we sped round the small loop near the end of lap one.

As the race went on, I found myself running with Bill Allison, a New Zealander who had joined ESH for the duration of his year's stay in Edinburgh. Running together, we encouraged each other and in the end I beat him, or perhaps he allowed me to beat him, to the line in 5th place, making me a certainty for Ostend

Fergus's bare feet propelled him to victory, the second of three consecutive wins, and between us came Jim Alder, Lachie Stewart and Andy Brown. My feet were so cold afterwards that I had to be half-carried into the changing room and my icy feet rubbed back to reasonable warmth – but it was worth it!

Alastair Wood (Aberdeen AAC) and DFM try for a dead heat at Helensburgh 1965.

At least that's what I thought till I got to Ostend to find that heavy rain, as well as the previous junior race, had turned Ostend racecourse into a muddy quagmire, very different from Hamilton. And so while Jean Fayolle of France battled it out with England's Mel Batty for victory, I struggled home in 100th place, Bill Ewing being 102nd out of the 125 finishers. Nor did Fergus run very well in his bare feet. I wore spikes this time but could have saved myself the trouble. After the race the three of us took ourselves off to a frites stall and sat looking mournfully out at the drizzle as we chomped Belgium's top item of cuisine. Later that evening we attended the formal post-championship dinner and did the usual things like signing each other's menus and larking about.

After that discouraging race I decided to have a go at the marathon. Through the late spring of 1965, three of us in Edinburgh Southern Harriers decided to up the mileage. The other two were Ken Ballantyne, a top class miler and good cross-country and road runner, and Bill Allison, the long-haired New Zealander who had helped me qualify for Ostend. Like a lot of distance runners at that time we were heavily influenced by the training methods of Bill's compatriot Arthur Lydiard, who had coached Peter Snell and Murray Halberg in 1960 to Olympic gold medals in the 800m and 5000m and Barry Magee to a marathon bronze in Rome. In 1964 world record-holder Peter Snell recorded a double win over 800m and 1500m, and John Davies went home from Tokyo with the 1500m bronze.

Lydiard had started training seriously in 1944 aged 27 and experimented over the next few years on himself, running every day and clocking up as much as 250 miles per week. He discovered that when he combined distance and speedwork his marathon times and also his track times improved. *Run to the Top* (1962) became a distance runners' bible. Lydiard divided the year into phases during which big mileage, hill training and track work all had a place. The part of his teachings that had the biggest impact was the concept of running 100 miles a week.

That was what Ken, Bill and I were aiming for. Bill was already knowledgeable about Lydiard's methods and helped us avoid mistakes, such as doing the runs too fast. As we would be more than doubling our average weekly mileage, it was just as well that Ken and I had Bill's advice. I moved from 63 miles in the first week in April to 101, 108, 85, 84, and 85 again over the next five weeks.

The high mileage paid off. By late April I had bounced back into form. In the Clydesdale to Helensburgh 16 mile road race Alastair Wood (Aberdeen AAC) and I ran the last ten miles in the lead and crossed the line together although the officials didn't like that, and declared me the winner. "Ye pair o' sharkers" said one of them.

I entered the SAAA 10 mile track championship on May 1ˢᵗ at Seedhill, Paisley, an event last held in 1948. There were only twelve starters, and after two miles the race turned into a duel with Alistair Wood, whom I eventually dropped with a 61 second last lap to win by six seconds. My time of 50:23 was not brilliant, but at least I was an SAAA champion. Bill Murray (Greenock) was 3rd in 53:52. The victory gave me new heart, and I carried on putting in the miles with Ken Ballantyne and Bill Allison as before. As we got nearer to June 12th, the date of the SAAA marathon over an undulating course from Westerlands (Glasgow University's ground), to Dumbarton and back again, I got rather nervous. On 29th May, two weeks before the marathon, I had finished a distant second to

Ken Ballantyne (ESH) Stage 4, Edinburgh to Glasgow Relay 1965.

Fergus Murray in the East District 3 miles in a time of 13:57.6 to his 13:25.4, which was a Scottish National, All-Comers and Native record. Fergus had run in the Tokyo Olympic 10,000m the year before and had been following a Lydiard based routine for some time. On 15th May he had run his first marathon at Shettleston and had beaten the two-time SAAA marathon champion Wood by 33 seconds with a 2:18:30 clocking. These were the first two sub 2:20 marathons run in Scotland. The East District race had shown that I was nowhere near as fit or as fast as Fergus, but it was worth giving the marathon a proper try.

The moment of truth was getting ever nearer. The Aberdonian Wood had been Scottish Universities cross-country champion as long ago as 1956, when it was held at St Andrews. He was a fine middle distance track and cross-country runner for the RAF and Shettleston Harriers, but only started running marathons in 1962. In that first season he won the SAAA title, and came 2nd in the AAA race, thus qualifying to run for the UK in the European Marathon Championship in Belgrade, and there he was 4th in 2:23:18.8. In 1964 Alistair Wood had set an SAAA championship record of 2:24:00.

In view of all this, and my own total lack of experience at the event, the only sensible strategy was to try to stick to AJW as long as I could, with no idea of a target time. In those days there were very small marathon fields, maybe a couple of dozen at most. Apart from Fergus, most of Wood's challengers in Scotland up to now had been runners with much slower track times, for most track runners believed that if they ran marathons or did marathon-type training it would turn them into plodders. All that was changing, and changing fast.

Nor was there much reliable information on pre-marathon diet floating around. A few marathon runners even still believed that it was best to deprive oneself of liquid as long as possible. Nowadays athletes have gone to the other extreme of full hydration, as we did, with ingestion of carbohydrate gels during the race, risky though these may be to the digestion. However as I had found myself during my long runs dreaming of a jug of orange squash, at least I went to the start well hydrated, but without thinking of manipulating my diet in any other way. In any case I tended normally to eat a lot of bread and jam or marmalade, potatoes: in short, plenty of carbohydrate.

It was a bit nerve-wracking to set off with so little idea of what to expect. Alastair and I were quickly in the lead. At 3 miles I was being encouraged by ESH team-mates, including Jack White with his bugle, a frequent accompaniment to our team's endeavours. "Come on, Donald!" he shouted between blasts. "Surely they don't expect you to be dropped yet?" said AJW, in an obvious attempt to psych me out.

If it worked, it took some time. We were still together at the turn, and on the first six miles or so of the long trek back towards Glasgow. The rises and falls in that long, long Great Western Road slowly but surely began to take their toll on my upper leg muscles, and at around 21 miles Alastair tried a surge and managed to open a small gap which widened little by little. My team-mates urged me to keep going, and without them I might have given up. But somehow I didn't, and crawled into the stadium to cross the line in 2:22:24. There was an audience of about a dozen people, including a Daily Record photographer. Alastair, who waited at the finish to shake my hand, had finished in 2:20:46. Charlie McAlinden of Babcock and Wilcox was third in 2:26:25. "Never again!" was my first reaction as Dunky Wright, the radio reporter, SAAA official and three-time Olympian who had run at Paris, Amsterdam and Los Angeles, grabbed me for a comment.

The Lydiard training paid off also for Ken Ballantyne and Bill Allison. On June 5th Bill recorded 4:05.1 for the mile, and 8:45.0 for two miles just two days later; and on 21st July Ken ran 4:01.1, the best ever for a home Scot at that time. So much for those who said all those long runs would slow you down.

The rest of my running year lacked focus and was interrupted by injury and periods of loss of interest. After the SAAA 6 miles on 25th June where I was 4th in 29:19.4 to Fergus (28:33.4), Andy Brown (Motherwell) and Joe Reilly (Victoria Park), I went on holiday to south Germany, where I did little training, and returned pretty unfit. I began to put in long weekend runs, once over a 24 mile "murder run" from St Andrews over the hills to Anstruther, (nearly 10 miles) along to Crail (4 miles) and back the last 10 by Kingsbarns and Boarhills, all on road and at a hard pace. It took me 2hrs 24 minutes. After 5 or 6 weeks of this sort of thing, I developed a leg injury and ran spasmodically for the next month with five or six days off at a time. It was surprising that I was able to run 33:37 for the long sixth stage of the Edinburgh to Glasgow relay on 20th November, in which ESH came a disappointing 4th.

Through December Ken Ballantyne, Graham Stark and a few other ESH runners picked up the distance again. At the end of January 1966 ESH were sending a team of four to Arlon in the southern, French-speaking part of Belgium (la Wallonie) to take part in the European Club Cross-country Championship for the first time. I ran 301 miles in December. Ken and

Winner of SAAA championship six miles, June 1966.

I brought in the New Year with 7th and 10th place finishes (69:12 and 69:47), in the famous Morpeth to Newcastle 13 ½ mile road race, following that with two weeks at almost 100 miles. We hoped for great things at Arlon on 23rd January, but all of us – Ken, Graham, John Rough and I - ran below par. I had my spike torn off after three miles and was forced to retire from the race. The Edinburgh Evening News pink sports edition had printed a photo of us posing on the aircraft steps when we left, but we came back anything but conquering heroes.

1966 was not a good year for me as far as running was concerned. The Arlon race turned out to have set the tone for the rest of the year. My target was to get into the Scottish team for the Empire Games (the last time they were called that) in Kingston, Jamaica. It was a very slim hope. I trained hard through March and April but somehow was not "on song", my best performance being second place to Andy Brown in the Clydebank to Helensburgh "16". 84:22 and 84:40 were our times. On the track I raced twice, both races on the same afternoon and both very poor. I kidded myself on that the training was going well, but it wasn't.

In the month or so before travelling to London for the Polytechnic marathon from Windsor to Chiswick, on the results of which the Scottish selection on a hot day, Saturday 11th June, depended, I had been doing regular runs with Ian Robertson (Dundee Hawkhill), the son of Charlie Robertson, a road running star of the 1940s who lived in Newport on Tay. For some reason I did a lot of training on the grass track at University Park, for instance sets of 12 x 220 yards in around 30 seconds and or 12 x 440 yards in less than 70 seconds. None of it helped.

Hope evaporated more or less at once as we set off from Windsor Castle in a temperature of about 80 degrees Fahrenheit, plus high humidity. I felt ropey right from the start and became more and more dizzy and overcome by the heat, so that the race turned into a nightmare and I dropped out at around 21 miles. I slunk home to Roger Cressy's house in the outskirts of London, and recall sitting shivering in the Tube, feeling ill and hoping I wouldn't throw up in the compartment. Meanwhile, Jim Alder had not been adversely affected by the heat and had qualified for Kingston, Jamaica. The Empire Games race was also held in hot conditions, and Jim performed miracles to defeat England's Bill Adcocks in the last lap, shouting "Geronimo!" as he went into the lead past an unresisting Adcocks. Alder had been well ahead approaching the stadium, but the marshal on duty had gone off to see the Duke of Edinburgh arrive and Jim had gone the wrong way before being re-directed.

My mileage went right down over the next 12 days as I recovered from the Poly experience. But the silver lining did come on the thirteenth day, Friday 24th June, when against any predictions, if anyone made them, I won the SAAA six miles title at Meadowbank in 29:28.6. The race was a struggle over the cinder track between Dick Wedlock (Shettleston), Pat McLagan (Victoria Park) and me, and the lead changed several times until I got away from McLagan with a lap and a half to go, winning by nearly 12 seconds. The time was a poor one, and ranked me only 5th in Scotland at the end of 1966. That was nearly two minutes slower than Alder's 27:30.6 set in London in July. But I was Scottish champion, and celebrated with my friend and fellow teacher Donald Mackenzie by downing a couple of Carlsberg Specials at the Murrayfield Hotel. It was there that I met one of our former gym teachers at Stewart's, Mr Mason, known as Andy, who said of me to Donald Mackenzie "He was one of my first". Well, maybe. And then again, maybe not.

I spent much of the summer in Loquémeau, a small fishing village in Brittany, where I had been invited to stay by Michel Cojean, a former French language assistant at school, and then went on to the Rhein-Mosel area of Germany to take part in a Goethe-Institut (Scottish-German Society) course for teachers. While there I kept training, but restricted what I did to fit in with the course. The Goethe-Institut is responsible for promoting the German language and culture round the world and organises many courses. This one was in Trier, a city founded 2000 years ago by the Romans. Its most famous landmark is the Porta Nigra, the Black Gate. An American Jesuit from New York who taught German in the Bronx had been assigned along with me to stay with a couple who turned out to be very pious, and almost venerated the Jesuit, who was a kind man who had a bad stammer and almost as bad spoken German. The language uses three genders and four cases, but the Jesuit had great difficulty with these. Our hosts, living as they did in one of the most Roman Catholic parts of Germany, didn't care – why should they have? – but I was clearly not in the same class as the priest because I was not a true believer.

After the course participants were offered a five-day visit to Berlin, including a day in the eastern part of that divided city. I did not on this occasion take the Goethe-Institut people up on their kind offer, but the Jesuit did. I heard later that he caused a minor incident at Checkpoint Charlie when he was asked if he had a visa. "Ich war noch nie in die…der Zone", [I haven't been in the Zone before] he replied, to the fury of the border guard for whom East Berlin was not "die [Sowjet] Zone" but "Berlin, Hauptstadt der DDR".

Back home, I gave up training seriously for the rest of the season and spent far too much time in the pub, despite my Madras colleague PE teacher Colin McLeod – himself not unknown to take a tipple – telling me to pull myself together and try for the 1968 Mexico Olympics. That was far from my thoughts after the Poly, but 1967 was to prove a turning point in my career as a marathon runner.

The AAA championship event was to be held at a remote location – Baddesley Colliery, near Nuneaton. The SAAA had sent a Scottish squad, accompanied by Hon General Secretary R.B. Forman, known as 'Rab', a bluff, loud-voiced, outspoken official who was a PE lecturer at Moray House teacher training college in Edinburgh. The race turned out to be a golden moment for Scottish runners, who took the first three places – Jim Alder 1st, Alastair Wood 2nd and me 3rd (2:17:19), encouraged by Rab standing in a car shouting "Come on, Duncan!". I found the energy to correct him.

How had I made this considerable improvement? I had trained pretty hard over the spring and early summer, but attendance at a summer course for teachers in Vichy in the Massif Central helped me to acclimatise to heat, and I put myself through sessions like 30x200m, or 4x600m downhill in the morning followed by a 15 mile steady run in the late afternoon. On return to Edinburgh I had a bit more speed than usual –in one session at Meadowbank's cinder track with Ken Ballantyne and Graham Stark we managed 5x400 in under 60 with a lap jog – much faster than I had ever done before. On Murrayfield's 5 lap to the mile grass track I ran an 8:58 two miles, just ahead of a 17 year old lad called Ian Stewart from Birchfield Harriers, Birmingham, and well ahead of Andy and Alex Brown (Motherwell YMCAH), and various others who normally beat me.

From 1965-66 onwards I travelled through regularly to Edinburgh at weekends to race, went to Saturday night parties round the Meadows, and took part in the long Sunday runs from 78 Morningside Drive, known as "The Zoo". The parties seemed mostly to be held at the flats of nurses, librarians, social workers, or teachers, and after the party had come to an end you (and sometimes me) either walked some girl home, parted on the doorstep, and then walked home yourself, in my case stopping at an all-night baker's near Haymarket to collect warm rolls and take them back to Kaimes Road, a further two and a half miles to the west. Sometimes I could buy an early edition of the Sunday Post. The bits I liked best in that newspaper were Oor Wullie, The Broons, and Merry Mac's Fun Parade, a collection of jokes.

The next morning I would take myself over to "The Zoo" ready for the long Sunday run at about 11 am. 78 Morningside Drive was owned by Professor Neil McCormick, an SNP activist, and let out to a group of students, who in the mid-to-late Sixties and early Seventies were all runners. The house was a magnet for other runners, mostly students but also including people like myself who could be classed as young professionals. I met John Bryant there, a young Oxford graduate from Somerset who had joined the staff of the Edinburgh Evening News as a sub-editor. I had been training with other "Zoo" inmates for about a year or possibly two. Fergus Murray, the hardest trainer, was known as "The Beast"; Martin Craven, "The Crab", who ran with us later had a curious running gait; and hairy-chested Chris Elson was known as "The Bear".

John has since told me that when the others said that I would be coming running the next weekend, they said he would like me because I was "brainy". If I was brainy, he was brainier, but in any case it was the start of a lifelong friendship. We met in late 1965, just around the time a gatecrasher to one of the Zoo parties pushed his way in and knocked out two of John's teeth when John tried to eject him. What worried John most was that two days later he was due to meet his fiancée Carol's father for the very first time, and was very concerned about the impression he would create if he turned up looking as if he had been in a fight. However Edinburgh's dentists saved the day and Carol and John married in 1966 and had two children. They did me the great honour of asking me to be one of the two godfathers of their first, Matthew, born on 7th July 1974. For the christening I travelled down to Haselbury Plucknett, where John had grown up in the Swan Inn, of which his mother was the licensee. His childhood involved drawing pints, checking deliveries of barrels of beer and cider, as well as milking cows, harvesting apples and other rural pursuits as well as winning a scholarship to a maintained grammar school and from there attending Queen's College, Oxford. There he had a distinguished athletics career over events from the mile via the steeplechase to the three miles and cross-country. He is a member of Thames Hare and Hounds, the oldest running club in the world (1875) but when he came to Edinburgh joined ESH.

A typical Sunday run from The Zoo started very slowly, after the previous night's excesses, and followed a route westwards through Currie to Balerno, then up a series of three hills known to us as "Baby Bear", "Papa Bear" and "Granpa Bear", or the toughest one just "Granpa", then through a gap in the Pentland Hills leading after about 15 miles in total to Flotterstone on the A701. From there we ran back towards Fairmilehead on the pavement or road, and the pace would often pick up considerably on the downhill section towards Morningside.

We usually ran for around two hours and covered 20-22 miles. The longest Sunday run I ever went on was about 34 miles and took me 3 hours and 40 minutes, at the end of which I collapsed on the carpet. That will give the reader a chance to go back in time to the 18th century while I recover.

Chapter 9

Talking about my Generation

Our family does not descend directly from the most famous of Macgregors, Rob Roy, the third son of Donald Glas (Grey or Pale) MacGregor of Glen Gyle. However there is a connection. A verifiable tradition is that Rob Roy, when a young man of about twenty, came to the aid of Patrick Grant, a flamboyant local chieftain much farther east in Aberlour and Knockando, and left two strong runners on Speyside to bear word to Rob Roy if the MacIntoshes annoyed Grant.

The MacIntoshes and the Grants had fallen out over the water supply to their mills. Around 1690 Patrick Grant had sent for Rob Roy when the MacIntoshes threatened to burn Grant's mill. Rob Roy appeared with a large band of Macgregors and between them they burned the MacIntoshes' own mill. All that reminds me of the old joke, quoted in one of my father's collections of humorous Scots stories, about the tourist who comes into the competitors' tent at a Highland Games held on a particularly dreich day and asks "Does anyone have a mackintosh to cover my wife?", whereupon a burly clansman steps forward: "I'm a Macgregor – will I no dae?"

The "planted" runners settled down as farmers, though it was not an easy life. The great-grandson of one of those runners was my ancestor James Macgregor, born in 1789. The manuscript of James's account of his life, and of 'My Northern Journey', a report of his trip back to his roots at Upper Ringorum Farm, Knockando which he had left for Glasgow in 1811, are in the National Library. My children and I have photocopies of the diaries.

As a teenager James made a terrestrial globe of wood, and took it to the local aristocrat, the Duke of Gordon in Huntly, who was initially doubtful that the boy had made it himself. Once convinced, he lavished praise on him and sent him for a term to the University in Aberdeen to study Natural Philosophy (physics). After that James returned to the farm, but saw that the jobs he had to do – repairing water mills etc – were old technology. The Industrial Revolution was beginning and he wanted to be part of the new age. So he took his globe and headed on foot through the mountains to Glasgow, where he found a job in the district of Tradeston with the firm of James Watt junior, son of the famous engineer. Macgregor eventually rose to manage it. He married twice, his first wife and two sons dying within a very few years. He "fell in with" a second young woman and married her, the marriage proving fruitful, as my existence indicates.

In the mutinous post-Napoleonic period in Scotland James was terrified of being thought a rebel. This was the period when keen Unionists liked to refer to Scotland as North Britain, often writing "N.B." on envelope addresses, though "S.B." is notable by its absence from the records. Plus ça change…but at least we have a Parliament. William Pitt's friend Henry Dundas, Viscount Melville, George III's viceroy, ruled Scotland like a police state – he was known as "Henry the Ninth" - until a financial scandal cost him office. To give him credit, he was active in opposing the slave trade, while on the debit side making sure that Scottish weavers and other workers continued to be treated not much differently.

A monument to Dundas, modelled loosely on Trajan's Column in Rome, stands in the centre of St Andrew Square, Edinburgh, from where he can look down on George Street, named for the monarch. Raised "by the voluntary contributions of the officers, petty officers, seamen and marines of these united kingdoms", the column was designed in 1821 by William Burn, who was advised by the noted lighthouse engineer Robert Stevenson (1772 - 1850), grandfather of author Robert Louis Stevenson (1850-94), after residents of the square expressed concern about the adequacy of the foundations to support a column of such height. A statue of Dundas was added to the top in 1828. The monument is 42.6m (140 feet) in height and weighs 1500 tons. By comparison Nelson's column in Trafalgar Square was put up between 1840 and 1843 and is 51.5m (169 feet) including the 5.5m statue of the heroic Horatio.

James became a member of the conservative "Auld Lichts" in the Kirk, and was elected an elder. He joined the militia, railed in a letter to his son about the dangers of joining a "combination" or trade union, of marrying someone who couldn't look after the household, of not praying daily or else Damnation and Eternal Hell Fire were inevitable. He suffered from black moods, especially in the mornings, which unlike his religious fervour and conservatism have partially been genetically passed on, though I have almost lost them, for which I am most grateful to whatever agency controls these things.

James's autobiography begins quite fully, but deteriorates in the last twelve years up to the final entries into an account of how much he paid for things he gave to various in-laws, relatives etc. The amounts expended on his trip North in 1836, such as the cost of coaches, tips, gifts to nephews, nieces, and to such as the "7 bastards – to each 1/-" produced by one of his sisters, are given precisely. He mentions the death of his mother but not that of his father. We can only speculate. He himself died in 1852.

Among public events referred to are the erection of the statue to Sir John Moore of Corunna in George Square, Glasgow, and to the execution of the 56-year old weaver James Wilson, sentenced to be hanged, drawn and quartered (though only the first was carried out) for alleged sedition and treason in 1822 on Glasgow Green. The hangman was booed by the vast crowd, though James doesn't mention that. He refers also to the smashing of windows during the riots prompted by the divorce of Queen Caroline and King George IV, who had just succeeded his porphyria-ridden father in 1820. The unhappily-married Caroline – her husband called for a glass of brandy when he first met her, could only bring himself to have sexual intercourse with her three times, and made a will leaving her one shilling with all the rest going to his morganatic wife Maria Fitzherbert - was a figurehead for the growing radical movement that demanded political reform and opposed the unpopular George.

In the years 1793 to 1817 Britain was at war with France, ruled for much of that time by Napoleon. The British governments were repressive and saw a French sympathiser at every street corner. A group called the United Scotsmen was formed to promote vote by secret ballot, universal male suffrage, the right to vote and annual elections.

With the end of the war came recession and unemployment. As in the 1930s, but much worse, wages were cut. For instance from 1800 to 1808 the wages of weavers were halved. Even bread was a luxury and it was folly to complain.

On Sunday April 1st, 1820, a bill was posted on the streets of Glasgow, Dumbarton, Paisley, Stirling and Kilsyth calling for a general strike to sweep away the present form of government. The British Crown had a rebellion on its hands. On Monday, April 2nd, the government called for all shops to be closed and everyone was to stay in their homes. Most of the weaving communities went on strike.

On April 8th a royal decree was posted at Glasgow Cross. It offered 500 pounds reward for the authors of the treasonable document of April 1st. The first arrest was that of James Wilson of Strathaven, a weaver who had been of a radical mind for years. He had carried a banner during the strike stating "Scotland Free or a Desert".

Wilson was taken from his home to Hamilton Barracks on a charge of high treason. On July 20th, 1820 he was formally charged in the high court of Glasgow.

The trial was a mockery of justice. He pled not guilty, but on the second day a verdict was already announced. The sentence was to be hanged, have his head cut off and his body cut into quarters. Wilson rose in the dock and said, "I commit my sacred cause, which is that of freedom, to the vindication of posterity." On the 30th August 1820, dressed in prison uniform, he was led to his fate on Glasgow Green. He was buried in Strathaven as a revered patriot.

Much more information about the background to the period is to be found on the website of The 1820 Society, which I commend to readers. The story of the weavers' rebellion survived only by being passed down by word of mouth within the families. Only recently did it become part of the history course taught in Scottish secondary schools.

After James, the Macgregors were engineers for two generations. James's son, my great-grandfather, worked for a biscuit manufacturer, Carr's of Carlisle, but Carr sacked him when he was found helping an aged fellow-worker sweep snow off the factory steps. "I pay you to be my manager, not to sweep snow", said "Ebenezer" Carr.

One of my ancestors on my grandmother's side met a sad end. On 7th May 1883 William Forbes, my great great grandfather, died at his home in Langholm at the age of 55, a year after being shot in the region of the kidneys by a sporting gun carelessly fired across the public highway where Forbes was pursuing his occupation of colporteur for the Bible Society of Edinburgh. The shooting party consisted of members and friends of the family of the Duke of Buccleugh.

William Forbes was known and respected throughout the Borders as a devout Christian and propagator of the gospel. The Duke and Duchess of Buccleugh spent part of each year at Langholm Lodge near the town. The Duchess was grieved at the accident and according to my great grandfather's account to my father, sent tokens of her sympathy to the widow in the form of hothouse grapes. There was no mention of money. The Bible Society awarded the victim eight shillings per week which may have continued to be paid to Mrs Margaret Forbes until she later remarried.

No criminal charge against whoever shot William Forbes was ever brought.

No wonder I'm a liberal with socialist leanings.

There is more to tell: on 18th October 1886, four years after the gunshot wounds to William Forbes, one of the shooting party of 1882, the Lord Eskdale, Walter Henry Montagu-Douglas Scott, Earl of Dalkeith, son and heir-apparent of the Duke of Buccleugh, was instantly killed by the accidental discharge of his own rifle while deer-stalking in Achnacarry Forest, Inverness-shire. He was 25 years of age.

On 18th September 1894 Viscount Drumlanrig, Francis Archibald Scott, a near relation to the above, was killed by the accidental discharge of his gun while game-shooting at Quantock, Somerset. The peerage became extinct on his death. He was 27. As he was only 15 at the time of William Forbes's death he may or may not have been trusted with a lethal weapon but he was probably of the party. But by another strange coincidence his grandfather Archibald William, Marquis of Queensberry, aged 40, was also killed by the accidental discharge of his gun while game-shooting at Kinmount, Dumfriesshire on 6th August 1858.

My paternal grandfather, David Macgregor, was also an engineer. He married an Edinburgh lass called Edith Forbes, whose father was a widower and lived in Edinburgh in a sandstone tenement off London Road. David and Edith stayed near Gretna and had two children – Forbes, born 13th July 1904 – a Wednesday's child born just one day short of four weeks after "Bloomsday" - and Margaret (Peggy), a couple of years later. In 1910 David their father was on an engineering job at Gareloch when he fell ill, supposedly having strained his heart helping a woman carry a sack of coal. He lingered a few days but then died, leaving Edith and her two children. She decamped back to Edinburgh and the three of them were looked after by the Old Testament figure of William Forbes, son of the Bible Society colporteur. He died aged

93 and his favourite sayings, according to my father, were "Owe no man anything but love" and "Tell the truth and shame the Devil". He might have had a third, from Paul's Epistle to the Romans: "Vengeance is mine; I will repay, saith the Lord."

Chapter 10

The Russians are our Brothers

The reward for our good showing in the 1967 AAA championship was that Martin Craven, who was also a member of ESH as well as of Kendal AC, his local club, and I were invited by the British Amateur Athletic Board to represent the UK in the historic Košice Marathon in Czechoslovakia on Sunday October 1st 1967. That only gave us five weeks to recover from the AAA race and to prepare for our first race in a British vest, which was not, in the light of experience, anywhere near enough. I should have just reduced the training to minimal levels, but instead fell between two stools by running 55 miles in the first week after the AAA run, then 80 miles with a 14.5 road race at Dunblane (second to Alex Brown of Motherwell but ahead of his elder brother the great cross-country runner Andy). There ensued a feeble week of 27 miles and a 70 mile week concluding with attendance at Ken and Doreen Ballantyne's wedding in Penrith, a very happy occasion. During the last week I eased off at last with 13, 7, 5, 6, and 4 mile runs in St Andrews and Edinburgh before flying to Prague via Heathrow on Saturday 30th September.

This was the 37th international race, billed since the Second World War as the "maratona mieru" [peace marathon] and had been first held in 1929. It numbered among its previous winners the great Ethiopian athlete Abebe Bikila. The steeplechase silver-medallist from Tokyo 1964, Maurice Herriott had been selected to compete in the "Grand Prix of the East Slowak Iron Works" steeplechase, part of the track and field meeting held in conjunction, and our team manager was a venerable north of England cross-country official. There were around 130 starters from 13 countries, most of them Eastern European, but with prominent entries from Ethiopia (Gebru Meravi, 6th in Mexico), Nedo Farčič (Yugoslavia), Jeffrey Reneau (USA), and Aad Steijlen (Netherlands), as well as the Soviet Union (Anatoli Sucharkov, Boris Dergachov, and Viktor Baikov) and Hungary (Janos Pintér and Attila Tormassi). I had heard of practically none of them.

Martin and I lined up in our tracksuits, mine a rather nasty royal blue nylon model that left friction burns on my neck after a long run, on a damp but warm morning (22-26 degrees C) behind a placard saying "Vel'. Britania", short for Velka Britania, wearing numbers 33 and 32. The traditional course started in

Košice October 1967.

the stadium and led through the outskirts of the town to the village of Seña on the Hungarian border some 13 miles away to the east, and straight back again. The route was more or less flat, so that the wind played a prominent role in determining whether or not the times would be fast. In 1967 there was a westerly breeze wind on the way out, so that the finishing positions would very likely be decided over the second half.

Košice is a very old town, situated at 211m above sea-level in a valley overlooked by the Slovak Ore Mountains (Erzgebirge) to the west and the Slanec hills to the east. It was at one time the second biggest city in Hungary. After the creation of the Czechoslovak Republic after World War I, the population grew from 50,000 to around 80,000, but during the period of the "Dictate of Vienna" [1938-44] when Slovakia was occupied by Hitler's Hungarian ally Admiral Horthy, Košice became a frontier town and lost one third of its population. In January 1945 it was liberated by the IV Ukrainian army and became the seat of the first Czechoslovak government on liberated soil. By 1967 there were 120,000 residents, several factories, three universities and many other cultural and scientific centres in operation, making the town the centre of the economic and industrial development of East Slovakia.

Over the previous 36 marathons there had been a distinguished cast list. The record for the course was held by Leonard ("Buddy") Edelen (USA) with 2:15:09.6. Edelen had held the world best for 364 days in 1963 with a 2:14:28 win in the Polytechnic Windsor to Chiswick race, a time eclipsed on the same course by Basil Heatley (UK) with 2:13:55. Other prominent past winners at Košice had been European champion Sergei Popov (USSR) in 1959, and double Olympic champion Abebe Bikila (1961). Only four men (Edelen and Popov, plus Viktor Chudomel (ČSSR) and Gyula Tóth (Hungary) had broken 2:20.

Tracksuits discarded, a group of 17, including Martin Craven and me, formed from the start and remained bunched together until shortly before the turn. By 20 km, reached in around 1:21:00, a cohort of five - Nedo Farčič, who was running in the colours of VIK Västeras, Sweden, Meravi, Sucharkov, Craven and Baikov – had taken 300m off the next group – Fink (GDR), Steijlen, Derkachov, Pintér and me. The wind was now behind us, and the pace crept up. The leaders reached 35km in 1:54:22, and Farčič and Meravi managed to break away from the other three. By the finish Nedo Farčič was away and clear for his biggest ever win, up to then or indeed later, in 2:20:53.8. The Ethiopian followed just over a minute behind (2:21:58.2) and then came a procession of nine further runners all under 2:25, the last being D.F.Macgregor in 2:24:54.2. Martin was 4th in 2:23.14.0. Somehow neither of us felt able to do more than just keep going over the last 15 km or so, no doubt because we had not recovered from Baddesley. I was disappointed and did not quite realise that the last stretch at Košice often has this effect even on runners a lot better than me. I would live and learn.

I thought I must have blown my chances of further BAAB selections. After Košice I eased right off, with a week in the Cairngorms with the school, then continued to train and race in the usual seasonal cross-country and road relays through October and November: the Kingsway relays in Dundee (3rd on 1st leg, team 6th); East District Relays at Newcraighall (6th fastest, team 3rd); the Edinburgh to Glasgow Relay (2nd fastest on stage 4, team 4th).

Fergus and I did a particularly long run of 25 miles the Sunday before the E to G, and the Sunday 21 from the Zoo continued. At the Madras 2nd year dance on 19th December, just before the Christmas holidays, the children were invited to guess how long it would take me to run round the 5 mile Mount Melville circuit. The pupil who guessed the time to the nearest minute was to win a

Gareth Bryan-Jones wins AAA title at White City 1968 (ED Lacey).

prize. I ran just outside 27 mins but hurt my foot and needed three days off training. More successful had been the stunt I performed the previous year at the 1st year dance, riding in on a child's tricycle in a Batman costume.

The club's disappointing fourth position in the 1966 E to G resulted in a changing room coup d'état, for we runners held the officials responsible by putting the wrong runners on the eight stages. These were of varied length, and it was possible to make a big difference to the result by not starting fast enough or by putting a weak runner on a crucial stage. The first leg was from outside Fettes College in Edinburgh to the Maybury Roadhouse, about 5.5 miles. The general tendency of leg 1 was uphill, for there were steady drags up the long stretch to the Queensferry Road and then from the Barnton Hotel to the Craigmount junction.

The second stage was regarded as crucial. A club could make up ground after a poor first leg, but a strong run over the second six mile relay along the A8 into Broxburn was essential if a team was to move up. Leg 3 was about 4.5 miles over a hilly stretch and was usually allocated to one of the weaker runners. It was then necessary to put another strong runner on the fourth stage and also on the fifth stage on high ground up to Forestfield Inn, frequently snow- or frost-bound. The Inn was one of the places where race officials used to foregather to take some well-earned liquid refreshment.

Next came the "long sixth stage" down to Airdrie Cross, supposedly 7 miles, and the traditional leg for a team's strongest runner. The record for the leg was gradually brought down over the many years I participated in the E to G from 33 minutes to under 31. Of course as in any point-to-point relay the wind plays a huge part, and stage records could only be achieved with a following wind.

The two final stages were relatively "easy", but many tough battles were fought out on them into Shettleston (5.5 miles) and over the final relay through the eastern part of the city of Glasgow, with many turns and twists, to Royal Exchange Square just up from what is now the Glasgow Gallery of Modern Art (GOMA).

After 44 miles the isolated runners would loom out of the gloaming, baton in hand, to cross the line in triumph, disappointment or resignation. Each year only twenty teams were invited, although occasionally one or two foreign clubs were permitted to run. The race had official sanction: the Lord Provosts of both cities, or their representatives, handed over a beribboned baton to the first runner from the previous year's winning team outside Fettes College and by some careful management received the same baton from the winning team's last runner in Royal Exchange Square.

Stewards or police were stationed at every roundabout or turn over the route and with very occasional exceptions no "incidents" took place. One that affected ESH was when Ken Ballantyne was accidentally touched by a car on stage 7 and forced to abandon the race. Miraculously no other accidents were recorded, for there was a constant stream of cars or mini-buses ferrying runners to the start of their stages in time to warm up, and that clearly interfered with normal traffic. The race had originally started from St Andrew Square near the Dundas column on a Saturday but was moved to a Sunday start from Fettes College main entrance so that the roads would be emptier.

Eventually the SAL Commission and the police had had enough of the stream of race followers dodging in and out of lay-bys or parking where they felt like it to permit supporters or athletes to jump in and out, and banned the race. Like the 12-stage London to Brighton, it was a great loss. The Scottish six stage relay championship that replaced it has never had the gritty glamour or excitement of the magnificent "E to G" which started in the 1930s.

Ironically, as journalists so often write when they mean "through bad luck", I had a persistent Achilles tendon injury from 27th October 1969 until 7th December – my longest ever period off training - and so could not take part in the E to G that year. However, John Bryant took my place in the team and won – at last – the coveted winners' medals, which showed Edinburgh Castle and the Royal Exchange.

1968 began with a very good run in the annual Morpeth to Newcastle 13.5 miler. Fergus drove down at 3 in the morning in his self-assembled kit sports car and won by 8 seconds in 65:01 from Jim Alder, who was well clear of John Caine (Gateshead H) (65:47) and Alistair Blamire (ESH) (66:00) That was just one second in front of me and 3 ahead of Keith Angus (Sheffield).

If I had hoped for great things in 1968, an Olympic year, the three Fates must have been listening and cackling away in the underworld. It turned out to be a year to forget. The 25 miler that Fergus took me round on February 4th above Carnoustie could have stood symbolically for the season ahead. We had barely covered three miles when a car driver covered us from head to toe in freezing slush; by the end we were chilled to the marrow and my fingers froze even in their gloves. 2 hours 26 minutes was a long time to be out at that time of year, but the mileage continued high, with weeks of 87, 85, 91, 91, 102 and 98 before the "National" at dear old Hamilton racecourse. But I was jinxed: despite finishing 6th over a course that included hurdles, I was only made non-travelling reserve for the Scottish team to go to Tunis for the "International". In the same way I had narrowly missed out on a trip in 1966 to Rabat in Morocco, or "Rabbit" as some of the Scottish officials pronounced it – rather like the groundsman at University Park, St Andrews who saw me scurrying round day after day and pronounced that "that Macgregor – he's runnin' roun' there like a fuckin' rabbit".

The selectors opted to pick Andy Brown, whom I had narrowly beaten. It was a sensible decision, as Andy was much the more experienced and reliable performer. I was not too disappointed, as I had experienced the start of the "International" at Ostend and knew I could never live with that sort of blazing speed. I would have been unquestionably "due for a bad'un", to use Jim Alder's marathoner's mantra – defeatist but true.

The target for the season had to be Olympic selection.

Font Romeu main building 1968.

After the National I started serious build-up training for the AAA race in Wales in the early summer, with 503 miles noted between 25th February and 31st March. Vaulting ambition o'erreached itself however when I went south to Loughbough for the AAA 10 miles championship and had to drop out after two miles with a sore back. The pace was just too fast and my weak lower back muscles couldn't handle it, but I was still able to run another hour and a half back for the 14 miles back to where I was staying! The mood was punctured though, and mileage fell away drastically as I tried to repair the back weakness through stretching and exercises.

Gradually I regained some form, winning a 3 miles against Pat McLagan (Victoria Park) on 27th April by 10 seconds in 14:18, and on the 11th May getting away from John Linaker (Pitreavie AC) over the last few miles of the Edinburgh to North Berwick 22.6 mile road race. The course had a generally downhill tendency and I was delighted to go under 2 hours, recording 1:59:46 to set a course record. John was 2nd 28 seconds back, well ahead of W.B.Mather, a tough Teviotdale Harrier, in 2:06:54. The gap between 2nd and

3rd demonstrates that it was a two man race. My time at 20 miles was 1:46:59, and I averaged 4:54 per mile over the last 2.6 miles. I felt full of confidence.

Adding to this was the fact that I had been invited by the BAAB to join a large group (over 60) of endurance athletes going to Font Romeu in the Pyrenees to help find out more about the effects of altitude training. The "management" was headed by R.B. "Rab" Forman, the SAAA Hon General Secretary, accompanied by the suave John Le Masurier ("Hello. I'm John Le Mas...") and Northerner Denis Watts, both senior coaches. We flew out on May 13th to Bilbao.

Squire Yarrow, the AAA President, Ray Watson (a physiologist) and I were delayed on arrival because we were involved in problems with the Spanish customs office. The Spanish and UK governments were caught up at the time in a crisis over Gibraltar, and the customs people refused to let us bring in a few cases of Complan or some similar cereal-based food. I recall arguing in French with an official wearing sunglasses about the matter, and him completely ignoring me. In the end he relented and we drove off to join the rest in Font Romeu. I was there also on interpreter duty as no one else spoke reasonable French.

The Font Romeu complex was built as a high-altitude complex for youngsters suffering from asthma as well as for promising sportspeople. The main building was a "gratteciel" of many storeys, with associated restaurants, gyms, and swimming facilities at lower level. The paths and roads round about gave access to reasonable running territory, though exposed. Foolishly I did not record much in my training diaries other than the runs I did, and so will have to depend on my memory for much else.

Rab Forman had an idea at the end of the first week that I did not agree with. He summoned the six Scottish runners and announced his plan that "the six Scots boys" should get together and go for dinner with him, leaving the rest of the party to eat in the refectory. I said I thought that might prove divisive, and didn't want to do it. Rab looked at me for a moment in disbelief: "Hmpph! You'd start a quarrel in an empty room!" The dinner did not take place.

We eased into serious running in the bright sunny weather, and as the days passed, so the lists of people I trained with grew: Jim Hogan, Dick Taylor, Ricky Wilde, Mike Tagg, Mel Edwards, Ian Stewart, Bill Ewing, Mike

General Strike, Font Romeu, 1968.

McLean, Maurice Herriott, John Hillen, Tony Ashton are all mentioned in my diary, people who all possessed running talent and potential.

Two examples: Jim Hogan had held Abebe Bikila for 30km in Tokyo in 1964, and after a series of drop-outs in big races had to everyone's astonishment and pleasure won the European Marathon championship in 1966 at Budapest – running for the UK instead of Ireland, in whose colours he had quite often dropped out. Maurice Herriott had dominated the UK steeplechase rankings for years and had won the silver in Tokyo, behind the great Belgian Gaston Roelants. The first Briton to "topple" Maurice from his perch was my friend Gareth Bryan-Jones after a riveting duel at Grangemouth in 1968, where my friends and I cheered him on.

As interpreter I was involved in more than one diplomatic incident. A member of our party decided one day in the lift to pinch the bottom of a young French woman. Her fiancé was standing beside her, and reacted with fury. I was summoned to a "summit meeting" to try to get the situation

Košice 1969: Demissie Wolde (Eth) leads from DFM, Chris Wade (Swe) and Hubert Riesner (FRG) at a feeding station.

defused. In such circumstances it's hard for the innocent messenger to avoid being tarred with the same brush as the offender, and I felt most embarrassed by the episode.

Worse was to come. Halfway through our intended three-week stay the weather changed. It started to snow, the temperature plummeted, and wet-weather gear from Adidas had to be rushed out from the UK. Then a national strike started in all of France following "les événements", the political upheaval of May 1968 that quite soon ended the reign of President Charles De Gaulle. The school kitchens closed, and so all 66 of us had to evacuate Font Romeu. Easier said than done, as no bus company could be found to break the *grève des transports* and take us out of France into Spain. Eventually a "blackleg" firm was found, and we loaded up the two coaches that conveyed us to the Spanish border. There we had to carry our luggage across and then another coach took us to the airport at Barcelona.

There we had lunch in a posh hotel, where I sat opposite Lillian Board, the Mexico 800m silver medallist who was not long after this to die tragically young of leukaemia. We ate tournedos steaks, the first and last time I have ever had that expensive cut of beef, and the first and last time I had a conversation with Lillian.

On return to Scotland the hard training picked up again, so that I was able to show good form on 1st June in the Dundee 12¼ mile road race, run round a two laps circuit near Caird Park and Camperdown, the first half in warm but very wet rain. The time was 62:29, a record, and my St Andrews training partner Alistair Matson, a former Zoo resident known as "The Bomb" because of (I think) regular digestive explosions, was second in 64:50.

That Dundee victory was the high point of the summer season. The following week I had sore calves, a sore throat, felt exhausted, fell asleep at odd times, felt bad, felt shattered: all that within a week of entries in the diary. I had picked up some sort of virus, but instead of resting until I recovered, I went on trying to train hard. "O brood of folly without father bred!" as Milton put it. On Monday 10th June I took to my bed and the doctor ordered me not to train till I felt better. I had five days off, feeling "fed-up, on brink of retirement". I was always prone to dramatic exaggeration.

The next race on my calendar was the SAAA 6 miles at Meadowbank's cinder track on Friday 21st June, and I dropped out with "tired legs" after only six laps in 7:06. On Sunday 28th I had my final run from the Zoo, and felt a lot better.

The rest of the story is soon told – even sooner than might be expected as there are no entries at all in my training diary between Saturday 29th June and the start of a new book on 20th July! I went into a phase of minimal training, drinking too much beer, and generally leading a meaningless existence for a few weeks. I didn't go to the UK trial for Mexico City, held at Port Talbot in Wales, where Bill Adcocks, Tim Johnston and Jim Alder qualified for the Olympics. In Mexico Bill was 5th, Tim 8th – both excellent results at altitude, Tim having spent more than a year in Mexico to acclimatise - but Jim sadly dropped out suffering from dehydration.

That summer I was invited over to Biberach near Ulm in Baden-Württemberg by Hans Wax, who had recently married and moved into a new house. I spent two weeks there, covering 93 miles, a mixture of slow running and speedwork, in the last 11 days of July, mostly with Hans, and 39 miles in the first four days of August, when I travelled back to Edinburgh. I was back in the usual routine.

The first race after this re-boot was on August 17th, a 2 miles at the Edinburgh Highland Games on the 5 lap grass track at Murrayfield. There I finished well down the field in about 9:30. The school session started on the following Monday, and in St Andrews my training partners for the next while were Ron Brown, a Canadian who was over on sabbatical with his family, Alistair Matson, and for a few weeks the loquacious Jim Haddow, who had run for St Andrews University in the late 1940s and was still an active athlete despite having had a few skiing injuries. Jim made regular visits over the next few years and always managed to fit in a few runs with us.

It took quite a long time to get back to full fitness, as I discovered when well beaten by Lachie Stewart and Pat McLagan in the Dunblane 14 ½ mile road race. Foolishly I led for the first six miles into the wind and was then rapidly dropped. Lachie won at a canter in 75:50, 1:40 ahead of me. A photograph taken near the start shows that I was still carrying half a stone too much.

As the cross-country season progressed my form slowly improved. I was clocking up between 70 and 90 miles a week and recording reasonable results, most of which I will skip over. The climax of the first half of the winter was a race at Camperdown Park, Dundee, between an SCCU select and the Scottish Universities on 14th December. After most of the first of the three laps, the tall Irish Edinburgh University student Dave Logue accidentally stood on my spike as we rounded a tight bend, and I had to stop to pull it on again, dropping from second to last. Ron Marshall wrote in the next Monday's Glasgow Herald that "the air turned blue" as I gave vent to my frustration. All that pent-up fury was turned into energy as I shot back up the field, running with considerable speed and power. In the end I finished 6th, less than a minute behind Lachie Stewart. It was a reasonable end to a disappointing racing year.

Just two days after that race, on Monday 16th December, a small 18 year old "professional" runner called Ian Grieve appeared at the university gym in Butts Wynd where Alistair Matson and I did our usual lunchtime session, and we invited him to go running with us. It was a 38 minute fartlek session on the hard, frozen sands and golf course. Ian worked as a junior technician in the Bute medical building, and we were to train together, on and off, for the next forty years, by which time he was a father of three and grandfather to rather more, the senior technician at the Bute, one of the extras in Chariots of Fire, originator and organiser of the St Andrews Highland Games, and President of the Scottish Highland Games Association.

Chapter 11

We'll keep the Red Flag flying here!

1969 started well. Gareth Bryan-Jones, whose wife Jan comes from Tyneside, Alistair Blamire and I all ran in the "Morpeth" again. Local boy Jim Alder had returned to form after his Mexico disappointment, and won in 64:30 from John Caine (Gateshead) (65:57), Alistair (66:03), me (66:38), John Hillen (67:06) and Gareth (67:18). We all then went off to a Happy New Year party.

Scotland was due to host the ICCU International Cross-Country Championships in March, and naturally there would be great competition for places. The choice of Dalmuir Park, Clydebank, with the co-operation of Clydebank Town Council, would mark a break with Hamilton Racecourse, where the very first "International" had been held in 1903 and every time it had been held in Scotland since, the most recently in 1960. The lack of suitable changing and washing facilities had made Hamilton unsuitable for modern needs, and 1968 had been the last year the SCCU Championship was staged there. For 1969 the SCCU Championship was moved to Duddingston Golf Course in south Edinburgh. That race was our target.

January had started propitiously. On the 18th I failed by only 3 seconds to beat Adrian Weatherhead (Edinburgh AC) for the East District title at Musselburgh Racecourse. Fergus and Gareth were 3rd and 4th and ESH easily won the team race. Then I caught 'flu and spent three days in bed and three more recovering. The National was on 22nd February, giving me just over three weeks to get ready.

The SCCU under its team manager J.C.R. Morton (Jim) had instituted regular training days for its potential team members. These were held on Sundays, usually at Lochinch, the Glasgow Police College HQ in Glasgow, but there was one at Fernieside, the ESH base, on February 9th. The morning session was occupied by a short run and a few hillclimbs, but in the afternoon we ran across to reconnoitre the course at Duddingston. The visit was moderately successful but to our hilarity we were chased off the park by a groundsman.

I combined training with a visit to a girl who lived in Darlington, a friend of Jan Bryan-Jones. I had met her at the post-Morpeth party. It was a rather scary drive through snow up to 6 inches deep, and in the last yard of the trip I managed to skid into a student, fortunately without causing injury. Once I was back in St Andrews, the snow had gone, and so had the girl.

That grumpy Duddingston groundsman can't have been very happy when he saw the conditions for the National. Hundreds of runners were going to be ploughing over his precious park through inches-deep slush and mud. I think those were the worst conditions I ever ran in. We warmed up in the rain, well wrapped up, and put our longest spikes in, dreading what it would feel like when we stripped down to racing gear. "Ice snow slush rain 5 ugh laps" is what I wrote in my diary. Colin Shields in his history of the SCCU *Runs will take place Whatever the Weather* (1990) says the Duddingston course was "icy, rutted and rock hard". It was icy, but soft, slushy and horrible.

Somehow, I ran well enough to take the final qualifying place for the Scottish team. The surprise winner was Dick Wedlock (Shettleston) from Fergus, Bill Mullett (Shettleston), John Myatt (Strathclyde Univ), Jim Alder, Jim Wright (both Edinburgh AC), me, and John Linaker (Pitreavie). The Scottish selectors did not want to select Linaker because of some incident on a previous trip, and so they positioned themselves round the final lap shouting me on.

When the team was announced, I was in, along with Dick Wedlock, Fergus Murray, Bill Mullett, Jim Alder, Jim Wright, Gareth Bryan-Jones, Ian McCafferty and Lachie Stewart. The selectors had gone on all-season form rather than a "sudden death" result.

About ten days later the Senior and Junior squads were taken on another reconnoitring run, this time to the International course at Clydebank. It was pretty obvious that the firm, steep gradients of Clydebank would not necessarily produce similar performances to those realised over the slush and mud of pancake-flat Duddingston. I did not fancy the course at all, and I wasn't the only one. If only they had stuck with Hamilton, or even better, moved the event to Musselburgh Racecourse!

Jim Morton's ambition was for Scotland to take away a set of medals from the Championship. The team had been prepared as well possible, and the selectors had chosen a good blend of youth and experience. As we paraded over to the start on Saturday 22nd March, wearing the rather silly-looking sky-blue knitted caps that Jim had obtained from a "sponsor", he looked both proud and expectant. I was less so, fearing that my weak lower back would not respond well to the steep inclines.

And so it proved. Ian McCafferty ran a storming race to finish third, and might have won had he not stopped to fasten his shoe-lace ("Ma lace is oot"), with Lachie, Fergus and Gareth backing him up excellently in 20th, 23rd and 24th.

Dick Wedlock (36) and Bill Mullett (54) closed Scotland's six counters in with 160 points to get us into 5th place out of 13 teams, behind England, France, Belgium and New Zealand. It was in fact one of Scotland's best team performances ever, but Jim Morton was disappointed. Of the other three runners, I was 74th, just ahead of Dave Logue who was running for Northern Ireland, while Jim Wright was 98th and Jim Alder did not finish. And that, apart from an outing at the Cross Internacional de San Sebastian a year or two later, was the end of my international cross-country years.

I wanted to re-launch the marathon career that had so badly stalled in the heat of the west London suburbs by running the Shettleston Marathon in the late spring. However fate, in the shape of the British Amateur Athletic Board, played an ace by sending me an invitation, even though it was only at three weeks' notice, to accompany Tim Johnston to represent the UK in the 3rd Karl-Marx-Stadt marathon in the GDR on May 10th. I accepted at once and sent off my passport for the necessary visa.

The weekly mileage over the weeks since Clydebank had been relatively modest: 87, 92, 37 (when I missed three days while on an unhappy car tour of the Highlands with a French girl) and 84. The prospect of international competition inspired me to put in a week at 90 and one at 79 miles, after which it was time to taper for the race. I was still a novice, and determined to learn as much as I could from Tim Johnston.

The weekend before the marathon, ESH ventured down to Leicester for our first attempt at the AAA 12-stage relays. Few Scottish clubs could or indeed can muster twelve runners of high standard, and it was lucky that all our runners were uninjured at the same time. The relays alternated a long (5miles 1277 yards) lap, and a short 3 mile one. I was put on the first lap, a long one. From the start outside Leicester Velodrome a sizeable group formed, spearheaded by Mike Freary (Bolton), Alan Domleo (Tipton) and me. I was able to hang on to Freary until just before the finish. Our team manager, Dick Ramsay, was agreeably surprised to see me so far up as my white vest with the two ESH bands had passed unnoticed at the checkpoints where our supporters stood. I was elated to be only three seconds down on such a fast runner as Freary, whose record on the roads and cross-country was outstanding. The team ran well but dropped a little on subsequent laps, so that we finished 11th out of 22 teams – a solid performance for our first attempt, and a confidence-booster for our trip east.

The visit to the industrial town of Chemnitz, as it was known before the Deutsche Demokratische Republik came into existence and again after its demise, coincided with the May celebrations of twenty years of communist rule. The lampposts were hung with huge red banners saying "XX Jahre DDR" and the streets and public buildings with flags bearing the iconic images of Karl Marx, Friedrich Engels and Vladimir Ilyich Lenin.

Our hotel was also used by prominent officers and political cadres from the GDR and other countries, and all the celebrations were reported on in the rather grey "Neues Deutschland" and other papers. Lead stories about Erich Honecker's welcome to the comrade president of the people's republic of wherever it was were as exciting as reports of UK party conferences, and just as predictable. In the hotel the waiters wore imperialist tail-coats and bow ties but took an eternity to bring the plates of toast and scrambled egg with onions for breakfast.

I visited the GDR briefly again in 1982 with our school exchange, when "Zwangsumtausch" (compulsory exchange of Western "Devisen" for non-exportable Ostmark) and other restrictions were in force. While there were some positive aspects to life in the "Arbeiter- und Bauernstaat", such as childcare and education and cheap subsidised staple foods, this was balanced by extremely expensive or difficult to come by "luxury goods" like cars, and more or less total travel restrictions on its citizens as far as travel westwards was concerned. Families from east and west Germany used to meet in the summer at campsites on Lake Balaton in Hungary specially set up for them.

Everyday existence was circumscribed by shortages, which were partly due to Western political measures imposed during the cold war. Walking through the streets I once saw three greenish oranges from Cuba offered for sale, and a notice in a stationer's offering as a special offer fountain pen repair.

For several years after reunification (or takeover as many Ostbürger saw it) I regularly visited Mecklenburg-Vorpommern, the region adjoining Scheswig-Holstein in the north, where previously our coach had had to stop at the Zonengrenze and stare at the bleak series of barbed wire fences, notices and ditches. There was a rapid programme of modernisation and westernisation. Many beautiful old buildings, for example in the capital Schwerin, were restored. A shortage of paint and other materials had made previous restoration impossible. In sport there were abuses (and just as many on the western side, not all of which have yet been exposed) but also great achievements. Is our approach to London 2012 so different?

Squire Yarrow was our team manager. "Squire" was his forename, though he looked every inch a country squire. In 1938 he had won the silver medal at the European Championship marathon, so that unlike most BAAB team managers he did understand the event. He was a very good companion for us, though there were no real difficulties for him to sort out.

The course was unusual - 8 narrow laps of a park. In the middle of the lap was a belt of trees, not quite thin enough to see through. The sandy grit surface was uneven and soft in places after recent heavy rain. That made it kind to the legs but as the race went on it grew increasingly harder to get much drive or bounce off the dead ground. Marathon rules state that races should be run on "made-up" surfaces, but the Germans, normally so observant of regulations, paid no attention to that

I should mention here the humanity and friendliness of the officials. Tim Johnston and I remember particularly Herr Naumann, who later sent Tim pictures of the race. The officials seemed to be enthusiasts, who had organised this event not for the greater glory of the DDR, but because they loved running. There was the same spirit at French, Belgian and German cross-country races. All over the world in cross-country, hill and road running particularly, then and now, you felt and feel you are experiencing a brotherhood (or indeed sisterhood) that cuts across frontiers and politics.

Tim gave every appearance of being confident, but said that four runners in the 70 strong field needed watching: Nicolae Mustata (Romania) and Jürgen

Busch (DDR) who had been second and fourth the previous year, plus Nedo Farčič, the 1967 Košice winner running for Yugoslavia, and Lajos Mecser (Hungary). Tim said that Farčič had impressed him in training in Mexico but that Mecser had been unable to handle the altitude at all.

The race started late in the day, at 5 pm, to avoid the midday and early afternoon heat. Nonetheless temperatures were around 20 C for the first hour though it grew cooler in the second half. I was in a large group of thirty or so, reducing gradually to a dozen by 20km (64:30). There was a sudden break by Busch and Farčič soon after that, and a second group of Johnston, Mustata, Mecser and Krebs (DDR) followed them at a distance. I was forced to drop back.

That 10km segment was the critical one in determining the leading finishers. Tim Johnston caught Busch and Farčič, but when the pace picked up again, the German dropped rapidly. After another few kilometres Mecser shouted something to the effect that Busch must have cheated by cutting through the shrubbery, but he made signs to explain that he had been "caught short" by digestive problems. He certainly looked all right again as he shot back up through the field.

Tim was well out in the lead by 30 km, but had also problems with his stomach and with his legs. He finished in 2:15:31.2, just 5 seconds outside his best, but had been too weary to force it over the last few kilometres.

When the break had come just after 20km, I had developed stitch, an unusual occurrence for me, and gradually fell back to around tenth, feeling rather sorry for myself. However by the time I was well into the seventh lap, the stitch had disappeared, and I picked off Mustata and Krebs, then two other East Germans, Leimbach and Veith. Squire Yarrow shouted to me with one lap to go "You're fifth now, keep it up!" which was encouraging. It was now too late to catch anyone else, Mecser, still grumbling about Busch, finishing fourth in 2:17:58.8 to my 2:18:51.

Busch came to the Maxol marathon in Manchester in 1969 – he was 8th - and I was assigned to him and his manager as interpreter. I remarked on the absence of private cars in the GDR, saying in a spirit of consolation that it might be nice to have relatively traffic-free roads. Jürgen shrugged and said he'd rather have a car. I expect he has one now.

Tim is still running, slowly he says, and has bought a house near Fenners, the Cambridge sports ground where he began with interval training so many years ago. He came up to win the Two Bridges (Forth and Kincardine) 36 miler in the 1980s and stayed with us in St Andrews. He was totally concentrated on the race and my wife Kim and I were instructed to give him cans of Coke, opened beforehand to allow the bubbles to escape, at regular intervals. He had deprived himself of caffeine for days before and hoped to get a boost. It worked, and he won impressively. Tim recollects that it wasn't an easy win at all. Going over the Forth Bridge after 34 or 35 miles, he started losing concentration, mainly as a result of the "stroboscopic" effect that the guard-rail uprights and possibly the caffeine were having on the view of the waves 200 feet below. He was being irresistibly drawn sideways – into the rail and – who knows? – over it.

As the time in Karl-Marx-Stadt was my second fastest, I could not be too dissatisfied. Over the summer I continued to train and occasionally race, but with no real sense of direction. I ran two 5000m in 14:33.6 and 14:27, the latter twenty seconds behind Fergus Murray and Alistair Blamire at Grangemouth. By now I was living at Boarhills and occasionally running into school, but the main sessions were done in Tentsmuir Forest at weekends and on the roads or at University Park during the week. On 11th June I got my 5000 personal best down to 14:15, again at Grangemouth and again only third, this time to Lachie Stewart and Gareth Bryan-Jones. I just wasn't fast enough. At the end of the month Fergus beat me by about 20 seconds in the SAAA 10,000m, my time being 29:54.5.

My training mileage was inconsistent over that summer, reaching 100 miles one week but averaging around 75. I had hoped to run well in the AAA Marathon in Manchester on 20th July, but finished a poor 28th in 2:32:09. I ran all right till 20 miles (1:46:20, but then crawled in at an average of 7:20 miles to finish dead beat. The only consolation was that I was staying at the home of Salford Harrier Arthur Walsham and his wife Enid, who were really hospitable. Together late at night we watched Neil Armstrong walking on the Moon. Now that was an achievement!

Things began to pick up after the Manchester fiasco: I came 3rd in the Kirkintilloch "10", which was closer to 11 miles as Fergus won in a record time of 55:43.6 from Ian McIntosh (Ranelagh) (56:00), my time being 56:09. The day was muggy and warm, and I came through over the last three miles.

On 16th August I travelled across the country to Ayrshire for the Largs to Irvine "20" road race. In 1968 it had been won by Hughie Mitchell (Shettleston) in 1:48:53. I took the lead from the start, and for some reason was able to "bomb it" all the way, although I recall long stretches of open carriageway that seemed to be the "long road that has no turning". I noted in the diary that I was "very tired at end. Last 4 miles eternal." It wasn't surprising I was tired, for the time was 1:37:20, and I finished 6 ½ minutes ahead of Mike Willis of Blackheath with Gray of Morpeth third. Hughie Mitchell was 6th. In all honesty I have to question the distance, but perhaps I had the wind behind me.

Metaphorically that was certainly true, as the BAAB had sent me a second invitation, this time to travel for another attempt to make an impression at Košice. This time I was the only UK marathon representative, but there were two steeplechasers, Ernie Pomfret and John Bicourt. I found this surprising as the marathon was of far greater significance in the athletic calendar. Our "team manager" was another long-standing north of England official, but he had little to do and could enjoy the days spent in Slovakia.

The political situation was of course very different from 1967. The Russians had overrun the country after the crushing of the "Prague Spring" and the removal from power of Alexander Dubcek, the prime minister. Soviet troops were much more in evidence, and the Soviets were extremely unpopular among the population in general. This was demonstrated during the race itself when the Russian runners were booed, at least until the demonstrators were enjoined to stop. It was a bit unfair to boo the runners, who hadn't invaded anywhere, but that's politics, I suppose.

The entry list for the 39th Medzinarodny Maraton Mieru (International Peace Marathon) on 5th October 1969 was made up of 123 runners. I don't know how many started, but 98 made it to the finish in times between 2:15:37.0 and 3:23:31.4. Many of the competitors came from Eastern Europe, but there were two Ethiopians, Demissie Wolde and Tadesse Medhin, as well as an English runner competing in Swedish colours, Chris Wade, brother of the celebrated tennis player Virginia.

It turned out that there were only about fifteen serious challengers for victory – those already mentioned plus Kalle Hakkarainen and Kalevi Ihaksi (Fin), Ismail Akçay and Canavar Hamza (Turkey), Vaclav Chudomel (CSSR), the

1968 winner in 2:26:28.4, Hubert Riesner (Fed. Rep. of Germany), Paul Krebs (DDR) whom I had beaten in Karl-Marx-Stadt, Gyula Tóth (1966 winner in 2:19:11.2), Janos Szerenyi and Denes Simon (Hungary), and me. The best of the Russians was Anatolij Sucharkov.

As in 1967 it was a damp day with little wind, and from the start I was in the leading group. Wolde and Medhin, along with Wade, Tóth and a few others kept up a good pace. At 10km and 15km Tóth was just in the lead (31:30, 47:44) but the rest of us were in close attendance. Gyula still had his nose in front at 20km (63:55) and at the turn, but I was credited with the lead at 25km (80:20.4).

The pace set by our group at 25 km would have produced a time of around 2:16:30, outside the record of 2:15:09.6 held since 1963 by Buddy Edelen (USA). However the leading pack split up soon after 25km, when the Ethiopians put in a burst and dropped Chris Wade and me. Wolde and Tadesse built up a big lead over that 10km segment, covered in close to 31 minutes. I ran most of the rest of the way with Chris Wade, and caught the fading Tadesse at the water station at 40km. Wolde scorched to victory in 2:15:37, and I was pleased to record a personal best with 2:17:33.2. Chris was third in 2:17:52, and Medhin in fourth lost over a minute to me over the last 2 km.

I returned to Scotland with my confidence boosted. OK, I had been beaten, but by the Olympic tenth-placer, and I had run away from his team-mate over the last two kilometres. Things were looking up again, or so I thought.

ESH won the Kingsway relays on October 18th, and I had the fifth fastest time of the day, just 4 seconds slower than Fergus Murray and Dick Wedlock. The next day, a Sunday, I did a 21 miler in 2:05 round a new "East Neuk circuit" from "Byways" in Boarhills past Bonnytown, down the Anstruther road, over to Carnbee, then to Pittenweem, Anstruther and along the coast to Crail and home via Kingsbarns. The next day I strained my foot at University Park, running on grass. It remained sore all week but I tried to "run it off". By the next Monday, 27th October I at last took the decision to rest. The next training run was not until Friday 5th December – five weeks without running a single step: it was my longest ever break from training.

Every cloud has a silver lining, or a golden one in this case, for my good friend John Bryant took that place in the eight-man ESH Edinburgh to

Glasgow squad, and helped them to their first ever victory in 3hrs 44 mins 57 secs, 3:09 ahead of Shettleston Harriers. That ESH team deserves to be commemorated. The running order was Bill Murray (position 6), Ken Ballantyne (5), Tommy Coyle (2), Gareth Bryan-Jones (1), John Bryant (1), Fergus Murray (1), Craig Douglas (1), Jack White (1). I didn't note it in the diary, but I'm sure I went to watch: at last the coveted medals were ours! It would be 1973 before I got my hands on one, and a second came my way in 1974. But that is for later. 1969 had been a better year: despite the five weeks off injured I had made progress, and recorded my highest annual mileage to date, 3510 miles.

Chapter 12

Messengers

He that runs may read: many books on running have been written over the centuries. In the pre-Christian period references to running abound from the Middle East to India and China, in Greece and North Africa. Runners were a regular means of communication, as names like "The Courier" or "The Messenger" indicate. The last running postman in Scotland was still working well into the 20th century. In 15th and 16th century South America the situation was similar, the most notable example being the chasqui (exchange, give or take) relay runners in the service of the Inca, young men whose national service was to carry and pass on messages in the form of knotted strings called quipu, sweep and clear the surfaces of a 3 to 10 km stretch, depending on terrain, for the year or two of their period of duty. The chasqui had to be available round the clock and slept in huts by the road, with food supplied by the royal household and prepared by their kinsfolk.

In 2088 BC King Shulgi of Sumeria, in the lands between the Tigris and Euphrates in what is the sadly abused country of modern Iraq, is said to have run from Nippur to Ur and back, 200 miles, between one sunset and the next, having promised to attend feasts of thanksgiving in both of these sacred cities. Records from Mesopotamia are among the oldest written documents in the world.

King Rameses II reigned in Egypt for 66 years from 1278 BC. At his inauguration he performed a ritual run on a track symbolically marking the frontiers of his kingdom, again thirty years later and every few years after that until he was over 90.

It is thus appropriate to place a wonderful new book by Thor Gotaas, Running – A Global History (first published in Norwegian in 2008 - English version by Reaktion Books, London 2009), at the forefront of my choices of athletics reading.

Thor Gotaas has produced a well-written and moderately sized book (348 pages of text in 32 chapters) that you can read in your armchair or in bed without effort.

Historic meeting: Helsinki 1952 – Hannes Kolehmainen, Joe Binks, Jules Ladoumègue, Paavo Nurmi discuss old times.

A notice in Glasgow's refurbished Kelvingrove Museum and Art Gallery toilets reads "Switch taps on and off by waving your hands at the sensor". That for some reason made me think of our sensitivity to language. In literature Tolkien (toll-kühn, madly bold) owes much of his popularity, I would speculate, to the names he chose for his characters and to our fascination with Nordic myth. Gollum spent his earlier existence swimming around gulping down fish, and the cosy world of Hobbiton and Bag End contrasts with the harshness of Mordor.

Germanic names gave Tolkien lots of ideas. At Madras College we once had a German language assistant called Gerlinde, whose name means the lime or linden tree who allows the warrior to return from the battle and lean his spear against her. Friedhelm means the helmet of peace, Siegfried the peace of victory – but no happy ending for him.

Trees have always been associated in Celtic life with clans and families. The Scots pine, symbol of Clan Gregor, has a sword stuck in its branches and a crown, and the motto 'S rioghall mo dhream, royal is my race. That is why I have reclaimed the name Pinetree Press from my father's legacy. The Macgregors claim descent from kings, as explained in his history of the clan, written for the Clan Gregor society (1977). Gregalach! was the clan war-cry:

while there's leaves in the forest, or foam on the river, Macgregor, despite them, shall flourish for ever. Or so runs the song.

My father Forbes published collections of Scots anecdotes as Macgregor's Mixture, a reference to Gregory's mixture which children once had inflicted on them if they had an upset stomach. The stories are historical, serious, but mainly humorous, divided into sections on education, religion etc. A typical example of word-play is the story of the pupil in primary school who had no rubber and was told by the teacher: "Use the boy's behind". Another is of the little girl who, when the class was asked who knew where God lived, answered that she did.

"What?" said the teacher. "How can you know where God lives if all the wise people in history…" Aye, but I do. He bides at 92b High Street. When I was coming to school this morning I heard the wifie there shouting 'Goad! Are ye no up yet?'"

Alexander Pope wrote in his Essay on Criticism that "Words are like leaves; and where they most abound/Much fruit of sense beneath is rarely found". I had better return to my theme. A good running book, like any good book, has to be written in an open style, demonstrate a certain luminosity, contain lots of detail and idiosyncratic information without becoming tedious.

People are fascinated by words. Ron Morrison's father David loved jokes, and one of his favourites told of the pupil who was asked to make up a sentence using the word "fascinate". The solution was "I had a coat with nine buttons, but I could only fasten eight." His other favourite was the story of the rubber blow-up boy who comes to school with a pin, and uses it. The headmaster, presumably using up his last breath on the floor, summons the errant pupil. "You've let the school down, you've let the teachers down, you've let me down…but worst of all, you've let yourself down!". My amusement can be imagined when I read a few months ago of a Dundee sheriff who used just this formula before sentencing a pupil who had embarked on a vodka-fuelled adventure of mayhem during a school excursion.

Language can be soft and caressing, echoing natural rhythms. Is it any wonder that "Burns" and "Bach" both mean a brook or stream? Larkin wrote of the vast moth-eaten musical brocade created to pretend we never die. Religion too has harshness and stillness associated with it, from the beauty of the Kyrie Eleison sung in 2010 in Crail during the interval of an Egyptian film festival to the staccato fascistic shouts about the Pope that occasionally infest football grounds and would not be out of place in the mouths of the twentieth century's Unmentionables. Headlines like Sink the Belgrano! and Gotcha! are not to my taste.

More melodic if equally insistent rhythms and chants were used by oarsmen from the time of Homer and no doubt before, to the Vikings and skalds in ancient halls and spectators in modern stadia. Why did that Latin professor, Erskine Wright, like to recite the lines of Virgil that I found so magnetic?

Mantua me genuit; Calabri rapuere; tenet nunc Parthenope: cecini pascua, rura, duces.

I recall them, without looking them up, from a lecture room in 1958. Mantova gave me birth, the Calabrians took me away, Parthenope holds me now: I sang of pastoral things, the countryside, leaders. I hope that's right!

Turning now to running literature: during the great period of Gunder Hägg and Arne Andersson's frustrated assaults on world records – their disqualification a slimy triumph of the blazers – crowds in Stockholm, Göteborg and other places used to chant at them:

Heja Arne! Heja Gunder!
lät oss se här verldens under!
slar rekordet om sekunder!

Heja Arne! Heja Gunder!
Let us see the world's great wonder!
Take the record seconds under!

We lay great stress on choosing children's names, and newspapers publish lists of the most popular every year. Our daughter was named for her grandmother and aunt, both long dead and both called Rosemary, and for her mother Kim. My stepmother Jean told me later she had always known I would choose that name if a daughter were born.

Kim's and my sons were named after archangels, Michael and Thomas, though I was unaware that either had a family connection until my father excitedly told me that he had had an uncle Thomas. My own first name, Donald, has little to do with ducks but means something like "ruler of all", which is as flattering as it is unwelcome, and my middle name, Forbes, is not only shared by my father, brother, and second son but the family name of my paternal grandmother.

Names can be magnetic. I went through a few years of being a distributor for Bioflow and Ecoflow products, magnets made in Saltash in Cornwall that have an effect on the health of human beings and animals, on fossil fuel consumption and even on alcohol, where magnetisation seems to "age" the wine, which is more than just imagined. I felt beneficial effects on energy and mood and only gave it up because I was in danger of becoming a Bioflow bore.

Versions of Arthurian romance offers numerous example of similar names: Arthur is the straight man, leading the quest, like Frodo or Harry Potter. We read of the adultery of the Queen with Lancelot, who casts his spear in her direction, and of the triple role of Morgan le Fay (fée, fairy) as Arthur's half-sister, enchantress, antagonist and finally supporter as he is carted off to the Isle of Avalon. The three Grail knights are the rather unexciting Sir Percival, Sir Galahad and Sir Bors, all a bit like members of the evangelistic Crusaders from my boyhood.

If we examine the sporting record of some of our leaders and well-known people, there is a strange correlation between their performance and what happened to them later. Nicolas Sarkozy and Jimmy Carter both collapsed while jogging, soon afterwards suffering a collapse in their popular support, and George W. Bush came off his bike, while Bill Clinton kept going despite the odd stumble. …and so on it goes.

John Bryant's books are spread randomly over two houses, and Volker Kluge's are classified and arranged in a specially designed archive in Brandenburg. I also have a large collection of running literature. It is held mainly in a big ornate bookcase sold to me for £15 by the former University Librarian, Dugald MacArthur, from whom we bought our family house at 8 Dempster Terrace in 1981. He felt guilty because he left us to clear out his study, left ankle deep in papers.

Here are some I have chosen. Sir John D. Astley's *Fifty Years of my Life* (1894) leads the field in the autobiographical section. He recounts a life as landed gent, backer of anything with legs (though he advises against betting too much on "a horse as can talk"). He was also an MP and general man-about town. Then there is Jules Ladoumègue's *Dans Ma Foulée* (In My Stride). Julot, the darling of the French athletics public, attracted a crowd of an estimated quarter of a million to his final run along the Champs Eliseés in 1946 after he had fallen victim to yet another epidemic of banning the best runners because they took too many expenses (MPs anyone?) Alf Shrubb's *Long Distance Running and Training* and *Running and his Cross-Country Running* (1908) give an insight into the determined regime of The Little Wonder, who broke numerous world records from 2000 yards to One Hour, the latter at Ibrox in November 1904. A modern biography of Shrubb by Rob Hadgraft (The Little Wonder, Desert Island Books 2004) joins others on Deerfoot, Walter George and Arthur Newton.

Next comes a little book by Gunder Hägg called *Hur jag blev Gunder Hägg* which I bought in a German version [*So brach ich Weltrekorde*, Olympia-Verlag 1948] and translated as *How I became Gunder Hägg* (not yet published). I should also note Ron Clarke's *The Unforgiving Minute - as told to Alan Trengrove* – it was ghosted but he admits it (Pelham Book 1966). It reads well and has a picture of my friend Fergus Murray on the cover. Brendan Foster and Cliff Temple collaborated on a fine autobiography (1978, Heinemann). Then there is a life of Gordon Pirie (*The Impossible Hero*, Dick Booth, Corsica Press 1999) as well as *The Lonely Breed* (Ron Clarke and Norman Harris, Pelham Books 1967, research on the Swedes by Tim Johnston). Alfred R. Downer's *Running Recollections* (1908), reprinted by Fraser Clyne et al in Aberdeen in the 1990s, gives a first person account of the career of the great sprinter and rather dissolute Watsonian as well as training advice from the stars of the fin-de-siècle period. And lastly the detailed autobiography to beat them all, Ron Hill's two volume *The Long Hard Road* (Ron Hill Sports Ltd 1981, 1982 – out of print), in which the famous "streaker" gives chapter, verse and footnotes to his every movement from September 25th 1938 to October 17th 1982.

Biographies: Volker Kluge's outstanding book on the atrociously treated multi-world record-holder Otto Peltzer, *Otto der Seltsame* (Otto the Strange) (Berlin 2000) richly deserves an English-language publication. I would join it with Peltzer's own moving 1955 autobiography, which Volker Kluge examines and clarifies, *Umkämpftes Leben* (Berlin [East]) (My Life as a Struggle). Otto was a multi world record holder, beat Douglas Lowe, the 800m Olympic champion, at Stamford Bridge in 1926 and the great Paavo Nurmi in Berlin over 1500m the same year (both in world record time). During the NS period Peltzer, who had homosexual tendencies, came into disfavour, though the national team doctor Martin Brustmann tried to intercede. Peltzer tried to settle in Scandinavia, but was forced to return by threats to his family who all died or were killed in the war. He was sent to the Mauthausen KZ, where he was greeted by the brutal commandant with "So! Der Schnell-läufer ist da! [Well! The fast runner is here!]" and badly maltreated. He survived and sought to be accepted as a coach in the Soviet Zone. Then he came west, but his enemies in the Deutschen Leichtathletik-Verband obstructed his attempts to be recognised and he fled to India. There he lived in a hut in the stadium in Delhi, fed by the families of the poor children he coached. Some of them reached Olympic level. It was while on a visit to Germany in 1970 with one of his athletes, Happy Sikand, that the man who had lived for sport collapsed and died. The DLV belatedly honoured him with a special annually awarded medal, and Otto-Peltzer-Races are held to this day on Sundays in Delhi in his memory.

Volker Kluge and I have been involved in several translation projects over the past six years, and I unreservedly commend any of his thoroughly researched works. His greatest achievement is the 5 volume set he has published (so far) of every Olympic result, winter and summer, between 1896 and 1996: every heat, every sport, historical and political backgrounds, voluminous footnotes. It took him 30 years, but it's worth it. There will be a richly illustrated book about the London Olympics, all being well, as there has been for all the past thirteen or fourteen Olympiads.

John Bryant's books are also well-written and thoroughly researched. Both *3:59.4*, dealing with the history of mile running until the breaking of the four minute barrier on May 6th 1954 by Roger Bannister, and *The Marathon Makers* are included. The latter gives an exciting and accurate account of the 1908 "Dorando Marathon" and the background to the White City Games. The main characters are the gallant Dorando Pietri who collapsed 5 times on the final lap, but won lasting glory, the tough but less charismatic Johnny Hayes whose team's protest brought him the medal, and the stiff upper lipped Scottish army officer Wyndham Halswelle, the only man to win an Olympic Gold in a walk-over because two of his US rivals – one was disqualified for forcing Halswelle off the track – refused to take part in the re-run. He still did 50 seconds.

I won't include Kenny Moore's colossal biography of his coach Bill Bowerman, running guru and inventor of waffle soles – with a waffle iron – on the grounds that it's too long. It goes into great detail, but the one that stands out is how Bowerman used to seal acceptance of a new athlete into the group by urinating on him as they stood in the showers. Kenny and his then wife Bobbie came to visit me in Dunoon, where we ran round Puck's Glen, a local beauty spot. They also came to us years later in St Andrews, and Bobbie rescued a dozen ducklings heading for the burn over a 10 foot wall without a parachute.

Finally in this section I include Peter Radford's book on Captain Barclay (*The Celebrated Captain Barclay*, Headline 2001). A reprint of the 1813 book *Pedestrianism* by Walter Thom, the first modern training manual, is now available (Pinetree Press 2010).

There is a limited number of good works of creative literature about athletics. I have picked the novel by W. R. Loader, *Staying the Distance* (1958)... ("Tigger Dobson was not content to remain average...") along with his autobiographical *Testament of a Runner* (The Sportsman's Book Club 1962). Then we have *Flanagan's Run*, by Tom McNab, based on the 1929 Bunion Derby organised by C.C. Pyle, plus Tom's other book *Rings of Sand* which concerns dirty work at the five ring Olympic circus. Peter Lovesey's *Wobble to Death* is a classic crime novel, centred on the six-day races that were a feature of late Victorian life and low-life.

An unusual novel (again in German, but deserving of an English language publication) is Hans Gebhardt's *Die 80 Tage des Gunder Hägg* (Autorenedition, Bertelsmann 1976). It tells of the journey of two journalists to investigate the background to the first banning of Hägg following his 1500m world record on 10th August 1941 in Stockholm where a delegation from Eskilstuna in northern Sweden engaged him for 400 kroner to run at a meeting there. The 80 days refers to one of the most prolific periods in athletics history in the summer of 1942 following his reinstatement. He and Arne Andersson set numerous records, Hägg alone ten of the thirteen he achieved between then and 1945. Tragically, both runners were disqualified, for a second time in Hägg's case, on 7th November 1945, a day of shame for international athletics among its many days of shame which still go on, as in the case of the South African women's Olympic champion Caster Semenya, now hopefully resolved in favour of the athlete.

Next, training manuals: apart from Thom, my list is headed by *Run to the Top*, by Arthur Lydiard, the Bible of Sixties runners onwards. Lydiard's methods are discussed in an earlier chapter. The eccentric Percy Cerutty (anyone remember what a "Stotan" was? - a cross between a Stoic and a Spartan) was the coach to the great Herb Elliott, undefeated over one mile throughout his entire career. Arthur Newton (1883-1959) was another LSD guru who took up running late in life for political reasons and ended up a long distance record-holder and the patron saint of the Road Runners Club. His old bicycle is probably lying in a hundred garages. Newton's simple, sometimes outspoken, language reflected his upper middle class upbringing and his admirable if sometimes overdone principles, for example it was bad form to sit in on a rival during a race. If you seek an amalgam of training methods, then either Fred Wilt (*How They Train*, various editions) or Toni Nett (*Modernes Training*, various editions) are your men. Jim Fixx, whom I interviewed for the Daily Mail in 1979 when the UK edition of *The Complete Book of Running* came out, wrote a best-seller that was easy to read, His new wife looked me up and down in his Hyde Park hotel before we went out for a long slow run and warned him that I looked fitter than the usual reporters. He gave a good interview and thanked me for the review. Sadly he died like his father before him of heart disease, but running if anything prolonged his life.

My final section is Off the Wall, a phrase which could be applied to just about any athletics book including this one. It is intended to include a few I couldn't fit in earlier. The 1966 European marathon champion Jim Hogan's autobiography, *The Irishman who Ran for England* (2008) is a model of its kind – it sounds like the man himself speaking, though without as much swearing as in normal life. Then there's Charlie Spedding's *From Last to First* (CS Books, Newcastle 2009). It tells how a modestly talented runner persuaded himself that he was as good as anyone – and won both the London Marathon and then Olympic bronze in Los Angeles in 1984. At that time I wrote to him asking about his preparation and have the six-page letter he wrote back. In my talk to the International Coaches Convention for the Dunky Wright Memorial Lecture that year I used Charlie's advice – I don't know how many were listening.

The wooden spoon goes to an instant paperback, *The Marathon Murder* by James Moffatt (New English Library 1972). It was written as a challenge in a fortnight, and reads like it.

Lastly, two poems: first, the classic *Song of the Ungirt Runners* by Charles Hamilton Sorley, who died in the First World War:

We swing ungirded hips, and lightened are our eyes.
The rain is on our lips, we do not run for prize.
We know not whom we trust, nor whitherward we fare,
But we run because we must through the bright broad air.

The waters of the seas are troubled as by storm,
The tempest strips the trees and does not leave them warm.
Does the tearing tempest pause? Do the treetops ask it why?
So we run without a cause 'neath the big bare sky.

The rain is on our lips, we do not run for prize,
But the storm the water whips and the wave howls to the skies.
The winds arise and strike it and scatter it like sand,
And we run because we like it through the bright broad land.

And second, and very immodestly, one of my own poems from "Stars and Spikes" (Nutwood Press 2004):

Running – a cyclical adventure that begins
When you first leave the house or changing room, and takes
You on a snail-whorled journey into time:
Jogging, trying to sprint, or steady with no pause
It doesn't matter if you're fast or slow, you win.
Just by being there, just by taking part…
The diary tells the story of the year,
Often unseasonal – mild February, May in snowy rage –
A day missed there, a long run stuck in here
And all the tiny numbers on the page
Explaining to the reader, if one comes
That you did six 800s on soft grass
On Monday, on Thursday ran an easy 10 –
Those jotted hieroglyphics as weeks pass

Are only relics, like the bony parts
Preserved by tar or mud in a great swamp
To be pored over, aeons hence, remote
From us as we are from the dinosaurs.

In Inca times young men
Ran carrying messages from post to post
Blowing their conch, winged on by sandals, then
Would pass the quipu on to the next guy,
And so on down the road: just as we do,
Running that relay through millennia.

Chapter 13

If it snows...1970 Edinburgh Commonwealth Games

The IX (9th for non-Romans) Commonwealth Games were awarded to Edinburgh at the city's second attempt at Kingston, Jamaica in 1966. Ten years earlier Edinburgh Corporation had voted by 34 to 18, a measure of the typical enthusiasm of my native city, to be willing to be the host city for the 1966 Games, which of course went - narrowly, by a 17-16 vote of the General Assembly of the British Commonwealth Games Federation meeting in Perth, Australia in 1962 - to Kingston.

Following that setback, a panoply of committees had been formed, and a huge amount of work had been done, much of it by the Games' Director of Organisation, Willie Carmichael, who lived in Gordon Road near my father's house. In the years and months leading up to the opening of the Games by the Duke of Edinburgh on 16th July the whole country, except for those to whom sport was of no interest as well as a minority of town councillors on Edinburgh Corporation, was dynamised by the prospect of Edinburgh as host to hundreds of the Commonwealth's top sportswomen and – men.

The Official History of the Edinburgh Games of 1970 was published that year by the organising committee. It is an extremely detailed 408 page volume, illustrated with many black-and-white photographs and four pages of colour ones, and a dust-jacket set out with dark blue lettering on paper of the light-grey tone of a typical Edinburgh sky. I recommend it to those who seek information about how those brilliantly successful Commonwealth Games were prepared – I say this even though there are several errors in the summary report on the marathon on p.155 and my name is mis-spelt as "McGregor, D." in the results on p169: but I'm getting ahead of myself.

The showpiece sport of the Games would, as usual, be athletics, and its theatre of action Meadowbank Stadium. The old cinder track had been torn up in 1968-9 and replaced by a modern Tartan track. The term "Tartan" referred to a product of the 3M company which produced all-weather surfaces, this one in a rather pleasing pinkish-brown. The stadium was rebuilt, and numerous other facilities were constructed, such as the Royal Commonwealth Pool,

Along the A1 : leaders at 20 miles in the SAAA trial for Edinburgh Commonwealth Games. L to R: Barry Jones (NZ), DFM, Fergus Murray, Bill Stoddart, A. J. Wood, Jim Alder.

now an A-listed building, near Holyrood Park and the velodrome adjacent to Meadowbank Stadium.

All of Scotland's athletes would be vying for the right to wear the bright blue vest with the Scottish thistle, and the chances were high that a large team would be "sent" to Edinburgh, the costs being relatively low. There would be three marathon representatives, and no shortage of challengers. Unsurprisingly, I made the securement of one of these three places the main target for 1970, regarding all other races until the SAAA championship on Saturday 16th May as secondary.

The Scotsman, at that time just about clinging to its proud boast to be "Scotland's National Newspaper", commissioned two series of articles on Commonwealth prospects in track and field and in swimming from Menzies Campbell and Bobby McGregor respectively. Menzies had recently announced his retirement from competition, saying that to sell his soul for a blazer with a thistle might not expose him to the fate of Faustus but it would be less than honest, adding that "for me the de Coubertin adage of competition being intrinsically more worthwhile than success has little validity…Those who compete at international level do so because they derive status as a result…it is a professional approach in a nominally amateur world…"

It was just a few days earlier in the same month, May 1979, that the IAAF had decreed that from then only white shoes without any makers' marks would be permitted in competition. "Et ta soeur", as the French say.

Menzies submitted a fortnightly series of well-written articles on many aspects of athletics, though it has to be said that the one on the marathon in which he said I came from Dundee did not get 10 out of 10. Sprinters, of whom Campbell was a distinguished example, tend not to have much understanding of what distance running is about, and vice versa. Athletics is not really one sport at all, but a coalition of the long and the short and the tall, or perhaps, to put it another way, of mesomorphs, ectomorphs and endomorphs all doing energetic things, sometimes beautifully and heroically, with their bodies.

For me, the first five months of 1970 were filled with mileage. From 28th December 1969 to 9th May 1970, one week before the trial race, I ran 1855 miles, an average of about 97.6 miles per week, with 11 of those weeks reaching a total of 100 or more, the highest being 112 ½ at the end of March. By good luck I was spared illness or serious injury. I raced only seven times over those five months, most of the results being mediocre: 16th in the Eastern District cross-country at Grangemouth in January, won by Alistair Blamire; 9th in the Scottish "Inter-Counties" the next week, with Dick Wedlock victorious; 12th in the SCCU "National" over muddy Ayr Racecourse where Jim Alder waded his way to victory; and second in the 8 mile Windermere to Kendal road race to Mike Freary (Bolton), who set a record of 37:20, 57 seconds faster than before, and 56 seconds ahead of me; 3rd in the "Tom Scott 10" from Law to Motherwell, on Saturday 4th April, in 48:52 behind Lachie Stewart (47:46) and Dick Wedlock (48:17); on

Monday 14th April against Queen's University Belfast I won a 5000m on the St Andrews grass track in 14:38 from Doug Gunstone; and finally I headed the field in the Clydebank to Helensburgh 16 miler on Saturday 25th April in 83:19 by 1:28 from Bill Stoddart (Greenock Wellpark) with Jim Wight (EAC) a further 19 seconds down.

During the period I attended the somewhat stuffy SCCU training days at Lochinch (twice) and at Fernieside, where I watched such peerless runners as Ian McCafferty, along with Jim Brown the most naturally talented athlete ever to emerge from Scotland, run effortlessly away from the cream of Scotland's cross-country talent as he had the previous year at Clydebank. At one session Ian was running in boots, and made four-minute miler Adrian Weatherhead look like a hack as the slightly built "McCaff" accelerated up an incline. I believe that only a slight flaw in his mental preparation, as exemplified in the 1969 "ma lace is oot" incident, held him back from winning an Olympic medal in1972, when he won his heat and went to pieces in the final.

I am deliberately abbreviating the account of the long preparation period so that the reader can avoid living though too many training runs with me. Apart from the SCCU sessions, I trained either by myself (over 100 times, a total of 1017 miles), with Ian Grieve (44 times, 228 miles), Ian and his 'professional' Games runner colleagues like Iain Whyte and Alex Kidd a further 5 times, for a total of 60 miles, with Ian Grieve and Doug Gunstone once, Ian and Bob Heron once, Ian and John Cunningham once, Ian and Alex Wight 3 times, Kenny Ballantyne twice, Jack White and Graham Stark 3 times, Fergus Murray 4 times, Doug Gunstone 8 times [once with Ian Docherty for 4 miles], twice with the "Zoo" people , twice with "wee" Tommy Coyle, twice with Gareth Bryan-Jones, 5 times with Bob Heron, 3 times with Alex Wight, once with Andy McKean, once with Craig Douglas, Mike Bradley and Eddie Sinclair. 62 miles were covered at the 3 SCCU sessions; races plus warm up and warm down accounted for 87 miles.

Fartlek and speedwork (mainly 300m and 200m reps, from 20-32 of the latter) formed a small proportion of the total, perhaps 5 per cent.

All that detail no doubt seems a bit anal, but it does give a different perspective on how the training was done. I only worked it all out for the purpose of this chapter – just in case you think I do that sort of thing all the time.

All-Bran Man: Jim Alder wins despite digestive problems.

I went home to Kaimes Road for the weekend (8th and 9th May) before the race, and became aware of a sore side, possibly a muscle strain, in the course of a 9 miler along the River Almond via Cramond and back by Cammo, where Robert Louis Stevenson sent David Balfour in "Kidnapped" with a letter for his uncle Ebenezer who lived in the desolate "House of Shaws" and tried to kill him by sending him up a broken external staircase without a lantern. In 1970, it was a windy, chilly day, and I wore a tracksuit and three layers; it was not spring-like at all.

On the Sunday the side was still sore, and I called off from a 5000m League race I was due to run in Glasgow, preferring to run a steady 15 miles in 89 minutes, but was uncomfortable if I pushed the pace with or against the wind. It was back to school on the Monday, where I followed the usual routine of a brisk 4 miles on the sands and golf courses with Ian Grieve at lunchtime, and a steady/slow 6 miles at University Park after school, following which I went to see physiotherapist Bill Thomson, the brother-in-law of P.E. Director Archie Strachan.

Tired but happy: Scotland's marathon trio – Fergus Murray, Jim Alder, DFM.

Bill's ministrations seemed to improve the injury, but at a school dance that evening for junior pupils I recall expressing despondency to the new head of English, Quentin Cramb, who encouraged me to go to Edinburgh anyway and "give it a go".

Saturday 16th was a very pleasant day, neither too windy nor too hot. The course had been tried out for the SAAA Championship in 1969, but the chances of doing well in consecutive years over the same course had seemed to me slight so that I hadn't entered on that occasion, and the race had been won by Bill Stoddart, the consistent Greenock man. He had entered again, and was a possible contender, but the most likely occupants of the three Scottish Commonwealth Games places were in a group including Jim Alder, Fergus Murray, Alastair Wood, Jim and Alex Wight, Alistair Johnstone (Victoria Park) who was in good form, and his clubmate Pat McLagan. Barry Jones from New Zealand was also in the field but definitely not bidding for a Scottish vest. And of course there was me, who definitely was.

After the customary easy few hundred metres in the stadium, we turned left on to the main London Road, the A1, which led us south-eastwards towards

Portobello, Musselburgh, and on for several miles farther before the route branched off left on to the A198 and we ran along just inland of the dunes and bents of the East Lothian coast before reaching the turning point on a minor country road and heading back into the breeze.

Over that first 13.1 miles, for the intermediate times were all given in miles still in Scotland and indeed in the UK at that period, the pace was "solid" without being excessive for the leading group of a dozen or so. The evidence of that is that we all stayed together through 5 miles (25:51), 10 miles (52:18 – 26:17 split), 15 miles (77:58 – 25:40 split) and 20 miles (around 1:44+ - a 26+ split). I remember being aware of a long East Coast train passing us as we headed slightly uphill towards the capital with about 7 or 8 miles to go, and of noticing some passengers at the windows: "What are these guys up to?"

At 21 miles things came to life as Jim Alder made a brilliantly timed break and kept it up for several hundred yards. By then he had dropped all except me. I had not just been train-spotting but had been keeping a close eye on the group, expecting a break. So I went with Jim at once. It was far too risky for any of us just to run along at a steady pace and rely on a fast finish, but I lacked enough confidence to make a sustained break myself. That one extended acceleration by the Clydebank-born Morpeth bricklayer determined the outcome of the race.

I stuck to Jim as we moved through the "Honest Toun" of Musselburgh, so called because of an incident in 1332 when the Regent of Scotland, Randolph, Earl of Moray, died in the burgh after a long illness during which he was devotedly cared for by its citizens. His successor offered to reward the people for their loyalty but they declined, saying they were only doing their duty. The new regent, the Earl of Mar, was impressed and said they were a set of honest men, hence "Honest Toun". That was far from my mind as we pushed our way up Willowbrae Road and then into the last seemingly unending traffic-filled stretch of Portobello Road, then London Road between tenements and petrol stations, opening at the last to a backdrop of the Castle on its rock, a mile or two away, Arthur's Seat and, our destination, the lighting columns and great bowl of Meadowbank Stadium. A Scottish Universities event was taking place on the track and infield, but there had been few spectators when we started and not all that many to welcome us back.

Hot van: Forbes with WWS551 at hillclimb.

Jim entered the stadium just a yard or two ahead of me, but I didn't notice that he had had an attack of diarrhoea a few hundred metres earlier and that the product was running down his right leg. Photos of the scene show that clearly, but I doubt if I would have made a greater effort to outsprint him. My old friend Ron Morrison, second in the Scottish Universities steeplechase to Dave Logue (Edinburgh) earlier in the day, witnessed the finish and says I was grinning an idiotic grin and didn't try to catch Jim. Certainly the pleasure at clinching a place in the team took precedence over becoming Scottish Champion. Rightly or wrongly, I didn't much care.

Jim had run a championship record time of 2:17:11, and my 2:17:14 was also a personal best. Fergus had uncoupled himself from Barry Jones to take the third spot with 2:18:25. Wood, Johnstone, MacLagan, Jim Wight and Bill Stoddart followed Jones home at respectable intervals. But the afternoon belonged to Jim, Fergus and me.

A mere nine weeks separated us from the Games Marathon on 23rd July, my 31st birthday. It was an exciting time, occasionally frustrating, as team members had to fill in forms, go and be fitted for uniforms, and so forth. We were all given blue blazers with silvery buttons bearing a thistle motif, except for mine which had a stag's head on them. White trousers were standard, though few could have had much use for them apart from during the opening parade, and the same went for the white hat. The Scottish vest was a bright blue essential as were the white shorts. Our tracksuits were nylon. Among the "extras" that appeared in our kit were pairs of paper underpants which the manufacturer had generously donated. I experimented with these to see how long they would last. Ten miles was about their limit.

Teaching and its associated tasks continued through May and June, and the summer holidays began on 3rd July. After recovering from the trial race, I stepped up the training again, recording 91 miles in the week 24th to 30th May, despite the Saturday being wasted at a Higher German markers' meeting after which I "felt lousy" and could only manage a dusty and windy 5 miles in tracksuit bottoms, and then ate too much.

The next day was also very windy, but Fergus and I managed a 2 hr 27 minute run (24 miles) in the Pentlands. Both that week and the next I was up to 103 miles. There was a team get-together at Tulliallan Police College near Kincardine over the weekend of 19th to 21st June. We were allocated uncomfortable army-style beds in the police barracks, with institutional food to match, and when we tried to run on the golf course just along the road we were chased off. Weekends like that, in unsuitable locations, are not team-building but dispiriting, and Dick Wedlock and I went through to Edinburgh on the Sunday morning to escape the mournful atmosphere and to get in a decent fifteen miler in the hills, after which we both felt better. Paavo Nurmi hated team get-togethers, because they upset his usual routine. I disliked them too.

Although the training included some speedwork, the first race I had was a 5000m at Meadowbank in the National League Division Two. Adrian Weatherhead (EAC) won in 14:17.6 from Fergus (14:23) and me (14:28.6). It was a windy day, so the times were not too bad.

The week of 5th-11th July was spent in Edinburgh, where I ran with John Bryant, Alistair Blamire, Dave Logue – who was running the Games steeplechase for Northern Ireland - and in St Andrews, where my companions were Jim Haddow, over from Canada again, and Doug Galloway, a 1:54 half-miler who lectured in Arabic. On Saturday 11th I moved like most of the rest of the Commonwealth Games participants into the Games Village, situated at Pollock Halls between the Commonwealth Pool and Holyrood Park, a majestic location.

The Village was under normal circumstances student accommodation for the University of Edinburgh. We registered and were given passes and other ID without very much by way of security being evident. In 1970 organisers did not think in terms of terrorist activity at big sporting events in the UK.

Alistair Blamire (Edin Univ) outsprints Ian Binnie (Victoria Park) on first leg of E to G 1965, Maybury.

There was in fact a plan during the Games by unknown parties to assassinate the Kenyan Olympic champion Kip Keino by shooting him from a flat overlooking Meadowbank Stadium. My friend John Bryant, at the time a reporter and sub-editor with the Edinburgh Evening News, found out about the plot and contacted the police.

It was good to be familiar with the area, so that training could be carried out with the least possible disturbance to the normal routine, the ideal scenario for athletes. Unfortunately however I developed a stomach upset and was out of sorts, so much so that when Gareth Bryan-Jones and I joined a few others for a drink in a pub near the Meadows on the Saturday evening, wearing our Commonwealth Games blazers, I embarrassed myself and my friends by being brusque with a couple of customers in the bar. The men had spotted that we were competitors and asked us quite reasonable questions as to what we were competing in, where we came from and so on. Downcast because I was worried that my stomach upset would prevent my running properly – in twelve days' time! – I gave monosyllabic, surly answers and soon went out. I was followed by Gareth, who suggested that I had been "unnecessarily stroppy". He was right.

The stomach was still upset at lunchtime the next day after a ten mile run with John Bryant, Dick Wedlock, and Alex and Jim Wight through Colinton Dell and the Hermitage of Braid. In the afternoon at 4pm John, the most inventive, amusing and encouraging of training comrades, came up with a cure for my nerves and by taking me on a very slow 50 minute jog in Corstorphine Woods, in full tracksuit. We chatted, joked and reminisced and worked up a good sweat as we padded along on the woodland paths. After a shower I felt in good spirits again. The next day was my father's 66th birthday: I was out for 5miles with Lachie Stewart and Dick Wedlock in the morning and ran a hard ten miles in the afternoon with Jim Alder, Lachie, Ian McCafferty and Ian Stewart. Again I wore a full tracksuit to help my body sweat out the bugs.

The next few days passed quickly. My stepmother was not too happy when I reported my unwillingness to attend the reception at the Palace of Holyroodhouse to which I had been invited as part of a cast of hundreds By Royal Command, one of many receptions held during the Games. I had already said good morning to Princess Anne as she trotted up the Queen's Park on her horse, in answer to which I was graced with a friendly smile; and I felt that was enough socialising with royalty. My stepmother said it was "all part of the Games", and she too was right. I just didn't enjoy these things.

That was true also of the opening ceremony on the afternoon of Thursday 16th July (my stepmother's birthday). In the morning I had done a 9 mile run with Gareth into the Village from Lasswade, outside Edinburgh, where he and his family lived. Gareth was technically sharing a room with me at Pollock Halls, where the fittings to the ropes attached to the national flags klirred against their flagpoles at night in the wind and kept people awake. Gareth preferred to stay at home, so that when Jim Hogan, the loquacious Irishman who was still reigning European marathon champion, came along looking for a floor to sleep on, I was able to offer him ours. The air was filled with the high-flown language, much of it beginning with f, b or c, that Jim only switched off, at least as far as I could see, when talking to women. One story of why he had left his previous athletic club related that he had been running round Richmond Park when a dog approached him looking aggressive. He kicked it, and the lady owner piped across: "Don't you dare kick my dog!" Jim replied very colourfully that she was lucky he hadn't kicked her. She turned out to be the club president's wife.

On the Friday eight days before the race I went back to Boarhills and ran a "not too fast" 16 at Tentsmuir with Doug Galloway and Jim Haddow, still feeling full of wind. After that I began easing down: a steady 10 with the Wight brothers and Andy McKean. That evening I made my only visit to the stadium to watch the 10,000 metres in which Lachie Stewart made himself immortal in the annals of Scottish athletics. It was raining slightly, but we shouted ourselves hoarse. That was a reason for not returning to Meadowbank on subsequent days, along with the desire to avoid getting too nervous and wasting energy.

During the 10,000m the veteran Scotsman reporter Jack Dunn took refuge in the bar from the rain, emerging only to ask "Who won?" At the press conference after Lachie's triumph, Ron Clarke, the multiple world record-holder who had been outsprinted off the home bend by the speedy dental technician, was asked if Lachie could win an Olympic medal (or it may have been "break the world record"). Clarke replied sensibly with his Australian twang "Who knows? Who can tell?"

As the race approached I had still not decided what shoes to wear. The reason was that my previous racing shoes were rather battered and I needed to replace them, but had not been able to find a pair that I liked. Puma had provided red racers rather like the white model Bill Adcocks had worn when winning the Marathon to Athens race in 2:11, but the soles were too thin, and I had passed them on to Dave Logue, who also took size 9 ½. Gareth came up with the solution by lending me a pair of well-used dark blue suede Adidas racers, which I was able to "run in" to my own specifications over the last three or four days.

"Race day dawned, and, thank goodness, it was not excessively hot" as Dunky Wright had said in 1968 in a BBC broadcast about the 1932 Los

Angeles Olympic marathon. That Thursday 23rd July 1970 was pretty warm, however, and for just about the first time anyone could recall, there was practically no wind on the course. The prevailing wind was normally from the west, but that day was wind still.

Dunky's sentence about the start of the 1932 marathon begins : "We set off at a steady six minutes to the mile on our watches". The 1970 field did not. There were only thirty starters, but they included several of the world's greatest marathon exponents, such as the Lancashire-born Aussie Derek Clayton, holder of the world's best (2:08:33.2), Jerome Drayton of Canada (who was born in Germany and had changed his Ukrainian name from Peter Buniak to Jerome Drayton "because I had always liked the name Jerome and felt it fitted well with Drayton" and had run 2:11:13 in winning at Fukuoka in 1969), Jeff Julian of New Zealand, one of Arthur Lydiard's original NZ stars, his team-mate Jack Foster, a late starter in running who was now 40, the English trio of Ron Hill, the obsessive Lancastrian, the 21 year old Don Faircloth from Croydon who had shocked the cognoscenti by winning the "Poly" to qualify for England's team, and Bill Adcocks the outstanding Coventry racer. Philip Ndoo of Kenya and John Stephens (Tanzania) were the main African challengers, along with Sinkala of Zambia, Rwabu (Uganda) and Dlamini (Swaziland). Mike Teer and Mike Cranny represented Northern Ireland, Mike Rowland, Dai Davies and Cyril Leigh Wales, while Harnek Singh and Y. D. Birdar started for India. Ken Grant, a former Dundee Hawkhill Harrier and S. Alecio wore the colours of Gibraltar. Fergus Murray, Jim Alder and I were of course the home candidates.

Jim had been put into a state of incandescent fury by an article in the Sunday Post under the headline "If it's snowing, put your money on Jim!" The basis for the headline was an interview with Derek Clayton in which the tall Australian had said that if the pace was fast, Jim would not have the class to keep up, but that if the race was run in extremely windy, hot or cold conditions, then and only then would he have a chance. Naturally, Jim resented that suggestion, and was determined to hit a fast pace and give Clayton something to think about, or die in the attempt.

The initial pace was well inside five minute miling. Four runners went through five miles in 23:31, these being Drayton, Clayton, Ndoo and Hill. Next came Harnek Singh in a very optimistic 23:57, 12 seconds up on Stephen, Alder,

Edinburgh Commonwealth Marathon July 23 1970: leaving the stadium.

Adcocks, Murray and me. By 10 miles, passed in 49:34, Fergus and I decided that the field was "bound to come back" as the leader, Ron Hill, was nearly two minutes ahead of us with 47:45. Unfortunately some of the field had no intention of coming back.

We caught a glimpse of Ron Hill soon after the turn as he headed westwards into the sunny afternoon. He passed 15 miles in 1:12:18, 59 seconds up on Jerome Drayton and 69 ahead of Alder and John Stephen. Adcocks, Foster, Clayton and Moore made up the leading eight. However by 20 miles we were seventh and eighth, both Clayton and Drayton having cruised to a halt by the roadside. Our time was 1:42:02 but we were 41 seconds down on Jack Foster whose pace showed no sign of slowing. It became a battle of mind over matter, and Fergus gradually drew away from me to finish in seventh place only 22 seconds behind Bill Adcocks.

Ron Hill, string vest and all, had set a new UK best with 2:09:28, an astonishing performance. He had to wait 2:36 before Jim Alder crossed the line in a much improved personal best of 2:12:04. So much for "If it snows, put your money on Jim". Don Faircloth was another who recorded a world-class time (2:12:19). Foster (2:14:44, Stephen (2:15: 05), Adcocks (2:15:10) and Fergus (2:15:32) paled by comparison, while my 2:16:53, Mike Teer's 2:17:24, and the other three sub-2:20 clockings of Andy Boychuk (Canada), Mike Rowlands and Cyril Leigh (both Wales) could all be classified as just "good". Even so, I took satisfaction from a personal best. Gareth, not long after finishing fourth in the steeplechase final, came out along the road to watch us finishing and was too tired to keep up with his own shoes as I headed towards the stadium.

That evening Jim Hogan was once again using our floor in the Games Village as his bed. He announced to me that he had arranged to go for a run with Ron Clarke at seven the next morning. I asked if I could come. "Sure you can!" And so with great difficulty I hauled my aching, stiff limbs out of bed and staggered out on to the concourse, where Ron Clarke met us. "Who's this?" he asked when he spotted me, but recognised who I was when Jim explained that I had run the marathon the day before, for he had been watching us come in. We set off, and as I had expected my strength lasted about a quarter of a mile – but at least I can say "I went running with Ron Clarke"!

That summer I had been invited to visit some friends in France and took a few weeks off serious training. The trip took me to Vernon-sur-Seine, then to Cusset and Chamalières in the Puy-de-Dôme, Massif Central. One notable run there was a steep climb up to the plaine de Gergovie (from about 400m to 744m above sea-level), where the Romans under Julius Caesar were defeated by Vercingetorix in 52 BC. I said au revoir to my friends in Chamalières and went south to Orange, to see Jean-Claude Martin, to Hyères (Jean-Pierre Hugon and his family) and finally to Lorgues once more, where I stayed with the Goberts – all friends I had made in 1961-2. Then I turned the nose of my white Renault 4 northwards again, and headed via the Alpes Maritimes and Gap right across France to Dieppe. I crossed to Southampton and, anxious to get home, zoomed the 471 miles back to Edinburgh overnight in 10 hours 40 minutes, arriving at Kaimes Road on the morning of August 16th, in time to get ready for school a few days later.

The rest of the year saw me in regularly quite good form on a training regime of almost exactly 400 miles a month, though by accident rather than by design, from September to the end of December 1970. Overall I had the best set of early season results before or since: starting with a 14:30 5000m win over Pat McLagan with a 30 second last 200 in the Scottish League on September 6th, I had second fastest time of the day at the ESH Fernieside 4x2.25 mile relays (11:48 to Adrian Weatherhead's 11:32), then won a Pifco Infra-Red Heater for fastest time at the McAndrew Relays on 3rd October. In fact Jim Brown ran 13:34, two seconds faster than me, but as a Youth he was ineligible for his team, Clyde Valley AC. The heater made up for a year's tenure of the fastest individual trophy, as Lachie Stewart had forgotten to bring it back, either through forgetfulness or presumption. Ron Marshall of the Glasgow Herald remarked on my exuberant response when he whispered to me that I had won.

I was beaten by Don Ritchie and Alastair Wood in a cross-country race from New Park playing fields in St Andrews the following week, but fastest again at the Kingsway Relays on 17th October with 13:30. Three weeks went by before the next race, the East District Relays at University Park, St Andrews, which of course I knew rather better than the back of my hand. Weatherhead and ESH's top Borderer, the stocky Craig Douglas from Hawick, were first and second on time (11:13, 11:16, both on the first of the four legs), then me with 11:17, but the highlight of the afternoon was that ESH finished its teams in the first three positions.

It may be of interest to mention that from 1968 or so onwards I was in the habit of running a very easy 20 minutes or so on the morning of a race. I felt this helped with getting my body race-ready and that combined with an extensive warm-up I could get more out of myself; and I always added a decent warm-down after the race to keep the mileage up. Some theorists of the 21st century pooh-pooh this as unnecessary, but I can assure you that they are quite wrong. Mileage, combined of course with other factors such as speed training of various types, diet, and sleep, has always been and will remain king.

On 14th November I took part in Glasgow University's open five mile road race but was hammered by Fergus (24:41), the phenomenal Jim Brown (24:44), and Andy McKean, younger brother of Bob (24:51). My 24:53 was also inside the previous record, but I did not feel good during the race.

The next Sunday a very strong west wind hampered the runners in the Edinburgh-Glasgow Relay, slowing the times dramatically. I was placed on the "leg of death", ie the sixth, from Forestfield Inn to Airdrie Cross. Somehow I managed to run the second fastest time, 35:13, and even caught 37 seconds on Commonwealth Games hero Lachie Stewart (Shettleston), though another hero, Jim Alder, was fastest with 34:46. ESH narrowly failed to beat the blue and gold-clad Shettleston men but came a close second. The next day John Bryant and I ran a pleasant though eventually very tiring 20 miler out from his flat in Mardale Terrace via Roseburn, Corstorphine Hill, Cramond to Turnhouse and Ingliston.

An SCCU team travelled to Guiseley (near Leeds) the next Saturday for a six mile match versus the Army and a Northern Counties of England Select. Jim Alder won from Kip Keino, who I assume was running as a very welcome guest, and Keith Darlow (North). I noted that there were too many fences, my excuse for coming only 13th.

It was freezing cold at Kirkcaldy for the second East District League race on 5th December. It was run over heavy but rutted country; in fact it was so cold that Gareth Bryan-Jones, Alistair Blamire and I all raced in tracksuit bottoms. Andy McKean won the race (wearing shorts), but Gareth and I were second equal and Alistair fourth – it was easy in those days!

The second week in December started with a 20 in Tentsmuir Forest with John Bryant and Bill Murray, as John and Carol were staying at Boarhills for the weekend. John was running very well, but it was still cold and I wore two tracksuit tops. The rest of the week was an ease-down for a new venture, an attempt on the world two-hour track record at Pitreavie Stadium by Dunfermline on Saturday 12th. I had no idea how I would cope with such a race. Would it be tedious to run for 120 minutes round and round a track? What if it were windy? The SAAA organisers, among them Dunky Wright, had assembled a good quality field including the doughty warrior Alastair Wood, his Aberdeen clubmate Steve Taylor, against whom I had also raced since my university days, the Wight brothers and a few more.

The race started at 11 am. It was a cold but bright day, and there was no wind to speak of. From the gun Alastair and I set the pace, but the first lap of 81 seconds was much too slow. Dunky shouted to get a move on, and we did, covering the next three laps in 78, 76 and 75 for a 5:10 first mile. By now the two of us were into a rhythm, and we alternated in the lead for the next 18 miles or so until I began to pull away from "the sardonic Alastair Wood", the

At six miles in the 1970 marathon:
Fergus Murray and I realise they're not all coming back.

description by Ming Campbell in that Scotsman article a year or so earlier. We went through five miles in 25:30, 10 in 51:06, 15 in 1:16:31.8. By 20, reached in 1:42:06.8, I was 13 seconds up.

The other runners provided helpful targets as we lapped them, and that continued even when I was in the lead alone. We did not know how close we were to Jim Alder's World Record pace. He had covered 23 miles 1071 yards at Walton on Thames on 17th October 1964. It was only with two laps to go that Dunky shouted that I was close to Alder's record, but by that stage it was beyond my powers to go faster. The last fifteen laps, that is, up to 1 hour 54 minutes 10 seconds were ticked off in 77, 76 or 75 seconds. If only I had knocked a single second off each of those laps, or indeed any others! I ran 77, 74, 75 and finally 72 for the 91st, 92nd, 93rd and 94th laps, and ran as hard as I could for the remaining 52 seconds…

It wasn't quite enough. 23 miles 971 yards was the distance achieved: 11 miles 1344 yards (18,932m) in the first hour, 11m 1387 (18,971m) in the second, finishing about 400 yards ahead of Alastair with Steve Taylor third. I had set a world track best for 35 km (a rarely run distance) of 1:50:59.8 and numerous Scottish Native, National and all-Comers' Records, some shared with AJW, some Native Records not achieved as they were held by Jim Alder, and the time was the equivalent of a marathon in around 2:13:30. I was elated but at the same time disappointed. Why had I not just run that teensy-weensy bit faster? If only... And yet it was one of my best runs ever, an almost perfect climax to the year.

Chapter 14

Who was this Zeus?

In 1970 I had run 4698 ½ miles, according to the training diary. How exact that half mile was I am unsure, but I usually round it up to 4699 – for some reason never 4700. In any event it was my highest year ever for mileage: 4048 in 1971 and 4254 in 1972 were the next best. The daily average was 12.874 miles per day, just short of a half marathon.

I was banging in the miles in early 1971, as I had been asked to go to San Sebastian with Dick Wedlock and Gareth Bryan-Jones for the international cross-country race there on Sunday 31st January. In December Fergus Murray and I had been due to represent the SCCU in another cross-country race in Luxemburg, but BEA kept us waiting at Edinburgh Airport in the fog from 11am till 5pm, when we decided to go home. Euan Murray (Garscube H), the SCCU secretary, later phoned us up to complain that we should have gone. Instead we went for a run to get the weary hours of waiting out of our systems.

After that non-event it was 100 miles a week or more for most of the month, easing down only for the last two days before I was due to tackle the racecourse at Lasarte. I was terrified of the hurdles, Gareth's forte but my faible. However fear lent me springs and I hurdled amazingly well, to finish 18th in a big field. Dick was 8th and Gareth 34th; some of the English lads even congratulated me on the unexpectedly good run.

In previous years Lasarte had been a happy hunting ground for "El Lachie", who had picked up numerous Basque berets, cups, prizes and no doubt bundles of "illegal" pesetas in appearance money, but I wasn't anywhere near his class, and so I only got a beret.

The next day Gareth and I, having missed our usual long Sunday run because we were racing, decided to set off an hour before the coach taking the British teams to Bilbao airport, the intention being that they would catch us up after about an hour and a quarter's running along the coast road.

Athens 1971: with Stelios Kyriakides (Boston winner 1946).

The best laid plans of mice and men gang aft agley: we set off as arranged, after putting our luggage on the coach, and were running along fine until it started to rain after 20 minutes. It was cold, and we were wearing tracksuits. The bottoms on mine were held up by thin elastic, and as the rain grew heavier the trousers began to sag and the elastic eventually broke. I had to run along holding my bottoms up with one hand –we had no gloves – and the run became one of the most miserable I have ever experienced.

The athletes' bus did not appear, though we kept looking round for it every so often. 1 hour 52 minutes had passed before it drew up just ahead of us. As the two drowned rats clambered on board, a great cheer went up from those within its warm interior. It turned out that the departure from the hotel had been delayed by around three-quarters of an hour. After the 29km or so we had covered along that bleak grey coastal road, we were very happy to clamber into the coach and towel ourselves down before changing into warm clothing.

The next big race was the SCCU cross-country championship on 20th February at Bellahouston Park, Glasgow. I was pretty fit because of the high mileage and managed to come 7th to Jim Alder, Alistair Blamire, Dick Wedlock, Fergus Murray, John Myatt (Strathclyde University) and Andy McKean (Edinburgh Univ) who was about to move up on to the high level plateau of his career that brought him four Scottish cross-country championships and made him more or less unbeatable in Scotland. Lachie Stewart was one place behind me and the top ten were made up by Norman Morrison (Shettleston) and Jim Wight (EAC). Doug Gunstone (Edinburgh AC) beat Jim but was disqualified for being a junior. It was a pretty good array of distance running talent – add on Ian McCafferty and Ian Stewart and it would have been a team hard to beat in Europe, England apart.

Despite my good barefoot run, I didn't get the chance to pull on the Scottish semmit (=vest, cognate with 'samite [velvet])) at the CC International, but I wasn't worried, as the British Amateur Athletic Board had invited Fergus Murray and me to compete in the IX Classical Marathon. It was held over the 1896 Olympic Games route from the seaside plain where the Persians had been defeated in 490BC, past the tomb of the Athenian warriors who had been killed during the battle, and up over the hills and then down for the last 12km or so to the Panathenaikos Stadium.

The stadium had been built in the time of Pericles in the 5th century BC and extended in marble by the Roman Herod Atticus in the 2nd century AD. It was upgraded for the first Olympic Games of modern times by Georgios Averoff, a shipping millionaire, who gave a total of nearly 2m drachmae to reconstruct the stadium and also to build a shooting range, velodrome, tennis courts, stands, and boathouses in Piraeus. There had even been money left to install new gas lamps and new pavements in Athens. In those days it wasn't described as "legacy" but that's what it was.

It is of course extremely doubtful that a messenger, and certainly not one called Pheidippides or Philippides, had ever run back over the hills through the blazing sunshine, met the god Pan in the heat-haze at the top, among the scents of thyme and rosemary and broom, and staggered on to collapse and expire on the Parthenon flagstones with the words "We've won" on his salt-encrusted lips. But it's a good story.

Someone certainly brought the news of victory. He was unquestionably a hemerododromos, or day-runner, a soldier trained to carry messages over long distances, like the Ethiopian "Cushi" in II Samuel Chapter 18 who was sent by the Israelite general Joab to carry the tragic news of the death of King David's rebel son Absalom – he had been caught by the hair in a tree while riding through the wood of Ephraim after the battle between the royal forces and his rebel army and had thus hanged himself - to David in Jerusalem.

One such hemerodromos was said by Herodotus, writing about 50 years after Marathon, to have been sent by the Athenian leaders to Sparta to ask the Spartans to assist against the huge Persian force led by King Xerxes. The Spartans were tough, and also superstitious or perhaps just religious and said the moon was not in the right quarter and they would only come to Marathon when it was. If only Tony Blair had said that to George W Bush. In the end the Spartans arrived too late for the battle but were able to help the Athenians pile up their own dead warriors plus those of the enemy.

The messenger was then said by Herodotus to have run back to Athens with news of victory, but no death scene was reported. The Pheidippides version only surfaced in the 1st C AD in the writings of Lucian about 500 years after the battle. It can't be regarded as an eye-witness account.

We were going to provide a 1971 re-run, helped to some extent by our team manager, the legendary Duncan McLeod Wright, or "Dunky" as he was universally known in Scotland. Dunky had run in three Olympic Marathons, dropping out in 1924 with blistered feet, finishing 20th in 1928 in 2:45:30, but coming good in 1932 when he was fourth to Juan Carlos Zabala (ARG), Sam Ferris (GBR), Armas Toivonen (FIN) in 2:32:41. "Four men on the track at the finish of an Olympic marathon, a sight seen never before, and for that matter, never since…" as he said in 1968 when he recorded his story for the BBC. It was a short broadcast that had tacked on to it excerpts of interviews with Fergus Murray, Lachie Stewart, and me. It all sounds incredibly ancient.

I had also done an interview with Dunky in 1969, published in Athletics Weekly. Although I had thought it covered his career pretty well over a double page spread, he described it as a "travesty", though I never found out why. Others seemed to regard it as interesting. ["My friends told me I spoke well."]

Dunky had won a huge number of races and taken part in athletics as runner, judge, timekeeper, organiser, official – just about everything. He was also a broadcaster on BBC Sportscene - or "Scotfoot" as I called it since it was 90% about football. Dunky was squeezed in – "I was at Garscadden today to see young Eddie Knox of Springburn Harriers storm to victory by 40 yards…" – if listeners were lucky, just before or maybe after the shinty results around 6:55 pm on a Saturday night as we sat in the dark coach heading back from some muddy cross-country race in the West. The sports programme was always followed by Scottish Country Dance Music, introduced by the familiar chords of "Kate Dalrymple' (DUM diddy DUM diddy DUM diddy DUM, DUM diddy diddy diddy Dum Dum Dum Dum).

Wright was also a journalist and wrote for the Scottish Sunday Express. He was a "character" – much loved, though not by all, as he had a ruthless streak and took himself too seriously, so that he was much imitated, especially by people like me. It is true that we were in a sense mocking him because of his working-class attitudes, education and background – he had worked for the railways – but the mockery was never malicious. Dunky had been notorious in his time as an athlete for changing clubs. He had been a member of Clydesdale Harriers, Maryhill Harriers, Shettleston Harriers, to name but the three best-known ones. This chopping and changing depending on the strength of the clubs was rather like the antics of the Vicar of Bray. Dunky represented Scotland 11 times in the cross-country International, a record only surpassed by Andy Brown and Jim Alder.

In early 1971 I started livening up my training diary (for a few months only) by recording at the top of each week's page any "Diner-Waiter" jokes that had appeared that week in The Sunday Post, a very popular if couthy paper of which the journalist James Cameron had once written that Scotland would only be free when the last Church of Scotland minister had been strangled with the last copy of The Sunday Post. It is a DC Thomson publication. In those days Oor Wullie and The Broons appeared in the Fun Section, which included a load of jokes headed "Merry Mac's Fun Parade". For some reason my brother Forbes and I decided to investigate whether the "Diner-Waiter" jokes were chosen arbitrarily from a central store or used in sequence. So it came about that future historians reading my training diaries will find gems such as "You'll find everything on the menu, Sir!" – "So I see! Bring me a clean one!" or "Waiter, you're not fit to serve a pig!" – "I'm doing my best, Sir!" above notes on the long Sunday runs.

In the build-up for Athens I ran 400 miles in February and 424 in March. For the first time I had decided to try the Saltin diet, as pioneered with such great success by Ron Hill. I note that I called the first phase "the Fat Diet", and I'm not sure just how effectively it was carried out. On Wednesday 31st March I ran three miles with Ian Grieve at lunch, then a depletion run of 16 miles in 1:48 from Boarhills with Doug Gunstone. On the Thursday I did three five mile runs, solo, with Doug, and with Alex Wight (up for the week on a course), Ian and Doug respectively. On April 1st I managed a five and an eight miler with Doug, a nine solo on Friday, and finally a "dreadful" six miles from Byways as the diet continued to weaken me. Then Fergus and I flew off with Dunky to London and then to Athens.

The IX Classical Marathon was held like its predecessors on 6th April, the date of the first modern Olympic Marathon in 1896. The race had been held since 1955 and in 1969 it hosted the European Championship. In 1971 it attracted quite a good quality field, headed by Japanese champion Akio Usami, whose best was around 2:10, by Jack Foster (New Zealand) who had run 2:12:17 at Fukuoka in December 1970 and by Australia's John Farrington, who had first swung across my rather remote horizon when he was one of the first four in the BUSF championship cross-country in 1963. He had since emigrated to Australia and was hoping for a place in the Olympic marathon, if his adopted country sent three runners.

There was an Ethiopian called Gizachev too whom no one could discount since the successive triumphs of Abebe Bikila, barefoot in Rome in 1960 and shod in white and black Pumas in Tokyo in 1964, and the victory of the veteran Mamo Wolde (birth date unknown) at high altitude in Mexico City in 1968. The Ethiopians and Kenyans had not yet developed the squad system later used, and women's marathon running was not yet fully established anywhere despite the efforts of Kathy Switzer and others at the Boston and the encouragement of Dr Ernst van Aaken, one of the pioneers of LSD, who had for some years organised an annual women-only race at Waldniel near Düsseldorf. Another pioneer of distance running for women was Dale Greig of Scotland.

Other leading contenders included Herb Lorenz (USA), Danny McDaid (Ireland), Nedo Farčič (Yugoslavia) and of course Fergus Murray and me.

We stayed at an international hotel called the "Astor" not far from Syntagma Square, and on the first evening after arrival the three of us were out for a stroll when my left arm was grasped very firmly by a tall well built man with a moustache who asked if I wanted a woman. I tried to explain why I had come but he ignored that reply and kept hold of my arm. Fergus and Dunky had not seen this and I was reluctant to create a scene by calling the police or drawing their attention to the man, who in the end faded into the crowd as I was about to signal for help.

Greece at that time was under the rule of the junta of "colonels" and one or two of my progressive friends expressed mild surprise or disapproval that I should seem to be offering support to their fascistic regime by running in the race. I have to say that the political aspect never crossed my mind until afterwards when they brought it up.

Dunky unconsciously provided us with elements of humour, and we mocked him affectionately, though not to his face. He was too remote from us in age and attitudes. Stelios Kyriakides, one of the race organisers and a man who had become a post war Greek hero by winning the "Boston" in 1946, said to us one afternoon to remember that Dunky was an old man and deserved our respect, we too would be old one day.

Dunky had been given two BAAB pennants, and told us confidentially that "Now the Greeks, you see, they have no presentation. I've two pennants here. Between you and me and the four walls I'm giving one of these to 'Karakides'". We visited a golf course where there were letters and photos displayed showing various well-known golfers. Dunky: "I know every one of these men personally". He told us of his early days training and how he bought gymshoes for 1/11 from Woolworths. He said he used to train with "Jimmy Mackay and his brother from the Eastern Rowing Club" in Edinburgh around 1930. " I knew the head chemist at Boots, and asked him for 10,000 wheatgerm oil pills for pregnant women. We used to train on a mixture of olive oil and Horlicks – very smooth, lovely". James Miller, a future Lord Provost of Edinburgh and a one-time runner, had been asked by DMcLW "How are you getting on towards being Lord Mayor?"– "It's in the pipeline now, Dunky, it's in the pipeline now...".

He had said to Princess Anne when asked what it was like running a marathon that "it's like your dad running home to Windsor to bring in the rolls and milk". When the Queen asked him when he won the British Empire Games [1930], he claimed to have replied: "You don't need to take your shoes and socks off, Your Majesty, I'll tell you."

We did some short runs on the pre-race days (Sat, Sun and Mon) and Dunky went sightseeing. He came to the evening meal once to tell us about his day. "Now what is the Partheenon, Donald? – You're the expert." He had been to visit the Akropolis: "I was there for two hours – I did it justice. It's quite a place". He then said to Fergus, who has a general science BSc from Edinburgh University: "Fergus, I thought you were a history teacher. Tell me, who was this Zeus?" Dunky was incredulous at the prices charged for the Daily Express (2/-) and for a glass of lager (3/6), but on the evening after the race offered to stand us an ouzo – "it's their brandy, you know".

The Ethiopian trainer Onni Niskanen was Finnish by birth and wore a white and blue tracksuit labelled SUOMI. Dunky had been reading the start list and confused the Finn with Usami, asking "How good is this Suomi?"

That evening at dinner Dunky offered us a bottle of wine. "This is my wee treat for you", he said, putting it on the bill. He told us something of his achievements: "Just ask me, any distance between half a mile and a marathon, and I'll tell you when I won it."

He told us he won the Morpeth-Newcastle "seven times on the trot" but said (wrongly) that by 1971 it was two miles shorter and that the steep Blagdon Bank had been eliminated.

At the Amsterdam Olympics in 1928 he had been running with the winner who kept forcing him over, and Dunky thought "I'll push him into the Amstel at the next bend", but he ran away, and Dunky didn't see him again till the end.

More recent events also involved him. He told us he had been in a pub in Rose Street with officials Ian Ross (ESH) and Rab Forman (SAAA Hon Gen Secretary) discussing the marathon selection for the 1966 Jamaica Games. Dunky said "I'm putting Jim Alder forward", but Rab (allegedly) didn't want to pick him. Of course Alder won.

On race day we were taken out by bus to the village of Marathon. The TV cameras were rolling and Dunky mingled with the competitors, officials and some Greek Orthodox priests with their tall headdresses, remarking that "if this is on TV I'll be in every picture".

The temperature at the start was around 21 degrees Celsius and there was a strong headwind blowing out of Athens along the Marathon road. The field lined up, each

Duncan McLeod Wright as team manager, Athens 1971.

runner having been given an olive twig. The tradition is that the runners make a detour to the tomb of the 192 Athenian warriors from 490BC and cast their twigs down there.

When the gun went off, so did we, with Usami and Farrington setting a fast early pace. Not all the runners had understood the significance of the twigs and a few held on to them till the finish. By 5km Usami (in 14:25!) was well ahead of Farrington, Foster and Farčič: the 3 Fs…

I once heard a drunk man at Edinburgh's Haymarket one Saturday night use the 3 Fs in describing to his pal his very ungentlemanly approach to women. And talking of Haymarket, whose central clock was erected by Heart of Midlothian supporters to commemorate the Hearts players who had fallen in the First World War, my father once wrote to the TLS to explain the sexual connotations of the phrase "to get off at Haymarket", used throughout the railway age to describe coitus interruptus as opposed to the delights of "going all the way to Waverley" through the Tunnel of Love under the former Caledonian Station. He traced the idea to the time of the first railway into Glasgow, and a Highlander approaching Glasgow via Paisley. The Times Literary Supplement printed it, I'm pleased to say. In 1963, I think. If not, it should have been, as Larkin enthusiasts will appreciate.

The Athens course stops being relatively flat soon after the warriors' tomb. Usami went through 10km in 29:39, 53 seconds in the lead and despite the wind seemingly aiming at Adcocks's record 2:11:7.8. I was running in cohort with Fergus, but we had been dropped by the first five runners and worked hard up the series of hills up to 30km, the summit of the course. Meanwhile the Japanese runner had gone through 20km in 61:00, 2:33 ahead of Farrington with Jack Foster on 63:43 and Fergus, Farčič and me on 65:00, just ahead of Gizachev (65:12) and Lorenz (65:18).The long uphill drag and the strong wind began to slow everyone down, as the road veered to the west, and the wind from side-on to full head-on. At 25km Akio's lead was up to 2:50 over John Farrington. At 30km it was 2:59, but his 5km splits had dropped to 17:50 and 18:16.

Everyone else was running at that pace or slower, a relative crawl. Gizachev had moved up quickly past Fergus and me, but had attacked the hills with too much vigour and by 30km was beginning to come back.

I had hoped that the diet would result in a boost in energy but when it came to the bit I was not able to raise my pace over the gentle slope from 32km down to the stadium and developed a stitch. Fergus, who had also been affected by a stitch on the uphill section before half way, pulled slowly away from me. It was frustrating. Up front, Farrington reduced Usami's lead at the finish to 2:31 (2:19:25 to 2:21:56.2), and Foster was an isolated third in 2:22:29.2.

I recovered enough to catch Gizachev with 9km to go (and took 9 minutes out of him!). Fergus Murray's time was 2:25:5.4 and mine 2:26:2.8. The only other runners under 2:30 were Lorenz, McDaid and Maurice Peiren (Belgium). Jack Foster, who had a sore throat and a cold, said afterwards that he felt his 2:22 was "at least equivalent" to his 2:12:17 at Fukuoka the previous year, adding: "When Usami cleared away at the start, both Farrington and I let him go. We thought he was going much too fast with a head wind and hill to battle. But he got away with it. I still think we used the right tactics to a degree. I think we would both have slowed right down if we had attempted to stick with Usami."

That evening we celebrated with the promised ouzo and Dunky told us that "It would have been a sitter for me. I'd have won that race". Asked how he could be so sure, he said he would just have sat in on the leader all the way and then sprinted off at the end! Easier said than done, though it's impossible to compare runners of different eras, and Dunky was a top runner in his day. Fergus and I were half amused and half hurt that he could dismiss us so cavalierly as second-rater plodders – o wad some Pow'r the giftie gie us, to see oursels as others see us! Before the race he had confided in us – I noted all this down at the time – "Remember boys, the race is not to the swift."

He added to the confusion of names by looking at the intermediate times and noting that "here you gained 15 seconds on Salome".

That evening we went for a drive along the coast and stopped at a roadside stall where I bought a hot dog. It gave me food poisoning and I threw up violently. Just as well it was after the race and not before it.

At the prizegiving each runner received as a souvenir of the race a copy of a relief of the original marathonodromos collapsing on the Akropolis. Our participation did bring one small unexpected benefit. On the lookout for inexpensive souvenirs Fergus and I went into a gift shop that sold small ceramic tiles and plates with reproductions of classical themes about the Olympian gods and ancient Greek heroes and heroines. The burly shop owner was offering the small tiles (about 5x5cm) for 7 drachmas. When we said we were in Athens to race the marathon we were greeted as marathonodromoi and he cut the price to 4 drachmas.

After returning to Scotland and taking it easy to try to recover, for some reason I decided to run the Edinburgh-North Berwick marathon only weeks later. Alex (2:15:27) and Jim (2:15:43) Wight took me to the cleaners. The course was slightly downhill, with a slight following wind, and it was a warm sunny day. The route led over the first half of the Commonwealth Games course and then continued along the coast road to the resort of North Berwick. The brothers ran really well. I recorded my "standard" 2:19 and just managed to beat Gareth Bryan-Jones, who ran 2:23:17, over the last few miles.

Even more foolishly I tried two more marathons that summer: at the Maxol in Manchester on Sunday 13th June I turned in another 2:19 for 28th place. The SAAA championship on Saturday 26th June on a wet day over the BCG course was definitely a race too many for me. The legs were just too weary and after 1:48:15 for 20 miles I was forced to drop out at about 23. Pat McLagan (Victoria Park AAC) went on to win in 2:21:17 by two minutes from Bill Stoddart (Greenock Wellpark) and Willie Day (Falkirk Victoria Harriers).

I had already decided to go to work for the Centre for British Teachers in Germany and take a year's leave of absence. So my season in Scotland came to an end after the SAAA race. In my newly acquired but not very new maroon Renault 16 hatchback, I went for a camping holiday in the Vosges with a lady friend whom I had met on the plane coming back from Athens, and ran a bit there. Our criterion for selecting camp sites from the Guide Michelin Camping et Caravanning was the red symbol denoting hot showers - not all sites catered for the sybaritic.

Then it was back to Boarhills and Edinburgh to pack and say "Auf Wiedersehen!" to the dear familiar places, and "Auf geht's!" to the Federal Republic of Germany and the Lower Rhineland.

Chapter 15

Im Westen nichts Neues

It's every marathon runner's dream to compete at the Olympics. For years I had thought it unattainable, but in 1972 fate or chance or whatever may control our lives helped me to get there – and to perform well. That last bit is important, because not many people get a second chance if things go wrong the first time, and then you have the rest of your life to reflect on what might have been. I always think in this regard of Jim Alder, who, despite his magnificent achievements in athletics in every other respect, had to drop out in the 1968 Mexico City marathon because of dehydration.

I had decided to have a year away from Madras College, particularly from the junior building at Kilrymont Road at the back of the town, which I felt restrictive and the atmosphere unstimulating. I applied for a job as teacher of English for German speakers with the Centre for British Teachers in Germany, which accepted me in the spring of 1971 and allocated me to a position at the Staatliches Gymnasium, Emmerich. I had never heard of Emmerich, which lies on the plain of the Rhine not far from the Dutch border. I was on a year's secondment, so that my job was safe if I chose to return to it.

At the back of my mind, or even a bit further forward, was the knowledge that the Olympics were to be held in Munich in September of 1972. Would living in Germany be a help in getting there? Logically speaking, no.

One of the directors of the Centre was Tony Abrahams, the nephew of Harold Abrahams, the 1924 Olympic 100m champion, later well-known as a BBC radio commentator and later still celebrated through the film Chariots of Fire. Tony had heard of me, or at least so he said when we met at the interview.

There were quite a few teachers assigned to the Niederrhein area, and we all met up in early August for a fortnight's initiation course in the historic Burg-Hotel of Volmarstein in the hills above the Ruhr valley. It was quite good fun, but my principal memory of it is of mine host, a corpulent chap, who was keen that we went to bed reasonably early, coming into the bar at around 10.30pm and crooning to us: "Die Engländer müssen zu Bette geh'n…" which was greeted with catcalls. During the course I established contact with a number of others who were to be working in nearby towns and who would come to constitute a new social circle.

I drove to Emmerich in my maroon Renault R16 hatchback on 25th August filled with trepidation. I was assigned a room in the "Hopp'sches Konvikt", which was not an internment centre, though I occasionally had my doubts over the year, but a residence for (male) boarders whose parents lived abroad or at some distance. The warden, Herr Gutschalk, lived on the premises with his family, as did two or three of the deputy wardens. My room in the Konvikt overlooked a "Katjes" liquorice factory from which smells drifted across when there was a west wind. The Konvikt lay on the edge of town, not far from a narrow wood, the Helenenbusch, where I went for my first easy run that evening.

The next day I went to the school to be introduced to Frau Quinders, head of the English department, who talked me through some of the complexities of the German exam system, which I won't go into here. Suffice it to say that everything in education – and indeed beyond – is graded on a 1-6 scale, from "sehr gut" through "gut", "befriedigend", "ausreichend" (all pass marks) to "mangelhaft" and "ungenügend". [very good, good, satisfactory, just good enough, not good enough and unsatisfactory]

On arrival in Emmerich I bought a new pair of training shoes – blue Adidas "München 72". No doubt the name attracted me, but I see I noted "sore" in my training diary after the first run in them, a 79 minute easy-steady excursion along roads, woodland tracks, and across fields from the Konvikt. Over the first weeks I did quite a bit of exploring, clocking up 94 miles in the first full week and 101 and 100 miles in the next two. I was worried I would have nobody to train with, but managed to track down a local runner, Udo Hennig, who was persuaded to join me on some runs. That benefited us both, as Udo, who was more a 1500m runner, had been doing considerably less training and improved his fitness considerably over the next months.

As the Dutch border was very close, and the Dutch woodlands much more extensive, we trained regularly "abroad". Once I had found my way about, I took to driving across to the village of 's Heerenberg and parked in the woods. That changed after mid-December when a thief broke the car window and stole my newly purchased warm red anorak, a watch and a towel. Fortunately he or she didn't find my passport, keys and insurance in the armrest locker.

I got back after 1hr 45 min running to find a couple of policemen peering inside and around the car. I had to follow them to the local station to give my details, shivering the while as anorak and towel were of course gone. Brrr! It took a long time to get all the little rectangles of glass out of the vehicle.

Through Udo I entered a 25 km road race in Düsseldorf on 9ᵗʰ October, which I won in 82:22.8 by around five minutes from Willi Roggenbach (ASV Köln). I had a stitch from 5 to 15km but tried to go hard all the way, sustaining an even pace of about 16:15 per 5km. At the race I met an official and a couple of athletes from Köln, and signed up as a member of their club, TV Refrath, so that I would be able to have more chances to race.

The 25km result encouraged me, but it wasn't always easy to keep up the training effort. One benefit of the German school day was that classes began at around 8am but finished at 1 or 1.30pm, so that I could spend much of the afternoon/evening training, inserting lunch and/or a siesta as they fitted in to the schedule. Teaching was very tiring, but not physically so, and somehow, despite remarks in the diary about feeling fed-up or tired, I kept up a reasonable mileage through October (339 miles). The month ended with a win in the Westdeutsche Marathonmeisterschaft (i.e. the western part of West Germany) in Köln in 2:19:00.2 from Wolfgang Gloede (Alemannia Aachen), who was 59 seconds down over the rather rough and twisty 3 lap circuit. The stony bits caused soles of my feet to "burn" in my old Yardley racing shoes, which were a bit boat-like and near the end of their active life. As I was a foreigner I was adjudged the winner "außer Konkurrenz" [out of competition] so that Gloede kept the title. My prize was a Schick electric shaver, which I must have given away as I always shave in the shower with a cheap plastic razor.

From then until Christmas I was on recovery mileage, running mostly alone but sometimes with Eric Wakeling, a fellow teacher who worked in Goch, a village not far away, or with Udo Hennig. Udo was a friendly but fiery man whose character was reflected in his driving. In early December I had one race, a 6-7km "Adventscrosslauf" in the Helenenbusch woods near the Konvikt, organised by Emmerich sports club (ETV), and I won there by a minute or so.

At Christmas I went back to Edinburgh and took up the chase again, covering 110 miles for the last seven days of the year. Over the holiday period I had

Das ist Emmerich…und das ist der Rhein, 1972.

sessions with George Brown, Alex "Ikel" Wight, Martin Craven and Gareth Bryan-Jones in Edinburgh and with the usual running mates – Ron Morrison, Doug Gunstone, Ian Grieve – in St Andrews. It was a good break, and I returned to Emmerich determined to keep up as high a mileage as I could, though without any specific focus on selection for Munich, probably because I believed without formulating it with clarity that hubris or over-confidence would be followed by nemesis. It was better to be privately confident, but to avoid tempting the gods by stating it publicly.

I pioneered a new long Sunday run, the "Zwei-Grenzen-Lauf" (two frontier run), that led me over a bridge in the woods into the Netherlands and out again at the official crossing just a couple of kilometres from Emmerich. Initially I carried my passport in a plastic envelope inside my tracksuit. Under the Schengen agreement nationals of the signatory continental EC members could cross each other's borders without passports, but the UK had not signed up.

I soon stopped bothering to take my passport with me. The customs officers never stopped me anyway, or so I thought until Tuesday 14th March. After about 1hr 40min of running I had just passed the control barrier on the other side of the road when a voice shouted to me to come back. I looked round, and saw a Dutch customs officer gesticulating. He had a gun so I went back. What was I playing at, crossing without showing ID? Where did I come from? Where was I going? I explained that I was British and that I was training in Holland because the woods were so nice, and that I was hoping to run in the Olympics if I got lucky. He let me go, telling me that I would never be successful at running if I got worked up and over-excited. After that I was careful to carry my passport with me on that route.

To achieve 100+ miles a week I have always found that it's necessary to do 10-12 sessions. In February I had run 356 miles (including wins in a low-key forest trail race series over 10/15km [on the same morning] and 20km in the Königsforst near Köln). In March I covered 453 miles (average about 14½ miles a day). Much of the training was done in the woods by Elten close to the Dutch border, so that the proportion of road running was relatively low. I was lucky that my work conditions allowed daylight training as the spring approached.

On March 19th I drove back (overnighting in the Rotterdam-Hull ferry which had delicious apple and sultana cake), accompanied by Ralf Hühne, one of the Emmerich English and sport teachers. I dropped Ralf off in the city centre and went home, to discover that my father had been diagnosed (wrongly, as it turned out) with possible cancer and was in a weakened condition from chemotherapy. I helped to take him out on a few walks down by the river Almond. Happily, once the mis-diagnosis had been established, he recovered quickly.

I split the time between Edinburgh and St Andrews. On 25th March I raced the ESH 10 miles club championship, winning in 52:09 by 1:26 from Tommy Coyle with George Brown 3rd in 54:01, though I had a "bad feeling" throughout the race. The feeling was to be replicated a few weeks later in the Waldniel marathon, which I was intending to use as a practice run for the Olympic Games trial, the Maxol marathon to be held in Manchester on June 4th.

Meantime I had arranged to pay a visit to Dunoon, where my old head of department, Ian M Hendry, was now Rector of the Grammar School. The principal teacher of modern languages post was vacant, and Ian had encouraged me to apply for it. In Dunoon I was interviewed by Ian and by the Director of Education for Argyll, Charles Edward Stewart, and formally offered the job, for which I appeared to be the only applicant. It was a great prospect, although I was sad at the thought of no longer living in St Andrews. I nonetheless cherished the hope of returning there some day.

Meantime there was training to be done, as well as fulfilling my responsibilities as Assessor at the Staatliches Gymnasium. The head teacher (Schulleiter), Herr Oberstudiendirektor Rudolf Reis, was a very conservative man, tall, grey-haired with a small moustache, and had a low opinion of the "Sozis" who were in charge of Nordrhein-Westfalen's education policy. One decree from the ministry he described at a Lehrerkonferenz as "eine Unverschämtheit ersten Grades" [a first-rank piece of impertinence], which made me wonder how you would decide what constituted an impertinence of the second or third rank.

All teachers had a titular grade in the hierarchy, from the probationer (Studienassessor) through Studienrat, Oberstudienrat, Studiendirektor and finally to Oberstudiendirektor. Someone like me, who had eight years' experience but had not taught under the German system, did not fit into any of the usual categories, hence Herr Reis's decision to list me as Assessor Macgregor.

In fact after some initial silly mistakes, I was working pretty well, though I did not enjoy the four or five hour staff meetings to decide on exam grades. Everyone had his or her own seat at the long table, and mine happened to be next to that of a pipe-smoker who puffed out clouds of tobacco fumes continuously. Runners are not alone in detesting passive smoking.

Although my German by now was good, it was hard for me to pick up all the allusions and inferences in conversations among the "Kollegen", my teacher colleagues. It was a male-dominated staffroom, with Frau Quinders, a lady of a certain age, being treated as an honorary male.

One gentleman, who must have been close to if not past retirement age and taught only part-time, struck up a conversation with me one day that made me wonder what decade I was living in. He asked, in German of course: Would it not have been a good idea, Herr Macgregor, for Germany, the greatest land power, and England [sic], the greatest sea power, to join forces against the Soviets?" I was so astonished at his question that I could only reply something to the effect that I didn't think it would have been such a great plan. I can still recall his rather high-pitched, old-fashioned tones: "Wäre es nicht eine gute Idee gewesen...?" But such views were rare. Herr Reis, for example, drove an Opel. I asked him if he would not prefer a Mercedes (which had been the car of choice for the NS hierarchy), but he said: "No Mercedes – I'm quite happy with an Opel."

The high mileage continued during my visit to Scotland for the Easter break, and when I returned to Emmerich on 9th April it was time to get ready for a practice race, the Waldniel marathon on Saturday April 15th, just seven weeks before the Maxol. The village of Waldniel was the home of Dr Ernst van Aaken, the race patron and one of the pioneers of LSD (Long Slow Distance), although he didn't invent the name. Van Aaken was renowned for his encouragement of women's long distance running as well as of LSD as a rehabilitation therapy for heart attack and stroke victims.

On this occasion I did not do a full carbohydrate depletion , because the Maxol was such a short time later and I thought my body would react unfavourably to being "tricked" twice in two months. Also I intended to train through Waldniel and use it as part of my build-up. Therefore I did the normal two sessions a day on the Monday, Tuesday and Wednesday, 37 miles in total including some speed work, before easing right back on Thursday and Friday.

The race was a bit of a disaster. The weather conditions were poor – wet, windy and very cold at the start. I shared the lead with Manfred Steffny and a runner called Peters from Aachen through 5km (15:51) and 10km (32:20), but at around 15km had an attack of diarrhoea and lost 100-150m through a quick pitstop. I caught up again and was back sharing the lead at 20km (65:50), then had to stop again. I ended up jogging the rest of the way to finish third (as was the TV Refrath team) in 2:25:18. Steffny had won in 2:20:39 just 15 seconds ahead of Peters.

Even before I analysed the reasons for my bad run, it was clear that a stomach upset was the main culprit. It had started on Tuesday, possibly caused by iron tablets I had been taking, and had got worse because of the chilly conditions. I had also started the race with stiffness and soreness at the back of my thighs, caused by the speed work (4x500m and some 90m strides) done on the Wednesday. I would avoid speed work so close to the race the next time and with luck wouldn't have a repeat of the stomach problems. I was not despondent, and carried on training, running 67, 92 and 71 in the following three weeks – including a few relaxing days in Göttingen where I visited old friends from St Andrews, Janet and Neville Osborne and their family. Neville was working at the Max Planck Institute there. Then came a stroke of luck that changed everything.

On Sunday 5th May, exactly four weeks before the Maxol, I warmed up with an easy nine miles in the 's Heerenberg woods for a 5000m track race in the afternoon on the cinder track just opposite the Hopp'sches Konvikt. There would be some spectators, including Herr Gutschalk and quite a few of my students. I hadn't used the cinder track at all over the previous months as I preferred to avoid tracks, following the Gunder Hägg motto "the track is for the race". The field was small, and included my training partner Udo Hennig and a runner from Ratio Münster called Gerd Mölders, whom I had never heard of but looked a good runner.

I led from lap 2 to lap 5 and then from lap 6 to lap 12, but Mölders took me with 100m to go and crossed the line a second or so to the good. I was timed at 14:32.8 and Udo was 3rd in 15:18.

During the warm-down I found out that Gerd had run in the Mexico Olympic steeplechase and lived just 20 minutes' drive away in Kalkar, on the other side of the Rhine. Udo told me later that Gerd had asked what sort of time I could manage for 5000m. "About 14:30" said Udo. "So schnell?" [As fast as that?] he had replied. Gerd and I arranged that we would run together with his spaniel Ossi the next Wednesday in the Reichswald, a huge area of forest near Kleve.

It was a crucial decision, or stroke of fate: on that first run we covered about 14 miles in 93 minutes, and ran together another 11 times over the following three weeks. Although we ran at a relaxed pace over the undulating forest trails, occasionally slowing for the little spaniel to have a drink or quick bath in a puddle, those runs built up my confidence in a way that solo training would not have done, and so I owe Gerd and Ossi – and of course Udo in

Emmerich as well – a lot. In fact, as runners do, we were all helping each other: Gerd had been injured for quite a long period the previous year, and during his enforced rest from training Ossi had had a heart attack. His owner adopted the van Aaken principle of gradual recuperation through slow, easy running. Gerd's gradual return to full training had been shared by the little dog, who was by now as fit as we were, though he tended to get too hot and needed to roll occasionally in those puddles to cool down.

The mileage for those three weeks, which included a four day visit to Brussels with a few other teachers, where I ran in the Forêt de Soignes, was 120, 110, and 82. I did another 58 miles in the four low-carbohydrate days before the switch to the three days of high-carbohydrate, hydrating and sleeping pre-race regime when I only jogged 6, 4 and 3 miles very slowly.

A month or so before I had written to Edinburgh Southern Harriers to ask if they would give me some financial help to fly to Manchester for the Maxol, and they generously agreed to give me £50 although they had not expected me to qualify, but had voted to give me some money because had been a member since 1963. I had also written rather optimistically to Adidas in Herzogenaurach, explaining that I had no suitable marathon racing shoes, as my Yardley racers were more or less done in and I had been unable to find any suitable shoes in visits to sports shops. To my delight a parcel arrived containing a pair of light marathon shoes in white leather with the famous three stripes and a thin sole. I ran them in thoroughly in the weeks before the race.

My flight to Manchester was on Saturday 3rd June, and Arthur Walsham of Salford Harriers had again offered to put me up, as he had done at the 1969 Maxol, at the house he shared with his wife Enid. That evening Arthur took me out for a very slow 20 minute jog. At that stage the emphasis was on minimum effort, full hydration, relaxation, sleep and topping up the carbohydrates. One of the side-effects of doing the diet as thoroughly as my contemporaries and I did that you went to the start carrying a few pounds more than usual, but those pounds were mostly water. As a result it took a few kilometres before you stopped feeling bloated and got into your running properly.

The Maxol Marathon races were sponsored by a US oil company of that name. This year the race incorporated the AAA and Road Runners' Club (RRC)

Championships as well as the trial for the team at Munich, and a guarantee had been given by Arthur Gold, the former high jumper who chaired the BAAB, that the first three Britons to finish would be selected. Several other countries were using the Manchester event as their trial – including, rather curiously, the Federal Republic of Germany, who could have shown greater self-confidence as the hosts of the Games by arranging a trial race in their own country.

The field was a strong one. From Germany had come Paul Angenvoorth, Manfred Steffny, Herbert Schu, Alfons Ida, Helmut Urbach and a number of others, including Lutz Philipp. I had last come across him in 1960 when he won the German Universities Championship 5000 in Göttingen when which I had come a distant third. South African Ferdie Le Grange was also due to line up at Manchester Town Hall, along with Carlos Perez and Agustin Fernandez of Spain, Armando Aldegalega of Portugal, the Dutchman Aad Steijlen and lots more. But the real excitement for British supporters was to find out which three of their countrymen would gain selection. Ron Hill (Bolton), born in nearby Accrington and a long-time resident of Hyde in Cheshire, was the popular favourite, but the UK's cast list included Jim Alder (Morpeth), Don Faircloth (Croydon), Eric Austin (Worcester), Alistair Wood (Aberdeen), Bill Adcocks and Colin Kirkham (Coventry), Ricky Wilde, Mike Freary (Bolton), Dave Holt (Hercules-Wimbledon), Keith Angus (Sheffield), Bernie Plain (Cardiff), Mike Rowland (Thames Valley), Alex Wight (Edin AC), Martin Craven (Kendal and ESH), Steve Edmunds (Sale), Cavin Woodward (Leamington) – to name some of the best-known. From Cambridge Harriers came the Tuck twins of whom one had said of the other "My brother's only going to run two marathons this year – the trial and the Olympics." And there was Don Macgregor (ESH) "currently teaching in Düsseldorf" as The Scotsman believed.

For some reason I did not feel terribly nervous as I jogged around in the sunshine just before 10 o'clock. Alistair Wood asked me what I thought I could do. Now usually my response to such a question would be non-committal, but on this occasion I said straight out to him: "2:15" Bearing in mind that my best was 2:16:53, that might have approached the Tuck brother's statement in hubris.

I commented briefly in my diary above the list of the first 30 finishers: "Felt OK 1st 5 [km] (slow), then it got too fast, then I tagged on to group, then by halfway felt better, had sudden surge which took me past one after the other. Gradually overhauled Alder, Freary, Adcocks, Faircloth, Spaniards, Angus, Wilde, Finns, Le Grange, Austin, Plain, and, finally Colin Kirkham, just after the last turn. Then home: amazed!"

I can't describe most of the course at all as I had no real idea where it went. I do remember that the effects of the diet kicked in – the "sudden surge" – not long after halfway and kept me moving forward right to the end. I had avoided any muscular or stomach problems, which was indeed lucky. Over the first half of the race I lay well back and could not have looked to any spectator as if I was an Olympic possible.

I do remember the last few miles of the course, however. Before entering the Old Trafford stadium we had to run past the entrance and a further mile or so along the road, before turning and heading back to the famous Manchester United ground, where we had to complete a circuit of the rectangular cinder path that separated the playing area from the spectator terracing. It was a cruel thing to do to runners after a couple of hours, but those extra miles gave me a chance to catch all but two of the runners, Lutz Philipp and Ron Hill, in front of me to clinch not just the third team slot but the second. As I ran in I could see Arthur Walsham jumping up and down in excitement, and as I crossed the line I clenched my fists in pure delight. It was hard to take in.

I was standing on the grass grinning broadly and rejoicing in the moment, when two Adidas representatives (international runners John Davies and Mike Tagg) came running over, no doubt noticing I was wearing my white Adidas racers, to offer me some gear – tracksuits, trainers and so on. Then Arthur Gold came across, wearing his dark blue blazer and a wide smile, to shake my hand and confirm that I would indeed be selected. "Well, Don, I pwomised that the first thwee would be picked, and they will be." he assured me with his characteristic rhotacism (word found in OED).

2 minutes 16 seconds ahead of me Lutz Philipp had put in a last minute sprint to take first place (2:12:50), with Ron Hill a mere second behind. Ron had been aggrieved (not for the first or last time) at the BAAB for making him run a trial at all, arguing that he had done enough to justify pre-selection on this occasion – and I agreed with him. This would be his third Olympics and he had a really strong chance of winning the marathon. He believed that running another marathon before Munich would be a hindrance rather than

a help, as he would need a long time to recover and get ready to peak again.

That consideration was far from my thoughts on that golden afternoon. I had beaten my previous best time by 1:47 and come within 6 seconds of achieving the time I had predicted with almost supernatural confidence in response to Alistair Wood's question. I had not run 2:15:06 by design, as I was not really aware of my splits until seeing them on the results sheet along with those of the other 230 finishers and 41 non-finishers.

The table below gives the comparative splits for the leaders and for me. I must have passed inside a group at 5 and 10km, as no times were recorded against my name in the results sheets. I probably ran around 16:20 and 31:30 minutes and lay between 25th and 30th.

Km	Leaders	Elapsed time	DFM	Elapsed time
5	16:02	16:02	?	?
10	15:44	30:46	?	?
15	15:10	45:56	?	46:43
20	15:12	61:08	15:37	62:20
25	15:31	76:39	16:06	78:26
30	15:23	1:32:12	16:01	1:34:27
35	15:38	1:47:50	15:08	1:49:35
40	17:40?	2:05:30	17.53?	2:07:28
42,195	07:20	2:12:50	07:38	2:15:06

The 35 and 40km times suggest strongly that the measuring point at 40km was inaccurate.

Eventually I found a phone box and called my dad. I hadn't even told the family that I was running in Manchester, so it came as a bit of a shock when I said: "I've just qualified to run the Olympic marathon." – "You've what!?" I explained what had happened and that I had to fly back to Emmerich the next morning. At last I've done something to make him proud of me, I thought as I limped back to the field. Later that afternoon Arthur and I went back to his house so that I could have a shower (I presume the United players fare better for facilities), a cup of tea and a rest. We were sitting watching TV in the same room we had watched Neil Armstrong stepping on to the lunar surface in 1969, when the phone rang. Did Don not know there was a reception and prize-giving taking place? No, he didn't, but we hurried across in the car and I received my medal and prize – an inscribed watch. It got lost a couple of years later at the first handover of the Edinburgh to Glasgow road relay when I put it in my tracksuit pocket and gave the suit to someone at the start of the 6 mile second leg from the Maybury roundabout to Broxburn. But the real prize was not something that could be put in a drawer or lost at a race.

Chapter 16

Maxol to München

On the Monday after the Maxol I flew back to Köln/Bonn airport and drove north-westwards up the E36 to Emmerich. Stiff-legged and exhausted, I ran a very slow half-hour that evening round the quiet streets in the half-dark, nursing my blisters. The next day I hirpled into school and slumped into my seat in the staffroom. There were few colleagues there. No-one said anything other than "Guten Morgen!", until after a few minutes Ralf Hühne came over: "Did you do it?" He was clearly expecting the answer no. "Yes." His face lit up with surprise and pleasure. The news soon spread round those colleagues who were interested (not very many) and percolated gradually to the pupils, though I never mentioned it in class as far as I can recall. Back home, the Scotsman chose a large font for its story "McGregor selected for Olympic Marathon", and the Herald mentioned in its text that it had been "the sign of Nero" for Jim Alder, a curious reference presumably meaning thumbs down. He had been forced to drop out around 25 km, and in fact was unable to extend his great record in any future Games, whether Commonwealth, European or Olympic.

Aad Steijlen, who had finished 85th in 2:33:23, had invited me to visit, on the weekend after the race, the Hoge Veluwe nature park near Arnhem, where the Dutch squad regularly trained over the hilly terrain. Even after an easy few days I found the moderate gradients too much and was unable to stay with the group as we ran round for about 16 km. I apologised, but they understood why I was so slow.

I now had a balancing act to perform over the remaining 13 weeks until the Munich Olympic race, scheduled for Saturday 9th September. The first objective was to recover properly, the second to build up my mileage again with the correct mix of distance and speed, plus a few shorter races thrown in to check on progress. I had to ensure however that I avoided injury and illness as far as that was possible.

I was due to return to Scotland at the end of term, leaving Emmerich on 21st June after a couple of weeks at 73 and 89 miles. My last run was the 10.5 mile route up to Elten and back which I completed that morning for the 62nd time

Qualified: crossing the line in 2:15:06 at the Maxol, May 1972.(Mike Brett).

(I must have counted them up in my diary in one of many idle moments). Auf Wiedersehen, Emmerich! Over the ten months I had lived there I had had a lot of fun with my training companions and, at weekends, with the other British teachers strewn round the neighbourhood. I said goodbye to the Kollegen, few of whom I had got to know well, taking with me a much increased knowledge of the German school system and a signed copy of a book on Emmerich by Rudolf Reis, the headmaster.

In the spring I had had a short visit from Willy Bloch, a venerable friend of my father's and of my stepmother's older sister Nancy. Herr Bloch was a learned academic, but looked like a mischievous gnome, with glinting rimless glasses and a yellowy-brown waistcoat. On a short sightseeing tour of Emmerich and environs I took him along the Rheinpromenade, with its pleasant houses and shops built after the almost total destruction of the town in the latter stages of the war. Gazing across the wide extent of the mighty river, Willy Bloch was silent for a moment, then turned to me and pronounced his verdict: "So! Das ist Emmerich – und das ist der Rhein!" That just about summed it up.

Once back in Scotland I moved between Edinburgh, St Andrews and Dunoon. I had to present myself in Argyll to prepare for the new post and to seek four weeks' leave of absence to attend the Olympics. It was an unusual way to start a job, but it would at least ensure that most of the staff and pupils knew who I was when I eventually turned up. Ian Hendry was keen, as was I, that I meet as many of the staff as possible before swanning off. Betty and Ian had offered to put me up at "Windrush", the house they had bought on the hill above the school. I visited a local solicitor to arrange the purchase of a two-bedroomed flat, at 96 Victoria Road, a long street parallel to Dunoon's main thoroughfare and which was lined with semi-detached, red sandstone, four-in-a-block villas. The flat had a view to the front over the roofs to Gourock via the Firth of Clyde, and to the rear of a steep, all too often rain-drenched hillside with a few well-soaked and bored-looking sheep.

By good fortune I was able to keep up a regularly high mileage throughout July (466 miles or an average of about 15 miles a day), aided by a number of training partners: Fergus Murray, Doug Gunstone, Ron Morrison, Ian Grieve, John McCabe, Graham Stark, Bill Murray, George Brown, Alastair Blamire, Alastair Matson, Jeff Graves, and, on the second-last day of the month, Dave Moorcroft, who at that time was being coached by John Anderson and had come up from Coventry to stay at John's house in Currie. Dave, later the world record holder for 5000m, was at this time a talented junior, but was very cautious about training with me that Sunday morning from Balerno up "Grandpa" and through the Pentlands. He was worried that he might twist his ankle running over the tufty grassland near Threipmuir Reservoir and back down the hill to Currie. We ran easily for about 82 minutes with no twisted ankles for either of us, and I slotted in

Rab Forman, John Le Masurier, Denis Watts in the Alps.

another hour and a half with "the Beast", Fergus Murray, at 4.15 pm – giving me 25 miles for the day. I wish I could do that now. In July I raced only twice. The first was a poor 5000m at windy Meadowbank, where Lachie Stewart (Shettleston H), the 1970 Commonwealth Games 10,000m Champion, won easily in 14:30 by 21 seconds from Jim Wight (EAC) with me a further 4 seconds back. I "atoned" for that run by doing an easy 54 minutes in the evening with Fergus and Alastair Blamire.

Atonement as an athletic concept originates with the great Finn Paavo Nurmi. He trained much more extensively, as well as harder, than any of his contemporaries. His belief was that an athlete "sinned" by racing, and that a lot of easy running was necessary between races if the athlete was to sin successfully again. That principle explains why during an indoor tour of the USA in the mid 1920s he was able to race 55 times and only be beaten once. The American journalists were astonished to see how much slow running he did between races; and that quasi-religious explanation was what he and his manager provided for them.

In the second race, the Gourock Highland Games 14 miles road race, Jim Wight's brother, Alex, got the better of me. Most people expected me to win, as I was in the Olympic team. By now I had had my letter from Prince Philip congratulating me on selection. Through rain and sunshine Alex and I set a fastish pace, pursued by Bill Stoddart (Greenock Wellpark), Steve Taylor (Aberdeen) and Jim Wight. The course started in the Games park on a hilltop plateau, then dropped down to follow the coast road westwards and back the same way. We stayed together up the hill, but I decided not to try to accelerate over the wet grass track in case I slipped and injured myself, so that Alex won by 6 seconds in 69:54, beating his brother's record by 64 seconds.

After a second quick visit to the Hendrys' I headed back east and of course kept up the training routine. I was doing very little speed work – some fartlek, an up-the clock session and 10x100 was about all that I had done before being requested by the BAAB to come down and run a 2 miles on Saturday 5th August on the all-weather track at Crystal Palace. The meeting preceded the departure of an endurance group of rowers, canoeists, walkers and runners in which I was included, for altitude training at St Moritz.

The Crystal Palace televised races were being put on so that those selected for Munich could show the public, and the sponsors, their form. I was not very happy about running such a short track race. I didn't think it would do anything for my morale to be shown up by genuine middle-distance stars, but also I had hurt my little toe on the Thursday and it had become so painful on the Friday that I couldn't wear spikes, though I was able to jog in training shoes.

Not for the first time the BAAB officials showed themselves in a very bad light. When I spoke to chief coach John Le Masurier and a couple of others, they were most unsympathetic. I had to run because the sponsors expected it. "You know, Don, Munich…" – that was a barely concealed threat to withdraw me from the team because I had a sore toe five weeks before the big race! I was incensed and then miserable. In the end I had to ask the team doctor to certify in writing that I was temporarily unable to race, before the officials stopped being so silly. It was a completely unnecessary and nasty experience which, alas, has been repeated over the decades time and again, though under varying circumstances, because some officials, in blazers and sometimes in tracksuits, have forgotten - if they ever knew - how athletes feel and think.

British endurance men at St Moritz August 1972.
L to R: Brendan Foster, DFM, Ian Stewart, John Kirkbride, Ron Hill,
Harry Wilson (Coach), Ray Watson (physiologist), Dr Peter Travers.

Fortunately I was able quickly to put my annoyance to one side and concentrate on keeping the training going over the next four days at Crystal Palace. Although most of the athletes who lived within a reasonable distance of London had gone home, I stayed on there in a hostel until the flight along with a small congenial group who included Lynn Davies, David Hemery and the Canadian high jumper Debbie Brill. These famous athletes were very kind to me. They insisted on including me in their photo-opportunities and interviews, which boosted my self-confidence even though I was not usually required to contribute to the interviews. Away from the press, we enjoyed hours of jokes, stories and serious conversation.

Lynn and David were going out to Munich with the majority of the UK teams, and Debbie of course with the Canadians, but I would be flying with the endurance squads to St. Moritz for three weeks at altitude. Before the

1968 Mexico City Olympics there had been experiments with groups of UK athletes to see how performances were affected by periods spent in the mountains. Mexico and later on Font Romeu in the Pyrenees were two venues for these. An important element of the success of East African distance runners was thought to be the higher concentration of red, oxygen-carrying corpuscles in their blood, brought about

St Moritz August 1972: Ron Hill and family, Harry Wilson, Ray Watson, and Bryan Smith.

by the fact that they lived at higher altitude where the levels of oxygen in the atmosphere are lower. The theory was that if athletes who normally lived at a lower level trained at altitude for an extended period, they would perform better when they competed nearer sea level. There were many imponderables: what was the ideal interval between return from altitude and the next competition? Was there an ideal period to spend at altitude? How would anyone doing the Saltin glycogen-depletion diet be affected by these factors? The last question in particular had never been addressed, or if it had, the answers had not been communicated to the athletes, as was clear from subsequent events. In short, the British Olympic Association (BOA), or, as it was sometimes known to the athletes, OBA, Old Boys' Association, was taking a risk in sending us all to St. Moritz.

We were accompanied by coach Harry Wilson, and by Ray Watson, a physiologist, and a team doctor, Peter Travers, who later published a jointly authored but inconclusive article in the British Journal of Sports Medicine on the results of our altitude training. Among the British distance runners were Ian Stewart (5000m), Ron Hill (marathon), John Kirkbride and Brendan Foster (1500m), Dave Holt and Lachie Stewart (10000m), and Joyce Smith who was running the 1500m. At that time the 1500m was the longest Olympic

High up at Corviglia track, August 1972.

event for women, though Joyce would have been more suited to a longer race. Dave Holt had qualified by sheer persistence as well as effort. At the AAA championship he had been allocated only to the B race, but felt so sure of his form that he had lined up with the field for the A race and refused to leave the track until the officials permitted him to start.

A public subscription had allowed Ron Hill's wife May and their two boys Steven and Graham to come to Switzerland and they were staying at a boarding-house down the road from our hotel. Also in St. Moritz were distance runners from other countries, such as the great Belgian cross-country runner and steeplechase winner from Tokyo, Gaston Roelants, who had turned to the marathon and was reputed to be doing ferocious amounts of training – up to 60 km a day, and 60 x 200m were cited, though I don't know if that was accurate.

The best running routes were over the network of paths that circled the lakes Champfèr, Silvaplana, Nair and Stax or ran along the hillsides on the way to Sils and Pontresina. To begin with I trained thrice daily, sometimes with Dave Holt, Lachie Stewart or with Brendan Foster and Ian Stewart, over short distances only, until we had discovered what the effects would be on our bodies. Still, it all mounted up: 49 miles for the first three days. On the fourth day, Sunday 13th August, Dave Holt and I, plus a Dutch runner for part of the way, undertook a 19 miler. Towards the end of the run I got very tired but, worse, I experienced pain in my right Achilles tendon. That was very worrying, so much so that I only noted in my training diary that I was "a little worried" but did not trust myself to write why. I had had tendonitis a few years before and knew from experience that it could keep me out for weeks. That afternoon I went to confide in Ted Chappell, the very experienced physiotherapist who had looked after British teams for years.

It was thanks to Ted that I was able to compete in the Games. For the remaining four weeks he gave me regular treatment so that I could continue to train. I could do practically no speed work: I can find only references to a 3-4 mile fartlek, and to 10x100m on a path over that whole period. The lack of speed endurance training was a definite disadvantage. More importantly, I was able to keep up a decent mileage: a total of 293 miles in those three weeks in the Swiss mountains. As Arthur Newton once said: "Every man-jack of us has sufficient speed for the marathon." It just depends how fast you want to run it.

On Friday 25th August some of us were taken up to a 600m sawdust-on-earth circuit at Corviglia, at an altitude of about 2400m compared to about 1800m in St. Moritz down below. I did 15 laps of the trail circuit, along with a few others, including one of the members of the West German team Paul Angenvoorth who had been 10th in the Maxol in 2:16:44. (The others were Lutz Philipp and Manfred Steffny.) I started my laps by joining the circuit about 20 metres ahead of Paul, which he took to be a bit of gamesmanship on my part. Maybe it was. After the session I felt a bit dizzy and had no desire to go up so high another time.

Apart from training, there was not a great deal to do. We didn't have the energy to go sightseeing or the money to go shopping, and St. Moritz was as lifeless as any ski resort in summer. We spent some time socialising with the other groups of athletes, or chatting among ourselves. Our minds were concentrated on the races to come. In my case I mentally ticked off every day I managed to keep up the training and never felt the injury unduly. Ted assured me regularly that it would hold out.

The altitude group was due to go down to Munich (itself at 520m or so above sea level) on Wednesday 30th August, 10 days before the marathon. As far as I was concerned one of the great advantages of arriving in Munich after the official opening of the Games was that we didn't need to take part in the procession of teams round the arena. A similar though smaller parade at the Commonwealth Games in Edinburgh in 1970, though popular with spectators, had been preceded by hours of standing around waiting, so that I had got a sore back.

In the Euro-Hotel, I had been sharing room 223 with Ron Hill, who decided that he wanted to stay on for a few more days to be together with May and the boys. It was to prove a decision with disastrous consequences for his gold medal hopes.

Chapter 17

"Bloody hell fire, it's Don, and I thought I was moving through."

Munich was en fête: pastel-coloured banners and streamers everywhere, adorned with the 1972 Olympic logos, specially designed sports symbols and mottos. The Olympic Village contained eight-storey blocks of flats with stepped balconies, so that it was possible for anyone so minded to pour water down on the occupants of the balcony below. The rooms were sparsely furnished, rather like a barracks, with a bed, mattress, blankets and a chair and cupboard. I was sharing with Ian Stewart with whom I got on well. The military atmosphere was reinforced by the presence, as floor orderlies, of Bundeswehr soldiers doing their national service, who had the job of bringing us any hot drinks we wanted from the kitchen alcove. There was a television lounge downstairs in the block, but I don't recall watching it at all on those first few days.

Around the Village there was an architectural feature shared with the le Beaubourg in Paris. The services were carried along the outside of the buildings in colour coded pipes. It was possible to find your way around with a map in your hand by following a certain colour of pipe, though I never tried it. Newspapers later reported on the enormous number of contraceptives that were used in the Village, but again none could be put down to me. Unlike a few more glamorous athletes, one of whom in particular looked as if he might one day walk down the high street patting all the kids on the head in case he had fathered any of them, I was too preoccupied.

The first run in Munich was a 4½ mile canter round the Olympia-Park with the self-assured and friendly steeplechaser John Bicourt. The centrepiece was the stadium, an international sensation with its semi-transparent roof, designed by Frei Otto, over the stands. Later it was obscured by algae and had to be repaired. We athletes had passes which enabled us to visit the stadium for any event, provided we sat in the ground area, the stands being reserved for the great and the good and for ticket-holders who had shelled out good DM for a seat in the shade. I went to watch the 10,000m, as I had in Edinburgh, but otherwise stayed away to avoid getting over-excited.

1972 Olympiastadion München.

Despite the kindness of Adidas in Herzogenaurach in giving me shoes for the Maxol, I decided to change to the blue suede Biwako racers offered to me by Onitsuka Tiger. These had a bit more padding, and the soft suede was more comfortable than leather and less likely to cause blisters. I tested the shoes and decided I would be able to wear them without socks if I taped up my toes with zinc oxide tape and put a little Vaseline inside the shoe at any rough places.

The race was still 8 days away, and my Achilles continued to respond to Ted Chappell's care. I did a bit of exploration of the course, travelling by U-Bahn to Bonner Platz to run for an hour or so in the Englischen Garten, through which the course ran. During the Games it wasn't necessary to buy a ticket on the U-Bahn, our athlete ID being sufficient, though it was never checked. The next day I bumped into Till Lufft, an old friend whom I had first met when I accompanied that far-off Glasgow and Manchester University tour to the Black Forest in 1963, and we ran another stretch of the course so that I could familiarise myself with it.

I'm going into considerable detail of that final week's training to show exactly what regime I followed and to explain the sequence of events. The Saltin diet started with a "depletion run" of 90-120 minutes to reduce the athlete's store of carbohydrate. Then ensued three days of minimal carbohydrate intake which left the runner trying to train normally but feeling weaker and weaker. A switch to a diet of sweet drinks, lots of pasta, chocolate, bread etc resulted in theory in super-compensation. The body would store glycogen which in its turn retained 2.5 times its own weight of water. It was necessary to drink plenty. The "carbo-loading" phase lasted 3 more days and left the athlete slightly overweight on race day. It was essential to rest up, do just enough jogging to keep bowel movements regular, and get plenty of sleep.

Tim Johnston came along, as did Till Lufft, for the first hour of my 90 minute, 13 mile depletion run on the late morning of Saturday 2nd September. I ran in full tracksuit despite the summer heat, and in the evening at 6pm added another 20 minutes with John Bicourt, including 8x100m strides on grass. As Ron Hill was the leading exponent of the Saltin diet, I was keen to see how closely he stuck to it, quickly discovering, for example, that evening at dinner time that he allowed himself a yoghurt and an apple on the low carbohydrate days.

On Sunday morning at 10.40 Ian McCafferty and I ran 63 minutes on the first part of the marathon course. I felt slightly stiff in the calves and had a blister on my big toe caused by having an over-thick insole in my trainers. In the evening at 6.45 I ran a slow 4 miles, also on the road, with a few bursts. For part of that run I chatted to an unhappy Nigerian marathoner whose federation had refused to enter him for the Games although he had run 2:18, the excuse being that he lived in the USA. He didn't know what to do about it and was considering making his own number and just lining up with the rest of us. In the end he did just that, but as he chose pink cardboard rather than cloth to make his number, the last I saw of him was when he was being led off by security staff.

By Monday the first phase of the diet was beginning to weaken me, but I managed 6 miles at 10.15 am and then at half past two the last 12km of the course "steady" with Colin Kirkham, the quiet man from Coventry. Tuesday was the last day of deprivation before I could switch to carbohydrate, and at 3 in the afternoon I ran 7 miles with Ron Hill and Dave Bedford on the first part of the course. We crossed the Nymphenburg Schlosspark, where Ron and Dave had to help me to climb over the high gates, adding not a few mocking remarks about my climbing ability. In the early evening I went to the Olympiastadion to watch Lasse Viren beat Emiel Puttemans and Miruts Yifter, not to mention Dave Bedford, who disappointed himself in 6th position. Then Ron and I went back to have our last low-carbohydrate supper, and I spent the rest of the evening reading. At midnight one of the Bundeswehr lads bought me a couple of plastic cups of hot, sweet lemon drink, and I devoured my first Mars bar for several days before going to sleep. When I woke up on the Wednesday morning the world was in shock.

That's why I can't say much about the events that preceded the murderous attack of the Arab "Black September" terrorists on the Israeli team and its tragic aftermath, even though the break-in, hostage-taking and shooting of Moshe Weinberg and Josef Romano all took place in Connollystrasse about 200m from our block. While millions were watching on television, I was asleep in our room. I have a copy of the "Village News for that Wednesday 6th September 1972, with its huge headline "Terror". The report included photographs of the "Bürgermeister" of the Olympic Village, Walter Tröger, and Munich police chief Manfred Schreiber negotiating with the terrorists, and of the "guerillas" penetrating the Village with machine guns. There was also a chronology of the night's events, and the paper carried statements from various athletes deploring the actions of the terrorists, some of them echoing the view of Avery Brundage, the anti-Semitic president of the IOC, that "the Games will continue". Brundage's "fact-finding" visit to Nazi Germany in 1934 had found no undue harassment of Jews and resulted in the failure of the move to boycott the 1936 Games. Willi Daume, president of the Organising Committee was quoted as saying that "the participants and organisers of these Olympic Games will demonstrate that the Olympic idea of peace is stronger than the political fanaticism of cynical murderers."

Among the athletes there was consternation about the night's events. This increased later when the news got out of the death of the hostages at Fürstenfeldbruck airport. The Games were halfway through – should the remaining events be cancelled? Brundage had made up his mind, but opinions were divided. Some athletes, like 10,000m runner Jos Hermens (Netherlands) [later a top agent for African athletes], just went home although he had already competed. Most of those who had not yet had the opportunity to compete had to weigh the situation up: if we withdrew, how would that help the victims? If we didn't compete, we would probably spend the rest of our lives wondering what might have been.

The official decision was a compromise: the IOC would mark their respect for the dead by a day without competition, so that the whole programme would be postponed by 24 hours.

The Games had rejoiced in the title "die heiteren Spiele" (the light-hearted Games), but they were light-hearted no longer. The officials in their sky-blue uniforms tightened up on the security so easily breached by the Black September group who had been spotted climbing over the fence into the Village. Witnesses thought they were athletes climbing back in after a late-night party after some internal curfew imposed by their team management. Shooting and kidnap had been unimaginable.

It may be that the athletes who did not want the Games to be called off were very selfish and thoughtless, but I can't agree entirely. There was no right decision, and the only possible wrong one would have been not to have any postponement at all. My opinion of Avery Brundage is low, but he and his colleagues had little real alternative. I was there to concentrate on the race for which I had been selected after years of effort and with a good pinch of good luck. To withdraw would be a meaningless gesture which those who had encouraged us and supported us would not all understand.

The IOC decision meant that the marathon would start at 3 pm on Sunday 10th September, leaving four days until race day, instead of three. That meant an extra day of the high carbohydrate diet for Ron and me, but we concluded that one day would not make any real difference to the diet's effect. I tapered down as Sunday approached: 4 and 5 miles on Wednesday, 4 and 3½ on Thursday, 3½ and 3 on Friday, 2 and 1½ on Saturday, all at a slow pace. Ron did something similar. We were going out twice a day to kill time, to keep our bowels in order and our muscles loose. I did a lot of reading and sleeping. During the final preparation time I cocooned myself from the world and talked to few other people except some of the other runners, to our team managers and to Ted, who was consistently full of encouragement.

Ron Hill, as everyone in distance running knows, kept a voluminous diary on which he drew to write his two-volume "The Long Hard Road" It is a classic of running literature. He devotes a 25 page chapter to just under nine hours of

Olympisches Dorf 1972 : scene of terrorist attack.

the marathon day, Sunday September 10th, 1972. The chapter is written with great immediacy and liveliness because he noted down so many details at the time, and is illustrated with 20 photographs (4 of them include me).

The film director John Schlesinger was making a short film that was part of an eight-part feature called "Visions of Eight" because it contained eight well-known directors' interpretations of different aspects or events at the Games. Schlesinger had chosen the marathon: Ron Hill as one of the favourites had the lead role. He had been filmed training over the Cheshire hills, walking to the Village restaurant, and so it went on right until the end of the race and beyond. During the filming of that scene in the Village the cameraman walked backwards, pushing people out of the way, then backed into a column and fell over, which Ron found funny but I didn't.

Presumably Schlesinger didn't care if Ron Hill won or lost as long as his film was artistically successful, but Ron did care. He had set his heart on winning. He had done everything to realise his dream, perhaps too much. Was it necessary to have gold metallic shorts to wear on the rostrum if he won? But I hoped very much that he would pull off the first ever Olympic marathon victory for a British athlete. A poignant note: it was not until he published his book in 1982 that I read about the prophetic dream Ron had had on his second night at altitude, Thursday 10th August, as he slept just a few feet to the right of me in room 223 in the Eurotel, St. Moritz: "I was back home and it was sometime after the Games. I had finished sixth in the marathon and suddenly it dawned on me that it was all over and there was no going back. I almost cried in my sleep."

I'm sure I had many vivid dreams too, but none about the race. I was ranked 35th in terms of best times among the 77 entrants. What could I realistically hope for? Alistair Wood had said to someone that I would be in the first ten, but I didn't find that out until afterwards. I was a little concerned about my lack of speed work forced on me by the Achilles problem, but I had confidence in the build-up otherwise and in the diet. Of course everyone else might be following it too, but what the hell? In a marathon you are competing against yourself as much as against others.

What did I have for breakfast that day? I'm not sure – probably toast and marmalade and a mug of coffee. During the morning I drank some more tea, and some more bread and jam about 11, and kept topping up with water. The intervening time was spent checking my kit: that the numbers were securely fastened with four safety pins to the front and back of my vest, that I had the stick-on numbers for my shorts. I lay down and read for a bit, and tried to relax. Along with Dick McColgan, a Northern Ireland official who had been assigned to make sure we got to the check-in on time, the three of us, Ron, Colin and me - gathered at the lift at 1.50 pm. We travelled to the stadium by car taking with us the large sponges made of sliced up foam pillow which at Ron's suggestion we had filled with water and put in plastic bags. On arrival we had a bit of a walk under the stands through the maze of corridors to find the changing room. We had to report to final check-in at 2.30, the first report having been done for us by throws coach Wilf Paish. We sat there in the strained pre-race atmosphere in that subterranean room, getting up only to go to the toilet, a very important consideration before any race, or to stretch our legs. There wasn't much chatting.

A full 15 minutes before the start we were released out on to the corridor and up the steps into the open expanse of the stadium. It was quite hot, humid and sunny (21°C), and after dumping the green bag with my tracksuit in it, I jogged slowly up the straight and round towards the start at the 200m point. I took the soaked bit of sponge out of the plastic bag and squeezed it over my head, then wiped down thighs and arms. I thought there were a few envious glances: "wish I'd thought of that". Was this gamesmanship? I wondered, and glanced across to the crowded terraces. A small figure in black stood up and waved to me. It was Eleanor Gunstone, who was there with her husband Frank and their daughter Penny, a doctor, whom I had known since as an 11 year old she had won a Fife Schools cross-country race over Madras College Kilrymont playing fields. Penny's husband Rob Rother, and Doug Gunstone and his wife Palm, both international cross-country runners, had not been able to travel to Munich. I had met the Gunstones a few days before at one of the entrances to the Village, and Eleanor had told me about the very strict warden of the camp site they were staying at, and how he had made her use a towel to wipe dry the wash-hand basin, saying she hadn't cleaned up thoroughly enough.

Much of this was going through my head as I waved back, forgetting that all these spectators would think I was waving at them. And indeed there was a huge cheer before I turned away and carried on with the warm-up, waiting for the mark steward to line us all up. There were 74 starters from 39 countries, and I was drawn in the third row. All of us had cut our cloth numbers (298 in my case) down to the minimum size (strictly forbidden nowadays so that the sponsors get their money's worth). I was wearing a standard GB & NI cotton vest and very short white shorts with red and blue edging, but had cut the bottom part off the vest to reduce weight. The Tiger Biwakos [it's a lake in Japan] (size 10 US) felt comfortable. As we waited tensely for the steward to retreat and alert the starter to fire the gun, I almost smiled when the steward said "Take it easy, it's a long way." Shades of Old Meadowbank and "Toes behind the line, lads!"

The gun went, and a couple of rash people shot off in the lead as we sorted ourselves out round the first two and three-quarter laps and out up the tunnel on to the bridge over the dual carriageway, then up a short hill and on to narrow black asphalt paths. Soon we reached the wider roads, following the light blue line that since Munich has become standard for championship and big city marathons. I was concentrating on keeping relaxed and making sure

I wasn't tripped in the closely packed group I found myself in. I was never up with the leading group and found the pace fast.

At 5km the leaders went through in 15:51, the time given for all 26 of them: Hill, Frank Shorter, Kenny Moore and Jack Bacheler (USA), Karel Lismont and Gaston Roelants (Belgium), Mamo Wolde, Demissie Wolde and Lengisse Bedane (Ethiopia), Seppo Nikkari and Reino Paukonnen (Finland), Colin Kirkham (UK), Jack Foster and Terry Manners (NZ), Akio Usami (Japan), Derek Clayton (Australia), Gyula Tóth and Ferenc Szekeres (Hungary), the Soviet trio of Yuriy Velikorodnikh, Igor Shcherbak and Anatoliy Baranov, Jacinto Sabinal (Mexico), Julio Quevedo (Guatemala), Lucien Rosa (Sri Lanka), and Richard Juma (Kenya).

The second big group, which included me, was timed at 16:06. By 10km Hill and Clayton had gone ahead (31:15) with ten others within 9 seconds. Colin Kirkham had dropped back, and went through in 32:03, just a second ahead of me, though with several others closely packed together I didn't notice him. After those first few kilometres my back began to hurt – was I "due for a bad'un"? It didn't bear thinking about. The only possible race tactic was now forced on me – to run from the back as at the Maxol. At 15 km Colin and I still lay around 30th (47:44). It had been a bit of a struggle until then, though my pace remained pretty even, with successive 5km splits of 16:06, 15:58, and 15:41.

Earlier in the week Frank Shorter had already run a heat as well as the final of the 10,000m, coming fifth in 27:51.4. He regarded Hill and Clayton as his main rivals, and when both of them failed to respond to a burst the American put in around 12km, he decided to just go on himself and passed 15km in 46:21, 5 seconds to the good over Lismont, Mamo Wolde, Foster, Nikkari, Usami, Paukkonnen and Roelants. Hill was already 24 seconds adrift of the lead in 46:45 (13th).

My pace slowed slightly between 15 and 20km (16:03) and my position was more or less the same. Then I began slowly to move up the field. By 20km (16:19, 1:03:47)) I was 25th, at 25km (16:15, 1:20:01) 19th, and at 30km (16:19, 1:36:20) 17th.

Far ahead, Shorter had increased his lead at 30km to 65 seconds (1:32:49). Next up, though they were not catching him, were Mamo Wolde, the reigning Olympic champion from the Mexico Games, and Kenny Moore, then there was a further 20 second gap to Karel Lismont. The order thereafter was Clayton, Bacheler, Nikkari, Foster, Kimihara, Usami, Demissie Wolde, Paukonnen and Hill. Another three runners, one of them being the Ethiopian Bedane because I recall passing him, separated me from Hill, but I am unsure who the other two were.

The Englischer Garten part of the course ran from approximately 30km to 35km. Soon after I came into the park, a helicopter swooped down low over the trees, whipping up dust from the paths, some of which were surfaced with very small, sharp yellow-grey gritty stones. Just at that moment I came up to and went straight past the best of the Japanese, Akio Usami, who was swaying about slightly, then Demissie Wolde; Reino Paukonnen also proved unable to resist my charge.

By 35km Shorter, refreshing himself with flat Coca-Cola, was well clear (1:48:40) of Mamo Wolde (1:50:04). Lismont was another 14 seconds behind and catching, then came Moore in 1:50:25. Bacheler (1:51:21) was fading and had the Mexico silver medallist Kenji Kimihara scurrying along only 10 seconds behind.

The rest of the field ahead of me was not so far away now. Foster (1:51:49), Nikkari (1:51:49) and Clayton (1:52:19) were all slowing. Ron Hill had staged a bit of a comeback and was alongside the world record holder, 16 seconds ahead of me (1:52:35). I was now 11th. A lot of competitors had started too fast in the sultry conditions and at last I was picking them off by running a steady pace – not that I had had much choice.

I emerged out of the gardens and back on to the streets. Around 36 km I went past Derek Clayton, the world record-holder, who looked in trouble. For me, things were looking up!

I overtook Seppo Nikkari just after 38km and as I came round a corner I made out a familiar figure with silver shorts a couple of hundred metres up the road – Ron Hill. What was he doing back here? I wondered. My first feeling was not exultation that I was catching him, but regret that he obviously wasn't going to win. However I was racing here too, and concentrated on catching him up.

I was within about a hundred metres of him when, as he wrote later, he looked round to see why the gap between the clapping for him and the clapping for someone else was diminishing: "I glance round and get the shock of my life; there, head on one side, black rimmed spectacles, grimacing face, it's MacGregor. I think "Bloody hell fire, it's Don and I thought I was moving through." He says he panicked a bit: "Hell, what if he should beat me. He can't, I can't let him." It's all very dramatic stuff, as if my catching him up were some sort of nightmare. But I knew none of this and kept my rhythm going.

Within a few hundred metres more, about 39 km, we were level, and I tried to indicate without saying anything that we should run together and work our way towards the front if we could. Rather than trying to break away from him, I thought it was a better tactic to run co-operatively because in that way we were more likely to catch at least a couple of our rivals. We only had about two kilometres to do it in, but I was still pretty full of running. The 5km between 35 and 40km turned out to be my slowest of the race (17:06) but I was still moving through, now "assisted" by Ron, on whom I had gained 63 seconds between 25 and 40km. We shared the same time at 40km (2:09:41).

Quite quickly we passed Seppo Nikkari, and then the tall Jack Bacheler. He offered no resistance. Next was 40-year old Jack Foster of New Zealand, whom I knew from previous training runs and from Edinburgh and Athens. Into my mind came a piece of advice from some book I had bought when I was still at school fifteen years before: if two of you are coming up on an opponent and pass him decisively on either side, he is sure to drop back. So in the Olympic Games marathon, for the first time ever, I was able to enlist the great Ron Hill to help me put this advice into practice. I gestured to him to pass on Jack's right as I scooted past on the left– and it worked. Jack didn't attempt to stay with us and we raced on.

Frank Shorter was meantime almost at the stadium, having gone through the 40km checkpoint in 2:05:31 with a lead of over two minutes on Lismont who had just passed Mamo Wolde. Moore was still 4th, well clear of Kimihara. The shine was taken off Shorter's triumph by a silly stunt. A student, Norbert Südhaus, had thought it would be a good idea to 'lighten up the atmosphere' by dressing as a runner and running into the stadium ahead of the leader. He didn't look much like someone who had almost completed a marathon and in fact not like a runner at all, being rather stocky. To begin with he was greeted with cheers but they quickly turned to boos as he was stopped and led away. Poor Shorter couldn't understand why he was being booed as he ran up the first straight, but happily normal service was restored by the time he got round the top bend. It was a glorious victory in 2:12:19.8. Karel Lismont was second in 2:14:31.8, half a minute ahead of Mamo Wolde (2:15:08.4). Sports journalist Kenny Moore (2:15:39.8) remained in fourth place.

As Ron Hill and I came down out of the darkness of the tunnel into the stadium I was perhaps a couple of feet ahead. I don't think either of us saw Kimihara only about 40 metres ahead up the straight. I still led Hill as we pushed on up the home straight with a lap to go, staying outside a line of cones until we reached the top bend. On the back straight I let him through on the inside and so into sixth place. I was happy to be seventh even though some of my closest running friends have spent the decades since then telling me I should have tried a bit harder.

Another of the many things I was ignorant about was that the first six received a certificate, but in all honesty it wouldn't have mattered. For all the stuff that Ron wrote in his book about my moving out to let him through in the back straight ("What the hell for? Gentleman? British?"), I felt sorry that he was not going to be returning to his job at Courtauld's - from whose staff he had three days before received a book of "Good Luck" signatures with over 17,500 names - with a gold medal or indeed any medal other than the stainless steel commemorative one we all had. Nor was I aware of Kenji Kimihara just a few seconds ahead of us on the track. I was concentrating on getting over that line – 7th place was better than I could have hoped for in view of my Achilles problem, and had been predicted by no one, as far as I know, except the sage Aberdonian A J Wood.

Ron crossed the line in 2:16:30.6, less than three seconds ahead, and 3.6 seconds behind fifth placer Kimihara. My time was recorded as 2:16:34.4. I caught him up as he was walking down the track, hands on hips, looking exhausted and dejected. Trying to console him, I said something like "Bad luck, Ron…I'm sorry you didn't win. But I suppose I did OK". Not very diplomatic perhaps. The Accrington lad replied vehemently: "Bugger **you**!" When I went to find Ted Chappell, he was more encouraging. He said the next day, in words which I certainly did not merit but which were nonetheless nice to hear: "Anyone who finishes in the first ten of an Olympic final is a great man." But I would not have been in the first ten, and probably not even got to the start, if it hadn't been for him.

Colin Kirkham had dropped back gradually over the second half and finished in 20th (2:21:54.8). Modest as ever, his account later in the Road Runners Club magazine said merely; "In my part of the field, I didn't see anything much."

Later that evening Ron (civility restored) and I walked stiffly into the restaurant to be greeted in memorable words (memorable not for entirely serious reasons) by the Roman-nosed Renault dealer Arthur Gold, our chef d'équipe: "Well, congwatulations Don and commisewations Won – that's mowe or less how it should go…". We reacted with appropriate diffidence (Don) and politeness (Won).

Why had "wee Ronnie" been unable to stay with Frank Shorter and the other leaders? In the last third of the race, the diet worked almost as well for him as it did for me, but something was clearly not quite right. Ian Stewart and Brendan Foster think that he may not have been not 100% fit, but my hypothesis is that he made a mistake by not coming down from altitude with the rest of us. The body requires a certain time to acclimatise again to produce top performance at the lower level, and I believe that by pure chance I got it right by having a full ten days in Munich, while the six days he had left didn't allow his system to adapt. The depletion phase of the diet would also have slowed his adaptation from altitude. And on top of that, to quote his own words: "Someone had said that at altitude, the glycogen content of the muscles can go down by 30%; I daren't think about that; I had to do what I had to do."

Top marathoners nowadays, follow at the most an abbreviated form of the Saltin diet we subjected ourselves to. Some of them ingest carbohydrate gels during the race to provide muscles with accessible fuel. An article in Athletics Weekly by Dr Jason Karp (June 3rd 2010) gives a longer account of the factors involved. I was always reluctant to drink anything but water, for fear of an upset stomach. I preferred to tip cups of water over my head to cool me. It was an initial shock each time but after a few minutes I would feel a bit of a resurgence. Sponges were always welcome as well, and I would squeeze them out over my head and cool my thigh muscles with them.

"The diet" was always a subject of interest to other runners who hadn't tried it. There was a story going about in the 1970s that one well-known experienced British marathon runner decided to experiment with it, but after trying it in a big marathon and slowing dramatically over the last 10km he decided that it was no good. He explained that as prescribed he had started with a long depletion run a week before the race, and had then had three days of pasta, potatoes and sweet drinks, changing for the last three days to a low-carbohydrate diet of fatty dishes, cheese, meat etc. – and had run a personal worst). Perhaps the story is apocryphal, but I don't think so.

As for altitude training itself, it may be questioned how far its scientific basis and effects, let alone its practical application to runners have been established in the intervening decades, though it is now generally practised.

In the evening the Games closing ceremony was held, unsurprisingly, in a rather subdued atmosphere. I was there, but don't remember very much about it, except that we "paraded, mixed and mingled", as the biography of Avery Brundage puts it. Like millions worldwide I noticed that the retiring IOC President's name was comically mis-spelt on the stadium scoreboard as "Avery Brandage". We didn't stay up late.

My diary entry for the day after the race is a name-droppers' delight: "Jog two miles with Gammoudi et al, Prefontaine" is all it says. And, lest you mock, they knew who I was because they'd been watching the marathon runners come in. But then I had shared a room with Ian Stewart, who finished only 0.2 seconds behind silver medallist Mahomed Gammoudi (Tunisia) and beat US college idol "Pre" into 4th place in the 5000m, and then was so disgusted at not having won that he "felt like chuckin' the 'bleedin' medal over the stand". But didn't.

That Monday afternoon we flew back from Riem airport to Edinburgh. On landing I realised I had left my Olympic vest, shorts and shoes, still in the sweaty and stained condition they were in when I changed after the race, in a small British team bag at the airport. My light tan suitcase came off the luggage carrel with all the rest, as did the set of Olympic posters we had all been given. I was sad at the thought I would probably never see my kit again.

However when I got home to Edinburgh and had been welcomed by my family (but ignored by The Scotsman, who had hailed my selection but when my brother rang them up didn't want to know I was back in Scotland – after all, Scots who are in the top eight in the world are ten a penny), I wrote to the manager of Riem Airport asking if by any chance…

Miraculously, I received not just a reply, but the bag, with its UK Team label still attached and its very smelly contents intact. I've still got them, in a drawer in the bedroom. I foolishly used the posters as wallpaper in the flat in Dunoon and then couldn't get them unstuck when I moved away. The commemorative medal is balanced on a nail in the living room above a photo of my daughter Rosemary running the Bristol Half-Marathon in 2007.

And a photograph of Hill and me entering the Munich Olympiastadion hangs out in the hall. I'm ahead of him.

Chapter 18

Macgregor-san

The invitation to Fukuoka came when I was only a couple of months into my new job as PT Modern Languages at Dunoon Grammar School, so that I had for the second time that session to ask for leave of absence, on this occasion for a week. It was generously granted with pay.

I must have received the invitation towards the end of October, because in the weeks after Munich I had only run low recovery mileages (26, 36, 48, 38, 48) and noted in the diary for the week ending 28th October "started again seriously after 6 relatively idle weeks", which had ended with 4 days off because I had two teeth extracted.

The 7th Fukuoka International Marathon was to be held on Sunday 3rd December, so I had only five weeks to get myself into shape again. In autumnal Dunoon it got dark around 4, and it was only possible to get a reasonable mileage by getting out for a short lunchtime spin, usually through Hafton estate above the village of Sandbank overlooking the U.S. Polaris base. Most of these lunchtime runs were solo, but sometimes Graham Clark, one of the 4th year pupils, came with me. David Martin, whom I had met soon after arriving in Dunoon, was also an occasional training partner in the afternoon or evening, as was Graham. At two weekends I went east for races – the East District Relays on 4th November at Penicuik where I ran badly, and two weeks later the Edinburgh-Glasgow Relay, where I managed 33:14 for the 6th stage into Airdrie and the ESH team came third. On successive Sundays I did 19 mile runs with Fergus Murray, then again with Fergus and George Brown in the Pentlands. After a party at the Bryan-Joneses in Stirling a group of us ran an 18 miler in the Ochils on Sunday 19th November. On Saturday 25th and Sunday 26th I stuck in two long solo runs from 79 Victoria Road, the first 1hr 51mins for a run mainly on road via Kilmun, Blairmore Lodge and Ardentinny, and the other 2hrs15 mins in the other direction over forest tracks up in the hills north of Innellan.

The second of these was my glycogen depletion run, and the low carbohydrate part of the diet started at 4.15 that Sunday, and lasted until the Wednesday, by which time I was on board a JAL flight to from London via Copenhagen, Anchorage and over the North Pole to Tokyo, where we changed aircraft for the one hour flight to Fukuoka, which is on the southern island of Kyushu and is a city of about a million people.

As ever, the British delegation was made up of athlete plus manager. Peter Luke was the secretary of the Scottish Schools AA and the immediate past president of the SAAA. He was an affable man with a moustache and blazer, very interested in rugby. His diplomatic skills were very effective, as the main one was distributing bottles of Black Label whisky to Japanese officials.

We were accommodated in the Nishitetsu Grand Hotel, where I learned that the only foreign runners invited were Frank Shorter and Kenny Moore, Derek Clayton, Seppo Nikkari, and me. Kenji Kimihara was running, along with 75 Japanese runners who had times under 2:30, but Ron Hill had turned the trip down, Akio Usami was studying in West Germany, and Yoshiaki Unetani was also missing from the top line-up. Two other foreigners were entered – John Farrington (Australia) had been part-sponsored by a newspaper, and Alfons Sidler, a 38 year old Swiss runner, who had come 44th in Munich in 2:29:09.2 and had paid his own way.

On arrival on the Thursday Peter and I attended a friendly reception from the co-sponsors NRR (the Japanese AAA) and the Asahi Shimbun newspaper. We learned that at last year's event there had been an estimated 100,000 spectators on the flat out and back course round the bay, and that the television audience was and would again be around 40 million. There would be complete coverage plus 50 minutes of highlights an hour and a half later, though I never saw one second of any of it. On the other hand I have recently found out that a picture of me finishing at Munich was used regularly in 1972-3 by a German building society in a tv ad – no word of remuneration!

After the 26 hour journey, which had included a two hour stop in Anchorage where we admired the snowy wastes outside and resisted the Inuit sealskin souvenirs inside, I had trouble acclimatising and felt a bit dizzy after walking about. I needed to catch up on sleep, so that my first five mile jog on the Friday was very slow – so slow that the watching journalists, possibly thinking I was not fit, asked me as I got into the minibus back to the hotel "How is your physical condition?" to which Peter Luke replied confidently that it was very good. I was by now two days into the carbo-loading part of the Saltin diet and would not yet expect to feel at my best –race day would be soon enough.

6th December 1972, Fukuoka start.

Conditions were ideal – 12 degrees Celsius, negligible wind, 55% humidity, and sunny. The start was at 12.30pm. I jogged around a bit in the stadium, being photographed by Tiger shoe people who later sent me some prints as they had in Munich. I wore their fantastic Biwako blue suede shoes in all the big marathons I ran from September 1972 until 1976.

There was a steady pace for the 2 and 2/3 laps of the track, then it got faster when we reached the road. A leading group of Shorter, Farrington, Clayton, me, Nikkari, and 3 Japanese soon formed, but I fell back after about 3 or 4 km of "having a go", passing 5km in 15:03. That was the beginning of a long poor spell. I had not done enough speed training to cope with such a fast pace and my next 5 km splits were 15:46 and 16:18. However I pulled myself together over the last 12 km and, thanks to the diet, moved through from 10th to 6th and clocked a respectable 2:16:42.4, for the second time in four months not very far behind Kimihara. My "physical condition" had lived up to Peter Luke's prediction, despite my being described in the race programme, under a mocked-up "photo" which made me look rather Japanese, as a "veteran runner". I was still only 33!

Fukuoka prize-giving.

Frank Shorter ran a personal best of 2:10:30 as did Farrington in second place (2:12:00.4), Kenichi Otsuki (2:14:00.6) and Nikkari (2:14:02.8). The 24 year old Finn looked set for 3rd at 35km but "died" as he did at the Maxol in June. Otsuki took over a minute off him over the last 7km and caught him on the track.

Derek Clayton early on looked as if he was out for a sub 2:10 run, but developed a sore tendon which forced him to jog before halfway, and he retired around the turn.

Kenny Moore moved up to fourth, then lack of training during his recent globetrotting journalistic assignments for Sports Illustrated reversed his progress and he did well to get home in 13th with his legs "dead", as he said. The prizes were charming silver cups of various sizes, each having a ribbon round the neck of its base. The inside of each cup was covered in a gold-coloured alloy so that it looked precious indeed. That cup was one of the most attractive I ever won, so that when, much later, I decided to dedicate a trophy to the memory of a running companion, that same Graham Clark who had started running at Dunoon Grammar School in 1972 and who died tragically young at 47, I had no difficulty in selecting the most appropriate cup. It is now competed for annually at the 10km road race held by Carnegie Harriers over the Knockhill motor racing circuit near Dunfermline.

On the evening after the race our hosts offered us a meal in the best restaurant Fukuoka could provide – a French one! It was a great evening, much better than the visit to a night-club which the foreign runners had been taken to before the race. That had been a sort of strip-club where we gaijin stood as near the back as we could, while a few locals wearing crash helmets gazed at the strippers from as close a proximity as the stage would permit.

In the restaurant we all sat at a long table, headed by our host and his interpreter, a pretty girl with whom I later exchanged a few letters and cards. He seemed to be not just her employer but also a father-figure. The meal was excellent, and we were all in the best of spirits, especially Seppo Nikkari who must have drunk the best part of a bottle of whisky. He had to be helped back to the hotel, and I remember that Derek Clayton and Frank Shorter loaded him into a luggage carrier to get him into the lift.

We had time the next day to go round the markets and shops. The markets offered live chickens and other birds for sale, as well live fish and numerous other living creatures for customers to take home. We visited a big store, where people dressed as pandas bowed a welcome as we entered. It was a nice change from Santa. I was most impressed by the delicate way in which even the simplest of gifts was wrapped and beribboned.

Seppo Nikkari was on the same plane to Amsterdam as Peter Luke and me. He had had a rough night after his excesses. He spoke no English, French or German, but demonstrated good miming skills as he showed how his wife (touch ring on finger) would be angry (mime slapped cheek) because he had been sick (mime action) on his clothes. All he wanted from us was a travel sickness pill, which was provided.

Fukuoka Dec 1972: in a French restaurant after the race.
L to R: Clayton, Shorter, Bobbie Moore, Kenny Moore, Peter Luke, Japanese host.

Back home, the Scottish selectors had decided that if there were to be any Scottish entries for the Christchurch Commonwealth Games marathon, one would be the 1973 SAAA champion, and any additional runners would be selected on the basis of performances and expectations. Clearly the safest way to ensure a ticket for the plane was to win the title. If I could achieve a good enough time to win, my rivals could be left to sweat it out.

On the basis of my runs at Munich and Fukuoka I would be the pre-race favourite, but that meant nothing if I didn't train hard and build up through the spring. The race was to be on June 23rd from Meadowbank and would follow the route of the 1970 Commonwealth Games course, out the A1 and A198 towards North Berwick and back in again. The outward half was slightly downhill andthere would thus be a bit of a drag over the last few miles through Musselburgh and Portobello.

I had eased off in the nine or ten weeks since Fukuoka on December 6th, running between a low of 33 and a high of 70 miles. This was deliberate, as I wanted to be sure I had recovered from the 1972 season. I was also working very hard at Dunoon Grammar School to develop the modern language department. I reckoned that three months of solid build-up would be more or less ideal, provided nothing went seriously wrong.

Dunoon was where I lived during the week, but I preferred to go back East most weekends, either to Fife or to Edinburgh. I note that seven of the eleven weekends following Fukuoka were spent away from the Cowal peninsula. In Edinburgh I trained with various residents or ex-residents of "The Zoo" (78 Morningside Drive) or with my ESH clubmate Graham Stark, and in Fife with Ron Morrison, and John McCabe. To get back east I had to take a ferry from Dunoon to Gourock and then follow the M8 motorway, or to drive "round the top" by Rest-and-be-Thankful, Arrochar, Loch Lomond, and Stirling. I had changed my car from a pale blue Renault 12TL to a rather sportier dark blue Renault 6TS, but the overland journey from Dunoon to St Andrews still took about 3½ hours. One wet winter Friday night on the dual carriageway through Greenock I was pulled over by a policeman who told me, when I asked quite innocently how I could help him, that I had been speeding – 40 mph in a 30 mile zone. Fined £8.

Race performances in this period were poor: I came 12th in an East District League race, 23rd in the East District Championships, and a pathetic 50th in the National over a snowy course at Coatbridge on February 17th. The next day Fergus Murray, who had come over to Dunoon for the rest of the weekend, accompanied me on a 2hr 4mins outing through drizzle and a chilly wind over the "Achafour 18", which included quite a bit of climbing up endlessly winding forestry tracks. My build-up had started.

During the next four weeks I booted up the frequency of runs to 12 or 13 per week, averaging about 94 miles per seven days. One of the problems about training in Dunoon was that it rained so much. I noted that I got soaked ten times between 18th February and 3rd March. The only race I did was the ESH Club 10 miler on 24th March. It was a windy day and I won in 51:27 by 2:08 from George Brown.

April saw me in Brussels, where I visited my friend Eric Wakeling who had worked for the Centre for British Teachers in Germany in the small town of Goch. I trained with him and with Tim Johnston, who was working at the European Commission as a lawyer. His place of work was the Berlaymont multi-storey building, into whose elevator some protesting farmers had the previous week tried to insert a cow. I ran in the Forêt de Soignes, a huge area with some paths marked for pedestrians and some for horses. The easy days were with Eric and the hard days were with Tim. I was pleased to notice that over the six days I ran with the Olympic 8th placer from Mexico I was increasingly able to handle the pace. On the way home I stopped off at John and Carol Bryant's in London and enjoyed a relaxing 19 mile run with John on Wimbledon Common and in Richmond Park, followed the next day by a tough hilly 18 mile effort with Fergus Murray in Edinburgh via the Hillend artificial ski slope, through the Pentland Hills to Glencorse and back by Dreghorn. Over the first two weeks of April the mileage rose to 101 and 112.

The Easter holidays were over, and I resumed the Dunoon routine, accompanied sometimes by Graham Clark, and by Ron Morrison, Doug Gunstone and Stuart Easton in Fife at weekends. The Clydebank to Helensburgh 16 on the 28th April attracted a very strong entry, and the field remained bunched until the last mile and a half. Lachie Stewart sprinted to victory in 83:04, just ahead of Colin Martin (Dumbarton) and Jim Wight (EAC). Then came Willie Day (Falkirk Victoria), me (83:31), Alex Wight and Doug Gunstone (both EAC), and Martin Craven (ESH). 40 seconds covered the first eight.

I eased back the next week from 93 to 59, but returned to better form on 6th May when I won a British knockout cup 10,000m in 30:12.2 from Alex Wight and Alastair Wood. That kept me going, but I reverted to the usual up-and-down, "fed-up" mood for a day or two every couple of weeks. Remarks like "useless run" occasionally find their way into the training diary.

I was doing a mixture of steady running and speedwork. At about 11pm one evening in late May I was stopped by the police when finishing off a run with a session of 10x100 along the front at Sandbank. They wanted to know what I was up to so late at night! That week I managed 115 miles, the highest in the whole build-up period.

On June 9th, with only two weeks to the SAAA marathon, I won a Scottish League 5000m at Meadowbank in 14:26, beating Jim Wight and Colin Youngson (Aberdeen) with a last lap of 61-62 seconds. The following week, the last before I started the depletion diet, I ran 96 miles, finishing it off by running 29:53.8 for 10,000m, my second-fastest ever, for 7th place in the SAAA championship. The winner was Lachie Stewart in 28:59. Lachie also had pretensions to a place in the marathon team, though he had yet to make his debut at the distance. Jim Wight was second to Lachie in 29:22 and would clearly be a big threat on June 23rd.

I decided to experiment by reducing the long depletion run on the Sunday, 6 days before the race, to a 14 miler, which I covered in 88 minutes. It was warm and I lost 4.5 lb. Thanks to having Graham Clark to chat to on the runs, I was able to get to Tuesday night, when I could start to "carbo-load", without feeling too stressed, and the last three days were just the normal few miles very easy running. I went through to Edinburgh on the Friday evening and spent the morning sitting around and going for a stroll.

Here are the notes I made about the race in my diary:

"1st in 2:17:50 from Jim Wight 2:18:24, Bob Heron (Brighton & Hove) 2:21:15, Tony Moore (Longwood) 2:22 etc. Alex [Wight], Fergus[Murray], AJW[ood] retired. J.Alder "anaemia", JLS[tewart] food poisoning. 25:53, 51:50, 77:20?, 1:44, 2:11. Felt OK (more or less) all the way."

Although I was never far ahead of Jim Wight, I did not feel threatened at any point and shared the lead all the way until the last 3 miles or so. According to Dunky Wright in the Scottish Sunday Express, I tucked myself in the middle of a tight bunch of five of the 44 starters to the 20-mile mark just outside Prestonpans. "Then he strode into a three metre lead, followed closely by Edinburgh brothers Jim and Alex Wight and Rob Heron (Aberdeen)[in fact Rab Heron, Brighton & Hove].

"Coming into Portobello, three miles from home, he made his real effort and …strode to a 500 metres win and a sure place in Scotland's Commonwealth team." As I was only 34 seconds ahead, it must have been a very short or very fast 500 metres. Dunky quoted me as saying that "Plucky Jim Wight should come with me". When the selectors met, they did decide that Jim Wight had earned his place. Jim Alder on the other hand was dreadfully upset when he learned that despite his first and second places in the 1966 and 1970 Empire/Commonwealth Games he had not been picked. I felt sorry for him, but he had not shown much form over the past year or two.

It was very satisfactory to know that all being well I would definitely be going to Christchurch six months down the line, even though I would have to ask for a further leave of absence.

High jinks: Derek Clayton blindfolds Seppo Nikkari.

That summer I did little racing, and again reduced my training mileage. I had been in regular correspondence with the interpreter Miriam who had looked after the British runners at Košice in 1969, and she and her fiancé Michael invited me to come over. The plan was to drive across Europe in my pastel blue Renault 12TL. I equipped myself with maps and guidebooks from the AA. The intention was to set off on Friday 29th June, and to stay for the first few nights with friends, all of whom I had met through athletics. So I slept the first night at Salford at Enid and Arthur Walsham's, then farther south to Cwmbran where I ran a 5000m in the National League, coming 5th in 14:35.6. Here my hosts were Lynn Davies and his wife Meriel, who lived in an attractive street in Marshfield, Cardiff.

I then headed for the Bryants' in London. John had arranged for me to be tested by Dr John Brotherhood at the National Centre for Physical Research at Holly Hill in Hampstead. For John and me the episode was to go down as the "Holly Hell" incident: John Brotherhood started by measuring my fat with callipers, and found that I had the lowest values he had thus far recorded in a UK runner. He then wanted me to breathe into a rugby ball bladder to test (I think) my vagal-venous reaction. I remember he talked about subjects puffing cigarette smoke into this rubber bag. He then wanted to take a blood sample, but I burst into hysterical tears and the test had to be aborted. The fit was only temporary, as I was able to calm myself down with a gentle 74 minute run on Hampstead Heath with John Bryant.

The next day the Renault and I headed by ferry to Ostend and on to Brussels where the Wakelings welcomed me, then I continued towards Köln to visit Heinz and Inga Monheim, who lived in the neighbouring town of Porz, and we enjoyed a run and a few glasses of the local beer, Kölsch.

The great adventure really started after that, as I headed down the Autobahn in the direction of Bavaria, eventually stopping at Weinsfeld near Hilpoltstein, where it was very hot. The summer of 1973 in Scotland was also a hot one, relatively speaking, and water restrictions had been imposed back home. The old lady who put me up in her Gastzimmer had read about this in her newspaper and commiserated with me on "die große Hitze von Schottland", as if it were the Sahara.

The next night I stayed in the village of Hamburg an der Donau, of which I recall nothing except the memorable name and that it was a great contrast to the Hamburg an der Elbe, known in North Germany as "Tor zur Welt", gateway to the world. I spent the following morning trying to get into Czechoslovakia, initially through Austria. However the border was closed "because of foot-and-mouth", and would-be travellers were directed to drive back to the Hungarian border, purchase a visa, and get through to the Czechoslovakian Soviet Socialist Republic that way. It seemed that the "Maul-und Klauenseuche" was very localised or possibly diplomatic, as this was still the Cold War era and East and West repeatedly looked for ways to score points off one another. The Hungarians were happy to sell me a visa, but I drove the 30 miles or so through Hungary in some trepidation, as I spoke not a word of Hungarian so that some of the road signs were incomprehensible to me. At last I got out unscathed, and into Bohemia.

As I travelled farther south into Slovakia, the roads got worse and worse. At one point a tremendous rainstorm flooded the windscreen so that the wipers could not cope even at double speed, and drivers had to stop by the muddy roadside until the storm passed. My Renault was not as a rare a sight as I had thought it would be. Every other car was painted an identical shade of pastel blue and looked just like mine. In fact they were Renaults under a different name, Dacia, this having been the Roman name for the province which was now (approximately) Slovakia.

At last I reached Košice, where I was warmly received by my hosts. I was able to go running the next three days in the woods, and then drove with my friends to their country cabin or "maša" in the Tatra mountains at the village of Muráň. The village was quite high up, and so it was an effort to train hard there. My longest run was a 21 km out-and-back on the roads to Tisovec, and I was also treated to a day in the mountains and a ride on a beautiful horse with a golden mane – though I was scared stiff of falling off.

My friends were like nearly all Czechs and Slovaks extremely hostile to the Russians, whose army was occupying the country and had imposed a crackdown since the "Prague Spring" of 1968. I was urged to tell people back home what the Soviets were like. During the few days we spent in Muráň there were Red Army manoeuvres in the area. A seemingly unending procession of tanks and Red Army lorries passed through the village square for a full 24 hours. The Russians had posted a single soldier on the square to direct the lorries, and it was noticeable that no one spoke to him at all during all the hours he stood there.

Another feature of village life that struck me was that loudspeakers were in evidence round the streets, and that through them blaring music was played when it was time to get up, go to work etc. On my last day in Muráň which was very warm, I had a nasty fall after about 25 minutes running without a T-shirt along a gravelled path, and got back to the house with bits of gravelly dirt embedded in my shoulder. It was extremely painful. Miriam and her mother were able to clean it up, and I learned a new vowel-less word, štrk [gravel] which I will never forget. We were due to drive the next day to drop off Miriam's mother at Jihlava. I did manage to get there but I had very great difficulty in changing gear because my shoulder was so sore.

I crossed the border into West Germany at Herbruck, Bavaria. The contrast between the Czech border post and the German one was very marked. On the Czech side you waited in the rain as the crossing place had no roof; my car was searched in case I was smuggling someone out. As I had a few crowns left and wasn't allowed to export them, I was waved towards a shop where I bought a few bottles of pilsner beer from the real Pilsen from which it takes its generic name.

The Germans on the other side welcomed us travellers courteously and waved us through quickly on to the smooth Western roads. The return journey was interrupted at Porz, where I got the chance to run a 3000m for my previous German club TV Refrath. The štrk incident can't have affected me too badly as I won by 8 seconds in 8:34.7. I continued my pilgrimage northwards via the Reichswald, where I met up with Gerd Mölders and his friends for the first time since Munich, and the next day repeated the encounter with Udo Hennig at Reeuwijk in the Netherlands, where he was now living.

Chapter 19

Now Mac is a Gold bet

It was now early August, and I had six months to get ready for Christchurch. Over the late summer I trained regularly but not excessively and had a few races. Dunky Wright organised a One Hour track run at the annual Cowal Gathering on 25th August in which Gareth Bryan-Jones and Bill Stoddart of Greenock Wellpark, a former World Veterans Marathon champion, also took part. I won the race from Gareth by 1½ laps but only covered 19.291 km, some 25m short of the 12 mile "barrier". Dunky was very pleased with the prize he had selected for the winner, a brown leather suitcase. Heinz and Inga Monheim were over for a few days from Germany and we were able to spend a pleasant evening with them, Jan and Gareth.

Graham Clark, now in fifth year, was my regular training partner in Dunoon and making good progress in his own fitness. He joined me quite regularly on fartlek sessions or up to 10 mile steady runs.

I won by about 5 minutes in the Dunblane 14 mile road race (81.25) but struggled with boredom and tiredness over the second half into the wind. I got my comeuppance the next week at the Monkland 5 where I was tanked by Ian Stewart, Andy McKean, Jim Brown, Lachie Stewart, Fergus Murray and Jim Dingwall: now that's what I call a classy field. The winner was 66 seconds ahead of me in 24:30. The next day Doug Gunstone, who had been 8th at Monkland, ran in with me in the fog at the Tay Bridge "10" in 51:29, half a minute ahead of the local boy Rab Heron, who was on holiday from his job as a librarian at a college in Brighton.

Training in Dunoon was good as long as the light nights continued, because there were many picturesque if tough forest trails as well as the gentler run up Glen Masson, practically traffic free. At weekends I could if I chose run "o'er the hill tae Ardentinny", which in the 1920s and 30s had been part of the long walk Dunky Wright had included in the hundred miles a week he claimed in a 1968 BBC interview to have done: "We too trained one hundred miles a week: ten miles a night from Monday to Thursday, 20 miles on Saturday, and a 40 mile walk on Sunday." Without going into too much detail, I did not quite average 100 miles a week that autumn and early winter, but ran

396 miles in October, 370 in November, and 409 in December, an average of 13.4 miles a day. I competed regularly for ESH in the usual seasonal events: the Kingsway relay, which we won; the Allan Scally relay, where hosts Shettleston beat us; the East of Scotland relay where we won again; and the "blue riband" relay, the Edinburgh-Glasgow in which we triumphed over Edinburgh AC and Aberdeen AAC. I ran the long 6th leg into Airdrie in 32:22, my best ever on the leg, but was only 5th fastest. EAC's Andy McKean flew along the road in 31:00, 15 seconds faster than Dave

Roommates again: with Ian Stewart at Christchurch, January 1974.

Logue (Edin Univ) and 22 faster than Ian Stewart, up from Birmingham to run for Aberdeen. Ian shot past me with a mile to go, moving like the wind.

The SAAA National Coach had in recent years been John Anderson, a top-class coach, and a red-head, who lived up to his fiery reputation by suddenly resigning from the post. He was succeeded by Frank Dick, also a very well qualified coach but one who had a different approach from John Anderson, who had once gone on a two hour training run at Tentsmuir, had earlier given me some training advice and was later the referee on "Gladiators". Dick was a keen student of Eastern European training methods, especially for technical events, and went in for structuring the year to allow "double periodisation" and the like. This was no different in essence from what Lydiard preached, but it sounded unsympathetic.

The SAAA arranged for the Commonwealth Games squad to have supplies of "Pollitabs", a supplement whose main ingredient was bee pollen. The effect of these tablets was supposed to be to allow us to recover more quickly from our training sessions and thence put more effort into the next. I tried them for a while, but am not sure if they worked. At least they were not one of the banned substances like the range of anabolic steroids that not a few athletes on both sides of the Iron Curtain had been taking since the 1950s. I may say at this point that at no time in my athletic career did I ever go beyond "Pollitabs" in dietary experiments – excluding "The Diet" and beer and wine of course. As for most distance runners, these latter two formed a regular part of my fluid intake. It is probably true that if scientists ever came up with a drug that would ensure an athlete could break the world record in his or her event, but that if he or she took it death would ensue within a year, there would be queues round the block: but I wouldn't be in them.

I ran only one race in December, a cross-country event for the SCCU versus the Scottish Universities held in the snow at Stepps, and came a modest 7th. On January 5th I essayed the "Nigel Barge" 4½ mile road race, by tradition the first race of the year. I finished an even more modest 11th but in a strong field which was mostly made up of speedy middle-distance specialists. I continued to pile in the miles, not forgetting regular sessions of fartlek to improve my speed.

We were due to fly out to New Zealand on Thursday 10th January, a full three weeks before the marathon. We would have ample time to acclimatise and were very pleased to escape the worst of the Scottish winter. We had long since been fitted out with our uniforms and training equipment. I was again using blue Tiger Biwakos, and the suppliers in Japan had sent me a spare red pair. Our team uniform, which we would use for formal occasions like the opening ceremony (groan!) included a bright blue blazer with silver buttons, white trousers and a white hat. While not wishing to sound ungrateful, I have often wondered why athletics teams are supplied with items most of which cannot possibly be used in normal life. What sort of person parades around in a Commonwealth or Olympic Games blazer? I suppose if you play cricket or go in for amateur dramatics the white trousers might come in useful, but the hat?

The team assembled on Wednesday 9th January in the Royal Scot Hotel, just a few yards from the Maybury Edinburgh-Glasgow changeover point. Ian Stewart persuaded me to go out at 7.10 am the next day, much earlier than I was used to. As the local man I led him on an 8½ mile circuit round the

Barnton and Corstorphine area, but it was hard to keep up. The pace was recorded as "steady", but in fact I was hanging on, in the knowledge that most of the next 24 hours or so we would be in the air and I could sleep. We boarded our plane and I discovered that I was sitting next to the athletics team captain, Les Piggott (Garscube Harriers), a very good sprinter. Behind us was a female official with a particularly penetrating West of Scotland voice. Both of us made sotto voce comments about it being lucky that we had headphones and a selection of eight audio tracks to listen to.

The plane landed at Singapore (very humid with warm rain) and at Melbourne, where immigration officials walked through the plane spraying everybody with insecticide to guard against any bugs that we might have picked up in Asia. Other UK teams were travelling on the same machine, and I observed the phenomenon of compulsive airport jogging at each of the stops by one or two of the more obsessive runners, including Ron Hill. No airport stop was allowed to interfere with the "streak".

We touched down in the early morning local time, emerging from the aircraft rather bleary-eyed to be greeted by a squad of Maori dancers performing a dance of welcome. Then we were driven to the Games Village, a series of three-storey student blocks in the quiet suburban garden setting of the University of Christchurch. The team medical officers had of course exercised great caution in giving advice about acclimatisation, and told us we should not do any running for a day or two until our bodies had recovered from the flight. Ian Stewart, with whom I was sharing a room, had been on long trips like this before, and said the quickest way to acclimatise was to go for a half an hour jog straight away and then sleep. We did that, and the next morning felt well recovered and were a day to the good over those who had done what the doctors advised. We got straight into training: a 10 mile run with Ian and Lachie Stewart, Jim Wight, Norman Morrison (5000m and 10,000m) through the streets looking in vain for Hagley Park which had been recommended as the best place to run.

That was Sunday 13th. On the Monday we were out for 50 minutes at 6:10am and this time found Hagley Park, where we bumped into one of my heroes out jogging, the triple Olympic gold medallist Peter Snell, one of Lydiard's great athletes, who won in Rome 1960 (800m) and Tokyo 1964 (800m and 1500m). At noon I did another hardish 59 minutes round the park, and piled it on again on Tuesday with a 90 minute steady run with my two marathon colleagues Lachie and Jim, plus Ian Stewart. We dropped Norman Morrison, who was clearly not at his best. Later that afternoon I added a short track session with Lachie, striding the straights and jogging the bends for five laps.

After all this I was a bit weary on the Wednesday, and only did a little fartlek and then steady running. Brendan Foster, who was running the 1500m for England but had trained with me a few times in St Moritz and in Munich in 1972, went out of his way to warn me that if I trained so hard with the Stewarts and the rest I would burn myself out. I had realised that and assured him I had just wanted to put in a few very hard days before getting into a less intense rhythm.

In conversation during our easy runs in St Moritz "Big Bren" had told me that about 85-90% of his training for his specialist distance at that time, the 1500m, consisted of 6:30–7:00 minute miling, though of course like Lasse Viren he threw in intense sessions of speedwork for the remaining 10-15%.

The men's athletics team manager was Eddie Taylor, a long-serving Shettleston Harriers official who richly deserved the honour. We had been given very light blue denim "leisure suits" with orange stitching and fashionably wide bell-bottoms. We all looked a bit ridiculous in these outfits, which did not suit Eddie who was a tall, very thin man. Together with Frank Dick, Eddie held regular team meetings to tell us what was going on in and around the Village. Some the talks from Frank were intended to motivate us, not that most of us needed any motivation. I tried to avoid getting too involved in these team meetings,

On Saturday 19th January we went to Timaru, the birthplace of our reigning Scottish Commonwealth Games 800m champion, Rosemary Stirling, for a local meeting. There I ran a 5000m on the grass. It was won by Gordon Minty (Wales) in 14:07, with Lachie second in 14:24, and Campbell of New Zealand 3rd in 14:26. Chris Brasher, then an Observer journalist, was watching the race, and confirmed that "that spastic Macgregor", as he put it in that pre-PC age, had indeed outsprinted the great Ron Hill for 4th place in 14:40, despite Ron's repeated refusal to accept that verdict.

In between training sessions we had the chance to explore Christchurch and its surroundings. Local people had offered their services as chauffeurs to show us the locality, and as hosts for tea and chat. I escorted one of our assistant team managers to a restaurant in the town centre, which was fun.

The outskirts of the town looked rather like small-town America, with long stretches of concrete shopping centres and gas stations, but the older parts were more like Britain, or rather England, of the 1950s, with streets of neat bungalows, each with its own garden and garage. In the streets you could see cars which in the UK had long since rusted away or vanished into motor museums or collectors' clubs: Standard Vanguards, Jowett Javelins, Triumph Mayflowers, Austins and Morrises, Rileys and Wolseleys, Hillmans and Humbers. Because of the mild winters salt was not used on the roads so that the cars were slow to rust.

From the 20th January to the 28th, before starting the diet, I decided to weigh myself every day to check how my bodyweight was affected by the low carbohydrate phase. It fluctuated over the pre-diet days from 64.7kg to 62.0kg, most readings being in the area of 63kg. Over the three depletion days it dropped as expected to between 61.6 and 61.2kg. During that period I became very irritable as well as tired. On Day Two Lachie told me cheerfully at dinner: "You're just weakening yourself with all that nonsense" [or words to that effect], and I'm sorry to say that I threw my cup of warm tea over him The carbo-loading days proceeded as I have previously described in respect of other big races, and I was luckily not affected by any digestive or injury problems.

As at any big Games, a huge head of steam had been built up in the press about how the team might perform. At Edinburgh in 1970 the brilliant running of Lachie Stewart in the 10,000m, Rosemary Stirling in the 800m, Jim Alder in the marathon, and Ian Stewart and Ian McCafferty in the 5000m, as well as the gold medal discus throwing of Rosemary Payne had brought some journalists and pundits to expect even better results in New Zealand. For example Harry Andrew, writing in the Scottish Sunday Express of December 30th 1973 under the headline "GOLD-STANDARD SCOTS SET FOR GLORY", claimed that team commandant Willie Carmichael "reckons we are in with a shout for TEN gold medals" and that Dunky Wright, the Empire Games marathon winner in 1930, agreed with him.

Thus David Jenkins was being "internationally tipped" to win the 400m, and was quoted as saying "I am in deadly earnest about this one". Harry

1973 French exchange, Dunoon: Ian Hendry awards certificate to French pupil, Christiane Riffaud (Esbly) looks on.

even thought he had a chance of a 200m/400m double. The only threat to Stewart McCallum and David Kidner in the decathlon was, "I am told", from Northern Ireland's Mike Bull. And then came the 24-year old language teacher from Dunoon Grammar School, who had not only shed ten years but was "strongly fancied" to become Scotland's fourth Games marathon winner. He said I had "come on a lot" since Munich, but could face opposition from Lachie Stewart who had "stretched [his] training to cover the marathon" and "COULD BE THE SURPRISE OF THE GAMES" before retiring to devote more time to his wife and three children.

Ian Stewart, "grimly determined to hang on to his 5000m title", and Norman Morrison, "an outstanding candidate" for 10,000m, were supposedly the other gold medal prospects among the men, and reigning champions Rosemary Stirling at 800m, and Rosemary Payne (discus) were given as the journalist's golden tips for the women's events along with Helen Golden (200m), Myra

Nimmo (Long Jump) and Ian's sister Mary Stewart (1500m) who despite being a teenager "has all the composure of a veteran."

Ten gold medals! That was a tall order. This time it was the New Zealanders who enjoyed home advantage. The Lachie Stewart role was played this time by Richard Tayler, who defeated David Black (England) on the first day of athletics to take the 10,000m title with a Games record of 27:46.1. Ian Stewart was 6th in 28:17.2, a personal best, Lachie 10th (29:22.6) and Norman Morrison 15th (30:25.8).

As the days passed, the Scottish gold medal hopes evaporated. Mike Bull won the decathlon; David Kidner was 4th but Stewart McCallum retired injured. Frank Dick had urged us at an early team meeting to encourage David Jenkins, if we met him round the Village, by saying things like "Looking good, Jenks!" to boost his self-confidence. Whether confident or not, the talented Jenks did not perform quite as well as he and most of Scotland's fans had hoped. He came 4th in the 400m final in 45.9, 0.7 sec slower than his best, and ran disappointingly in the 200m final, coming in 7th in 21.0 (best 20.7). In the 5000m Ian Stewart lost contact with six laps to go but fought back to take 5th in 13:40.4 behind Ben Jipcho (Kenya) who won thrillingly by 0.2 sec from Brendan Foster in 13:14.4. Mary Stewart, Rosemary Stirling and Myra Nimmo competed well but were not in the first three. In fact the only Scottish track and field medallist was Rosemary Payne, who took the silver in the Discus.

Back home the press was having a field day attacking the failure of "our athletes" to fulfil the journalists' expectations, and comparing the athletics "prima donnas" with relatively unsung Scots in the wrestling, shooting, weightlifting, bowling, boxing and swimming events who had been picking up medals of all colours – 2 gold, 4 silver and 11 bronze in total. The Scottish hero was swimmer David Wilkie, double gold medallist in the 200m breaststroke and 200m medley races.

As news of the critical articles written by some of the converted football writers who were reporting in the absence of any knowledgeable athletics experts on their papers – though there were a few honourable exceptions – my fellow team-members and I got a bit annoyed. One Daily Record journalist so irritated us by the contrast between his sycophantic approaches to us and the tone of what he wrote in the paper after talking to us that he very narrowly escaped being thrown in the river that flowed through the university campus.

The happy mood of the team darkened. Outside it was hot and sunny; inside it was warm but the tone subdued. At the team meetings that I attended the management seemed to be fighting an uphill struggle. I stopped going to these "pep-talk" sessions and concentrated on the race, saying to John Rafferty of The Scotsman that "pessimism is infectious". John wrote: "He can say that again."

It was perhaps as well that I was unaware of what James Sanderson had filed on Friday 25th January, six days before the marathon, to the Scottish Daily Mail under the heading "Now Mac is a Gold bet". I had become favourite to win, he wrote, because "a sudden change from sweltering sun to chill wind has brought predictions from African and Australian coaches that Macgregor is the big gold hope. "As a former pupil of his school [Dunoon Grammar School] I could be prejudiced. But Mac is earning huge respect here…"

The huge respect was not particularly obvious to me, nor had I noticed "the worst summer for 35 years" becoming "like something from home…biting cold, rain and north-easterly winds…freak Arctic-like weather" which could "say met men, go on for a week". It was slightly less torrid for a few days, and there was a slight breeze. I noted only on the day before the race that it was "windier".

Sanderson had the support of "local marathon expert Larry Saunders" who opined that "this is one race New Zealand would not mind losing to Scotland, believe me." I believe you, Larry, but I'm still not sure why they wouldn't have minded.

Although all seemed fine with the last stages of the diet, I was more nervous before the race than I had been at the Olympics. Perhaps I sensed in some paranormal way the weight of expectation that some of the Scottish "fans with typewriters" were placing on my fragile shoulders. I don't think so, but some part of me almost wished I had just stayed at home.

This is, word for word, what I jotted down on a sheet of paper about three-quarters of an hour before going down to the stadium on Thursday 31st January 1974:

"Pre-Race: the time of hypermanic depression, up and down like a spirit level on the road to Ardentinny, now full of calm confidence & sure of having a good run, now wondering what the attractions of making the team could possibly have been, sure you're going to freak out in the first 3 km from nerves. Times when superstition can easily prevail + must be firmly controlled, when the pulse can be regulated by measuring it calmly, where last minute drinks are taken, + expelled, where music relaxes, while the body churns away, manufacturing chemicals which, you hope, will help drive you on for two hours.

"Spent some time after lunch discussing with 3 NZ runners and Clayton the possibility (improb.) of 2 hr mara – need about 20-25 sec per mile off the present time – maybe in several generations, seems hardly poss. with our type of man. Change cassette (Ian S. classical) to Simon + Garfunkel's greatest hits. Lying on mattress (beds removed cos sore back), all around relative disorder – order rooted in disorder stood – 2 telegrams + a letter …

Palms sweating slightly – why? Not so hot today as yesterday – hope wind gets up. Lachie is confident, absurdly? Jim wants a p.b. I could do with one too. Avoid stitch if poss. Is it?

My thoughts cover many days, years, many races. Intellectually I perceive absurdity of this racing, my body takes it seriously as does the everyday part of me. Re-read Cat's Cradle, a gd.bk before running.

We're going at 3.30, it's 2.48 now. Race is at 5. Reckon I should have another wee drink of electrolytes now. Go and mix it. Mix it in the race!

Where is the deathless prose? Paralysed out of me, in me? Does the nonsense gain in value by being written down? The thoughts of a sheep on its way to the bloody knife, of Armstrong stepping on to the moon. Easy for spectators, hard to go out into the afternoon, like a matador – or a bull? Have been reading The Oldest Confession – R.Condon. My memory's going, can't remember even book titles, names of place on the Edin mara route etc etc. Jack Foster tells me 2:12 doesn't feel any different from 2:20. Hope it comes today. Simon & Garfunkel have gone off, think I'll change them over. Nervous writing this is. In a few hours it'll all be over!! Joke."

All I can recall now about the "few hours" is that when we got to the Queen Elizabeth II Stadium, we were taken to a changing room and then led about 20-30 minutes before the start to a small rather cramped room where a small man with a scarlet blazer checked us off, asking "Everybody heppy ? Everybody heppy ?". Few of us were happy to be kept in there, but in the end we were released and jogged round the track. Did the starter really say "Toes behind the line" and "It's a long way – no need to jump the gun"?

When he fired, we shot off, but I did not have the speed to go with Ian Thompson and the other leaders. My training diary entry just says:

"Commonwealth Games – 6th in 2:14:15.4 to Ian Thompson, Jack Foster, Richard Mabuza, Terry Manners, John Farrington. See AW for details. Felt smooth but no speed. Had plenty power over last 2km – ran too much solo. Quite pleased." And in the "Day Week Month" totals column: "c. 27 - 52 - 383."

Athletic Weekly's report states that there was a cool breeze at 5 pm when the race started. I don't recall that, but it was definitely less hot than on previous days. There were 33 starters, but after the first five minutes twelve had broken away, including Derek Clayton (Aus), Ian Thompson (Eng), John Farrington (Aus), Colin Kirkham Eng), Bernard Plain (Wal), Richard Mabuza (Swaziland), Terry Manners, Jack Foster and John Robinson (all NZ). I was already 400m down with Malcolm Thomas (Wal) and Ron Hill, who this time was wearing a backless vest and Union Jack shorts.

Ian Thompson had twinges of cramp in the first few miles, and was attacked by a dog, but he took off quite early on and won very convincingly by 2 mins 6.6 seconds from Jack Foster. Ian's time was 2:09:12.00, a European best performance and the second fastest ever to Clayton's 2:08:33.6 (Antwerp 1969). The Antwerp course had however not been officially ratified as being 42,195 m so that Clayton's time was never universally accepted.

I had no choice but to run solo after the fast group had dropped me. They must have been fast as I went through 10km in 30:45, 20km in 62:00 [31:15], 30km in 1:34:09 [32:09] and 40km in 2:07:15 [33:06]… and so must have run the 21.1 km to the turn at Christchurch airport in around 65:40, which incidentally would be my fastest ever half-marathon time.

But I couldn't keep that pace up as we ran on through the warm late afternoon. For a while I found myself together with John Robinson in about 10th place, but he suddenly veered off into a suburban garden to make a toilet stop, and I saw him no more. I seemed to have quite a bit left over the last few km and overtook Bernard Plain not very far from the stadium, but had no chance of catching Farrington.

My teammates did not fare well. Lachie Stewart's optimism was unfounded, as became apparent after his disappointing 10,000m performance. The general view, expressed forcibly by members of the bowls team coming home in the bus after a reception, was that he was "a prima donna" who was "just out here for the trip". He went through 20 km in 63:30 and dropped out just after half-distance. The quiet Jim Wight, who had trained so hard but was somehow not on form on the day, maybe because of nerves, or the weather, or lack of experience of big Games, dropped out somewhere after 30km, where his time was 1:51:40. I have always felt sorry for athletes who have earned selection through effort and hard work and who then perform well below form or worse drop out. I can imagine only too well how it must feel.

While in New Zealand I would ideally have wished to do some more touring and especially visit the North Island. I had been invited to do so by George Brown, my father's old hiking companion who lived there with his Malaysian wife Chelo. Unfortunately the demands of training for the race, which after all was the reason I had come to New Zealand, made it impossible to accept the invitation, and I regretted that.

A second invitation was turned down very stupidly. Arthur Lydiard had invited a couple of the other runners to come with him on a flight round Mount Cook, leaving at 4 am on February 1st. I had the chance to join the small group, but the marathon the evening before had sapped my energy and I failed to wake up in time. What an idiot! The chance to meet Lydiard never came again.

For a change the marathon was not on the last day, so that we had the first two days of February to relax before having to fly home. The closing ceremony was held on the late afternoon of Saturday 2nd February; earlier I was in the packed Queen Elizabeth II Stadium to watch the young Tanzanian Filbert Bayi break American Jim Ryun's 1500m world record by nearly a second with a time of 3:32.2. John Walker (NZ) was only 0.3 seconds behind, and the first five beat the Games record. It was a magnificent finale. Filbert Bayi had given this admirable reply to a journalist's question about his chances: "If I don't win, the sun will still go up tomorrow."

The closing ceremony was a complete contrast to the stiff opening parade. The atmosphere was relaxed and happy, the tensions were gone, and a colourful mob of athletes and officials, draped in flags, some in exchanged tracksuits, surged round the track and jogged with linked arms over the infield as fireworks whizzed and sparkled under the southern skies.

One member of our team, Norman Morrison, was so enamoured of New Zealand that he decided to move there, and I was also mildly tempted to emigrate, but did not take it any further.

When we eventually got back to Scotland, cold and windy weather awaited us. I stayed with my parents for two nights before heading to Dunoon, but the nation's transport system did not prove up to the task of getting me there without hitch. There were train delays, and high winds had cancelled some of the ferry sailings from Gourock. Eventually I was able to unpack and prepare the auld claes and parritch for the next day at school.

Chapter 20

Trailing Clouds of Glory

In 1974 I had the chance to apply for the post of principal teacher of German at Madras College, as the languages department was to be split. Dunoon was a pleasant place in summer, but I found the long dark nights and the restricted area for training frustrating. Graham Clark had gone to Southampton to work for the Ordnance Survey and I had to train alone during the week.

Once again I underwent the interview ordeal in Kirkcaldy, and again the stentorian janitor announced me as the successful candidate. This time it was Dr Thompson who welcomed me back to the staff, where I was to inherit the Kiel Exchange from Mike Wills, the new head of French. The flat in Dunoon was sold at a profit and I bought a Wimpey house in Carron Place on the extreme western edge of town – sight unseen, relying on the judgement of my old friend Duncan Monteith. I acquired a cat and moved in.

The 1974 Scottish marathon title fell to me, probably the easiest win of my career, and in 1976 a third, one of the hardest. For the sake of brevity: in June 1974 I had reduced my average mileage a bit, but had done the diet again. The morning was spent doing a pencil sketch of 17 Kaimes Road. In the race I went off with Rab Heron and we swapped the lead till about 23.5 miles when he had "a weakness" – not surprising, as his second son had been born in the early hours of the day before, though I didn't know that – and I kept going to finish in 2:18:08, he was second in 2:19:15. I recall coming into the stadium and feeling not too bad.

In 1976 Fife Athletic Club had just been formed. Along with long-jumper Susan Hay I became one of the club's first two Scottish champions, of which I was proud as it brought recognition for the club. The race was described by third-placer Alistair MacFarlane as "a survival job", for the start was at 1.40 pm, the warmest time of the day.

Alistair and I shared the pace for 5 miles (25:48) before the Springburn runner realised it was too fast for him and fell back temporarily. His training partner – mine too – Doug Gunstone (EAC) passed him at 8 miles. At 10 I was about a minute ahead of Doug and the gap remained more or less

SAAA marathon champion 1976 – a first for Fife AC.
Joe Walker (Scottish Marathon Club) holds the tape.

constant all the rest of the way, as we sought shade from a distant row of trees along the A168.

I staggered into the stadium in 2:24:12, Doug in 2:25:23, and Alistair in 2:30:14. I don't know about the other two, but I was all in. My friends Agnes McKane had accompanied her daughter Ursula (Fife AC) who was running the 1500m and they stayed to watch the marathon finish. Ursula said I had deserved the applause - for once.

Over the next couple of years. I just got on with my job, ran regularly and raced regularly. One sad event was the death of Dunky Wright, born 22nd

September 1896, on 21st August 1979. He embodied all that was good about Scottish distance running. Like everyone else, he wasn't perfect, but he is greatly missed.

For a couple of seasons when I was 38 and 39 my running performances notably dipped. However the prospect of moving into the "Veteran" category (over 40) on 23rd July 1979 lent me new wings, and I determined to have a go at the IGAL World Veterans (or Masters) track and field champs, which included a marathon, in Hannover, Germany. Graham Stark, George Brown and I were the three intrepid ESH members who drove out to Lower Saxony in Graham's car. We crossed on the Hull-Rotterdam North Sea ferry and stopped in 's Heerenberg, just inside the Dutch border, for a run in the woods where I had trained in 1971-2. I found the run we did pretty easy, but the other two told me afterwards they had been toiling. We had booked up at a campsite in the country near Hannover, but tents were all exiled to a field at the foot of the site near the lake, the main park being for caravans. Although I had been told we were camping, I somehow omitted to bring any equipment with me, such as knife, fork and spoon or plates. My mind had been so focussed on competition.

The tent area had a big disadvantage: there was no curfew although in theory "Nachtruhe" was supposed to prevail after 2200h. That did not prevent a group in a neighbouring tent from playing Simon and Garfunkel till the small hours, despite George going to complain to the warden. If I never hear "Bridge over Troubled Water" again, I won't be sorry.

Somehow I slept enough to feel OK when we went down to the track. The other two were running earlier in the 1500m, but were eliminated in the heats. I had entered both the 10,000m and the marathon. The track races were run in 5-year age-groups and mine, the youngest, was the last to be run off. I covered the first 5000 in 15:10 or so. By that time I had a clear lead, and sped up gradually, finishing 53 seconds clear of Aldelagala (Portugal) in 30:04.2, my best for fifteen years.

In the marathon a few days later, I decided to take it reasonably easy, and coasted along in the leading bunch for about 10km, then headed off by myself. No-one came with me, and I waited for John Robinson (NZ) who had been far behind me in the 10km and whom I had last seen before that in Christchurch in 1974. We ran along happily, and as we got into the last

Filming Chariots of Fire, West Sands, St Andrews 1980.

few miles I suggested that we should just run in together. I thought he had agreed, so was a little disgruntled when he took off with about 100m to go and sprinted to the tape, subsequently denying that we had agreed to anything. I wasn't very annoyed as I had my medal, and had no problem with them being shared out. However I swore that in 1980 in Glasgow, where the IGAL road 10km and Marathon championships were to be held, I would have his guts for garters. The newspapers back home printed the story about my having lost out in the marathon (we only ran 2:22:50), with a photo of Robinson and me. My superior effort in the 10km was ignored.

A year went by, and I prepared carefully for this "grudge match". I had arranged through Ron Morrison to stay overnight at his father David's flat in Airdrie, the start being at 8 am on Sunday 24th August. I travelled through in the afternoon, and did a 15 minute jog at Bellahouston Park, where I was able to watch my host win the over-65 10km road race in 42:12 – a really fantastic time. Davie was thus in good spirits for the dinner that evening at the Sports Centre. However, I decided that if I went to the dinner my energy would be dissipated by having to engage in conversation about the race. I said to Davie that if he didn't mind I would just sit in the car and read a book. He should just enjoy the evening and stay as long as he liked. He wasn't in fact very late. In view of the 8am start few competitors and race officials were anxious to stay up longer than they had to. We drove home and I had a reasonable sleep, getting up at around 5 am so that I could eat the usual couple of marmalade rolls and have a cup of coffee. Over the previous day or two I had made sure I was well hydrated

It was a bright sunny morning. I went through the routine of a very short jog, then lay down to talk myself into a positive frame of mind – in my imagination I was back at Tentsmuir, coasting along with not a care in the world. I wanted to run. I was here to do my best. Then I got up, jogged around a little and went to the start.

The race was over a pretty flat lap which we had to cover three times. We lined up in wide Bellahouston Road, and would finish in Pollok Estate. I'm not sure how many starters there were – in the hundreds perhaps – but there was a group of very evenly matched contenders for the title, including Derek Fernee (England) and the winner from Hannover, John Robinson. A leading group of 12 formed early on, and stayed together till around halfway. I was always in or around the front, but about 32km Robinson got away and built

Extras line up, April 1980.

up a lead of around 100m. I thought I had lost it, but, encouraged by the shouts of supporters – many of them friends and rivals from the past decades – I pulled myself together and ate away at his lead. It was hard work, but after a few kilometres the lead was clearly diminishing, and when we left the streets and entered Pollok Estate with about 3km to go, I was at his back and accelerated to pass him. He fell away a little, and I crossed the line in 2:19:23, just 13 seconds up, absolutely delighted to have won – on home soil, and against the man who had sneaked the win in 1980. He said afterwards that he had developed a sore leg with a few miles to go, but who listens to excuses? Derek Fernee was 3rd in 2:19:41, a mere 3 seconds behind the New Zealander.

On the podium, I was presented with the trophy by a Glasgow bailie accompanied by organiser Bob Dalgleish. I also was handed a bottle of champagne, and in true Grand Prix style I shook it up and sprayed it over all those around, though I don't think Bob Dalgleish liked it falling on his blazer!

The world champion tag got me some kudos in Scottish veteran running circles, and I'm glad to say that Davie Morrison was delighted. He had followed the progress of the race closely, appearing at various place to encourage me with others like Bill Scally (Shettleston H), notably when I had been dropped and looked like settling for the traditional Scottish position

294

of gallant loser. The St Andrews Citizen printed a photo of me wearing a dark blue soft velvet pullover edged with white, rather like a cricket jumper in reverse.

In the winter of 1979/80 I was contacted by Sandy Sutherland, a freelance sports journalist, He had longstanding involvement with athletics through his being a Scottish shot putt champion and his marriage to a Commonwealth Games hurdler, Liz Toulalan from Cupar. He was secretary of the Scottish International Athletes Club and I was president one year. Sandy asked me to assemble a group of about a dozen local athletes from Fife AC and the University to be extras in a forthcoming feature film.

I swiftly agreed when Sandy told me that the film was to be directed by David Puttnam and the subject was the 1924 Olympic Games. It was a fascinating period of athletics history. The marathon had of course included our Athens manager Duncan McLeod Wright

The protagonists in the new film, provisionally entitled "Runners" and then "Clouds of Glory", were to be Harold Abrahams and Eric Liddell, winners of the Paris 100m and 400m respectively, though the most memorable athlete at those Games in most people's eyes was Paavo Nurmi of Finland who won the 5000, 10,000 and cross- country, the last held in torrid conditions so that many dropped out (though chemical fumes from the terrain run over contributed to the dropouts.)

The runners I approached were keen to earn £20 for the day's work. They would be wearing T-shirts bearing the 1924 team insignia of the British Olympic Association, a Union Jack embroidered on the left breast, and baggy 1920s style long shorts. No footwear would be supplied, as the actors were to run along the fringes of the surf that has been breaking for millennia on the mile and a quarter long West Sands, St Andrews. It is a magnificent stretch of beach whose backdrops, depending on your orientation, include the fragile dunes, the Royal and Ancient Golf Club and the (public) Old Course, and the historic town skyline and to the south east, as seen in the famous film sequence, the Eden estuary, Tentsmuir Forest and the cold blue-grey North Sea.

One or two of the runners asked were less eager, including my old friend Ron Morrison, professor of Software Engineering and later an Fellow of the Royal Society of Edinburgh as well as a distinguished athletics coach. Ron had a luxuriant beard at the time and didn't want to look like a short haired 1920s clean-cut chap like Lord Burghley ("Lord Lindsay" in the film, a role played by Nigel Havers), or like Harold Abrahams (Ben Cross) or Eric Liddell (Ian Charleson). He regrets not having a part in 8 Oscars now.

The themes represented were to be anti-semitism - embodied by John Gielgud as Master of Trinity College, Cambridge, allegations which the College denied - towards Abrahams; and evangelistic "muscular Christianity" as demonstrated by Liddell.

Those who wanted to be extras included "professional", i.e. Highland Games runners Ian Grieve, now President of the Scottish HGA and a training partner of mine since 1968, and Terry Mitchell, who had been "reinstated" into the so-called amateur ranks at the second attempt in the 1970s, with help from FAC, and went on to win international and Scottish distance titles from 10km to the marathon. Another runner was late recruit Angus MacIntosh, secretary of the Scottish Universities Council on Entrance, who later featured in the Courier as a guinea pig in the run up to the second Dundee People's Health Marathon in 1984. Student stars like Nigel Annett, a 1:50 800 runner, and Derek Easton, now a respected distance coach, and several others like Jim Stevenson, Doug Hendry and Gifford Kerr joined as well.

As a teacher at Madras College I was reluctant to seek a day off to take part in what might be a disappointing B movie. That hasn't stopped St Andrews people and others believing that I did "star" in it and was one of the white-vested elite striding with Georgian power and nonchalance through the breakers toward the Nirvana of the putting green and the Scores Hotel, to the accompaniment of Vangelis's Olympian trumpets – perhaps we could take the tune over and adapt it as Scotland's anthem instead of Flower of Scotland, St Andrew being the patron saint of both countries.

Incidentally I think of it as inaccurate when athletes who have previously competed at Olympic level are referred to as "ex-Olympians". It's like the Nobel Prize - you aren't called "ex-Nobel prize winner" after the ceremony. By that careless use of language I would have been an Olympic athlete only for 2 hours 16 minutes and 34 seconds, and Usain Bolt for 9.68 seconds plus what he ran in the heats and finals of the 100, 200m and relay. A swift farewell to greatness! In St Andrews we have a two-time water-polo

Plaque unveiling 1999: Ian Grieve, Angus Mackintosh, Terry Mitchell, DFM.

Olympian (1952 and 1956) in Jack Ferguson, former depute director of P.E. at the university, who over many years helped organise hundreds of sports events, and I suspect he might agree.

Members of the "extras" squad assembled for haircutting and kit inspection on the early morning of a fine Thursday, 24th April 1980. There ensued a long day of repeated runs along the sand - the stars were let off with fewer. The surf was freezing, so cold that teeth were chattering and the athletes given brandy. Some tried to stay warm by wearing tracksuit trousers under their baggy shorts, but the legs however tightly rolled up tended to come unrolled at the wrong moment.

At the end of a hard day's filming it was discovered that the camera, mounted in the dunes on long wooden rollers, had not been functioning. All had to be redone the next Thursday, 1st May, including repeats of payment, of the hire of the driver of the wee 1920s car that tootled past along the West Sands road going Parp! and of the man and his dog walking in solitary splendour along the dunes and pausing to gaze across at the university–educated aristos (as most of them in reality had been, the distance runners being an exception) disporting themselves unhistorically along the strand.

The crew disappeared and we heard nothing more until the first screenings were announced. The showing was on the day in April 1981 (I didn't note the date in my diary) my wife Kim and I had put in an offer (of £41,100) for our first house - sold in 2004 for around 9 times that figure. But we bid all we could afford and more.

We were very impressed by the film, though a loud cheer went up when the West Sands appeared over the words "Broadstairs, Kent, 1924". The roar was much louder when the film came to St Andrews. The film had a few longueurs, but the triumph of Liddell as depicted on screen moved me to tears, as it does every time I see it. I am an agnostic at best, but believe there may be underlying patterns in life: "There's a divinity doth shape our ends, Rough hew them as we will."

The filming was commemorated on a plinth erected by the Scottish Film Council in 1999. The date of filming is a year out, stating that part of the film was shot on location there in April 1981, rather than 1980. The plaque was unveiled by me as Community Council chairman, and I was accompanied in the photograph by Ian Grieve, Terry Mitchell and Angus Mackintosh, all standing in exactly the same positions as in a similar photo taken at Rufflets Hotel after the Dundee Marathon in 1983.

In "Chariots of Fire" there are numerous historical inaccuracies, mostly deliberately inserted to create dramatic intensity. The question of competing on Sunday is dramatised in the film in a scene in which Liddell stands by his beliefs as he is summoned to meet the Prince of Wales and some high ranking officials and is accused of arrogance. In fact he knew of the Olympic programme over a year in advance and changed his training to be able to move from doubling up over 100 and 200m to abandoning the 100 in favour of the 400. Nor is it mentioned that he won a 200m bronze just a day before the first heat of the 400m. The track at Colombes was 500m long, a not uncommon distance in big arenas on the Continent, reducing the distance that he required to run in lanes.

298

Whether Liddell was as strict a Sabbatarian in later life as he is made out to be is also open to dispute. In a Radio 4 broadcast called "Captured by Pirates", based on a book by Janie Hampton (Dampers and Doodlebugs: how the Girl Guides won the war, August 2010, Harper Press) two women who as girls found themselves in a Chinese internment camp in Tientsin province in the 1930s remember the benevolent "Uncle Eric" who regularly refereed football matches on Sundays and other days among the children, few of whom had seen their parents for years.

Other errors of fact include the detail of the run round the Great Court of Trinity College, Cambridge, within the twelve strokes of the clock. The feat was accomplished by David Cecil, Lord Burghley, later the Marquess of Exeter. In her fine book about the House at Burghley, Exeter's daughter Virginia Leatham says her father was hurt by the version portrayed in the film where "Lord Lindsay" is beaten by the Harold Abrahams character. Burghley it was who performed the feat - Coe and Ovett failed to achieve it - and as a result of the film falsification he apparently fell out with David Puttnam.

Virginia Leatham also recounts that according to the Burghley House gardener in 1928 (not 1924) it was matchboxes that Cecil positioned upright on the ends of each hurdle, rather than full champagne glasses. The matchboxes were a clever idea, the intention being to clear the hurdle in such a way as to knock off the matchbox with the leading leg while not knocking over the hurdle. The gardener is said to have asked him when his next race was. "Oh. I'm off to Amsterdam to the Olympic Games in a couple of days." He came back with a gold medal for 400m hurdles.

Team get-togethers in Broadstairs or anywhere else along the lines depicted did not take place in 1924. Training camps were rare in those days at least among British teams. Twelve years later Arthur Turk, the British team manager, returned from a poor series of performances at the Berlin Games. He was quoted in The Times as saying the team had in fact performed well and had been facing foreign athletes "many of whom had trained specifically for the event". I say, you chaps! That's hardly cricket!

Chapter 21

A family

Just after the World Veteran Championships school re-started, and among my tasks was to look after the welfare of our German language assistant Raimund (other name forgotten). He was a pleasant young man though hardly a soul-mate and I suggested to him he could stay at 16 Carron Place for a while until he found a more permanent place to live. We drove into school together in the mornings, and met up again at night, and of course our paths crossed at school as well.

One Saturday in September, Raimund said he had been invited to a student party in North Street near the Cathedral and did I want to come. Initially I demurred but in the end I went along.

When we got there I could see there was a general crowd of people, few of whom I knew, and we got ourselves drinks and started to chat. There was one person who looked vaguely familiar, a tall red-haired girl on the far side of the room. Someone had suggested we each do a party piece, and when it was my turn I recited the lament "Nänie" by Friedrich Schiller, Ian Hendry's favourite poem which I had with some difficulty committed to memory.

Of course few at the party knew the poem and certainly there was no one there who could have had much idea of the references and allusions to classical legends. I'm not sure I did. But it sounded good if gloomy, and I was moved by it (and still am) as it concerns the death of various types of beauty. Schiller maintains that to be mourned by those whom you loved and who loved you is "herrlich" [splendid, magnificent] and thus offers some form of immortality to "das Schöne" in all its forms while condemning "das Gemeine" [mean-spirited] to extinction.

I glanced at the red-haired girl as I recited, and we later got into conversation. She was called Kim Boxell (not Boxall, she stressed, the more common variant, and her father Ron had been stationed at Leuchars with the Royal Air Force. She had been at Madras but it must have been while I was in Germany or Dunoon.

Renaissance: 1983 win at Dundee in 2:17:24.

She had just cycled back all the way from Spain, where she had been camping with her boyfriend. They had fallen out and she had just got on her bike and set off through Spain and France and back to Scotland where her best friend was Fiona Alexander, daughter of Mr Robert Alexander, a well-known local butcher. Kim was staying with Fiona and her husband Alan Lockwood, a New Zealander and pilot. She asked me for advice about running. I suggested we go for a short training run together. That run took us though Spinkie Den, and through to the back road to Balone, south of St Andrews, about 4-5 miles in total.

Gradually we became closer, and after some weeks Kim moved in. I proposed and we had several of those conversations with parents where you advise them to sit down, as you have something to tell them. I was 41, she was 24. She told me she had agreed to marry me because I was already established and could look after her, or words to that effect. I recall being in my classroom one day (without the class) and being so overcome with emotion and joy that I almost fainted.

We booked up for a trip to Paris in the October holiday. En route we met Carol and John Bryant at Gatwick en route to Charles de Gaulle, then to our hotel. It was a very enjoyable if tiring few days, walking all morning, then lunch, running a little sometimes, having a siesta, eating out somewhere. Once we went to the famous restaurant Chartier where we had arranged to meet Isobel and Donald Mackenzie – on their first trip abroad for decades – and we sat at long tables. The waiter, when asked for the bill, proposed that we work it out for ourselves! It was a fun trip, wandering down the autumnal Jardin du Luxemboug, and by the bridges of the Seine near the bouquinistes, dry leaves at our feet and happiness in our hearts, at least for a long while.

On our return Kim discovered she was pregnant, which excited both of us very much. She went to see our doctor, George Cunningham who practised in 5 Dempster Terrace – you'd think he'd have been good by then with all that practice but he still said "he's going to be a footballer" in his attractively squeaky voice when the baby kicked. "What are you going to do?" He asked Kim. "I'm getting married in December." "Who to?" "Donald Macgregor." "Well done – congratulations - I never thought he had it in him!" Thanks, George!

Concentration: 5 miles, Dundee 1983: DFM, Richie Barrie, Murray McNaught. Masked: Sam Graves, Rab Heron, Craig Ross.

Kim had a difficult few months at the start of the pregnancy, and had to stay lying down for some weeks, when not working as a cook at the Pancake Place. I had to persuade her, with the zeal of a man who had always wanted to be a father, to rest up.

Happily things improved, and we started to look around for a bigger house. 16 Carron Place was an up/down 1970s Wimpey job but we preferred something more old-fashioned as a family home

First we had to arrange the wedding. I suggested Boarhills Kirk, out in the middle of the country, with Peter Douglas, the local minister and old friend to officiate. We went to see Peter who asked us if we really wanted to marry, etc. I explained that I was no believer but felt it was good to marry in Boarhills for nostalgic reasons – not the more picturesque Dunino as Peter assumed.

The reception was to be at Rufflets Hotel – with whose manager Peter Aretz I later had contacts through his sponsorship of the Fife AC relay team that won the St Andrews University 6x2 mile relay up the Grange and in by Cameron and Lumbo, start and finish in the Scores.

A guest list was assembled, and Kim's mother Joyce sent out the invitations. Kim's matron of honour was Fiona Alexander and the best man was my brother Forbes. The Bryants came up for the weekend, including Matthew, my godson, aged 6, who clutched a toy Rupert Bear throughout the weekend.

Kim's parents were there of course – I met them for the first time just the day before the wedding. My dad in his kilt, and our stepmother were also present in the small wood lined church on that day, Saturday 6th December 1980. We had invited around 40 guests, most of them people I knew, though some of Kim's friends were able to come. Among lots of others Ron and Ann Morrison were there, Ian and Evelyn Grieve, and the most of the McKanes. Willie McKane junior (11) played the pipes at the reception.

It was a sunny but cold day, and snowflakes were whirling in the wind as Kim and I walked quickly up the drive from the church, ahead of all the guests, to reach the silver Alexander Volvo driven by Al Lockwood. He took us to the cathedral where Peter Adamson, the University photographer as well as a neighbour, took more photographs. The complete set was put into a very well padded and expensive album costing about £70 – the most expensive book in

Happy family: Kim, Mikey, DFM, Rosemary pose with cup, April 1983.

the house. The reception, shared in defiance of tradition between Ron Boxell and me, cost £486 – I still have the receipt. That was fair enough as I was not the typical bridegroom, if there is such a person, for I was established in my career and he had only just met me.

It was a pleasant afternoon and evening, but we had decided not to stay at Rufflets but to spend the one-night honeymoon at Kings of Kinloch, a Perthshire hotel. By the time we got there we were too full to properly enjoy the dinner we had booked. Jan Bryan-Jones had put lipstick on the car windscreen so that we drove off in the black Alfa-Sud ASC18W with a smeary windscreen. And so started our married life.

Several months passed as we tried to adapt to being in a permanent relationship. I wasn't always very good at it. The big events to look forward to were moving to a new house and of course the birth of our first child. We looked at several houses – one was too much like an RAF house, of which Kim had had enough over her schooldays as her parents moved around;

another was too close to the Kinness Burn and prone to flooding and damp. Finally we decided to put in a firm offer for an 1891 ashlar built mid-terraced four and a half bedroom property in Dempster Terrace, just a few minutes' walk from the town centre. The owners were Dugald and Violet MacArthur, Dugald being the retiring University Librarian. He had been involved in the preliminaries that preceded construction of a new Library of modern design and the removal of all the stock from the old Library in St Mary's Quad. That was where I had sat for hours before heading to the Criterion at twenty to ten all these years before. The house was on the Kinnessburn, but sat high enough above it to ensure that we would be safe from flooding unless there was a tsunami. In fact in one of the great floods of the later 1980s the water on one occasion lapped up to the stones of the rockery at 5 in the morning.

After the first showing in Edinburgh of Chariots of Fire Kim and I squeezed into a red phone box on the corner of Lothian Road and phoned the solicitor. Tension, then: We had the house! Joy was unconfined, even though we could hardly afford it with mortgage interest rates heading up to 13 and 14%.

We moved in on May 8th 1981. Kim was heavily pregnant with Rosemary, though we didn't know the child was to be a girl, and so I moved most of our rather restricted possessions in a hired van. I carried them up the flight of stone steps and into the house where Kim decided where they should go.

On August 20th I drove Kim across to Ninewells when she told me it was time. It wasn't quite, for she had to wait a bit before being induced, then Rosemary Kim Macgregor was born on Friday August 21st at 2 a.m, 7 lbs 7 oz, dark haired and beautiful. I was in attendance at the birth, as with our other children, though I could only hold hands and try to say helpful things. When I could hold her, our daughter, it was the best moment of my life up to then, and I am sure Kim felt the same, tired as she was.

For some reason the 21st of August has been a significant date in my life. The 21st was the day I started teaching at Madras, the day my first employee in my later poetic/political work, Lesley Moffat, was born, and now the birthday of our first child. A red-letter day!

Kim was exhausted, I was tired but rather less exhausted. It was the practice to send St Andrews mothers, if they wished, to "lie-in" at Mount Melville

Glasgow start, Tron 1984.

House, Craigtoun, about two miles from the centre of St Andrews. It was a hot August and after a few days Kim was quite pleased to come home, where I had been trying to get things organised in between teaching and training.

It was great to have Rosemary around, even though she didn't always fall asleep when we wanted her to. A good way of inducing slumber was to take her for a "hurl" in the very well-sprung pram, which responded to a touch so that Kim and I could run miles pushing it – about 5 was the maximum we did. The Dundee "Evening Telegraph" published a photograph of Kim jogging on the path outside the front garden with a smiling baby.

Within a year and a half another trip to Ninewells Hospital was called for, and a few days later I took Rosemary in to see Mummy and her new baby brother Michael (Mikey), born on the 17th February 1983. He never took to the pram, and so when he was old enough to sit up we procured a very snazzy two seater push-chair so that the two of them could sit in it and be pushed (when they weren't fighting).

That is very unfair, as they were both very good children, though showing a stubborn independence that was occasionally exasperating to their parents but boded well for their future lives. Five years later, on January 2nd 1988, the coldest day of the year, Thomas Forbes (Tommy) came into the world and our family was complete.

Chapter 22

City of Discovery or "Eh'll Heh a Peh"

In 1982 the news got out that the City of Discovery was to go down the same route as New York, London, Chicago and Glasgow by holding a "People's Marathon" to be sponsored by Radio Tay, The Courier, the Health Education Council and the City of Dundee. The organisation had already been set up in skeleton form under the direction of the genial Alex Stuart, who had earned his spurs in the hurly-burly of lower divisions football management, and under the leadership of the chair of Leisure and Recreation, Cllr Michael Duff, who was small but enthusiastic and wanted to run in the race too. The race referee was to be the experienced Alistair Falconer who lived in Newport on Tay, and the medical and other support teams were equally well qualified.

I had already competed by invitation at Aberdeen (1981 – 4th) and Glasgow (1982 -10th). Edinburgh also intended to have a People's Marathon but characteristically when it came along it was relatively low key and unenthusiastically supported by the populace along stretches of the route. I remember an empty infinity of road between Portobello and Meadowbank where more or less the only person around was a woman with a pram, who understandably ignored the runners. It put me in mind of my choice for "Worst Postcard Ever", a photograph of a woman wheeling a pram along a Glenrothes pavement with the sole skyscraper, Raeburn Heights, towering above her. In reality Glenrothes, so often called a blot on the horizon, is a modern town of parklands and flowers, sheltering beneath the beautiful Lomond Hills, and a shimmering river runs through it. It has its problems and its deprived areas, but these are small in comparison with Edinburgh, Glasgow or Dundee.

I determined to do well in the race and trained seriously for it, though averaging "only" 70 miles per week over the late winter and spring, with regular group sessions at Tentsmuir on a Sunday (the church of the open air) where the Fife AC people were joined by Dundee Road Runners and others including a Courier journalist called Sandy McGregor, later to write local bestsellers about murders in Dundee, and an acerbic Wednesday opinion column as "J J Marshall",

Loches en Touraine (Anny Descoubes).

When interviewed I tried to place the burden of favourite on others such as Murray McNaught, the rather exotic architect who had spent time in Spain and could easily get confused about race starting times or dates – "Jeez-o – is it on Saturday?", or Terry Mitchell, twenty years younger than me. Inside myself I was pretty confident that I would be there or thereabouts. Others cited as challengers were Rab Heron – the man who as St Andrews Univ CCC secretary had failed to keep the minute volume with its race reports up to date and was now a librarian in Brighton. Craig Ross, a man of many clubs, was another favourite. He has competed over the years for Dundee Hawkhill, Aberdeen AAC (as in 1983) and Fife AC depending on location and mood, or so it seemed. An outside bet was Richie Barrie (DHH), son of Alistair who had been a year ahead of me as a student (at Queen's College Dundee) and who had risen to be Dundee's chief planning officer.

Kim, Rosemary and Mikey – only two months old – were to come across for the finish in the Alfasud. I went over early. It was a greyish but not very windy day, not too cold – ideal for running. There was a huge field of around 3500, and all of us lined up in City Square, then still not entirely pedestrianised. The course would lead us in a small loop then westwards towards Invergowrie, back to Broughty Ferry past HMS Victory and the shipyards, now used for assembling oil platforms.

We would then go off in a wide arc north of the Kingsway – Scotland's first dual carriageway – and past the Dundee University playing fields at Downfield, before rising to the highest point about 21 miles, just before Lochee. Then the course descended in swoops towards the city centre before flattening out into the main street and the finish gantry in City Square.

Bang! A group of a dozen rapidly formed, going at quite a good pace – all the predicted favourites. I stayed in the group for five miles, taking it cautiously, then Richie Barrie and I found ourselves breaking away from Sam Graves (FAC), McNaught, Heron, Ross and the rest. Ron Morrison was spectating and he recalls a young female Radio Tay journalist who thought it was a good idea to collect Craig Ross's thoughts as he passed at about 11 miles an hour. "How are you feeling?" she asked, holding out the microphone to the sweating Craig, who had a bad stammer.

"F…f…f.. off!" he replied rather forcibly, and ran on.

Richie told me he would keep going till 15 miles and in fact kept up his helpful pacemaker role as far as 16, when he drew to a halt. Then I was on my own and had ten miles of mental concentration to go. I don't think runners who are aiming to run four or five hours (which I don't think I could handle) realise how great is the concentration required to run under three hours let alone 2:20. You have to stay focussed all the way. It's possible to exchange remarks for a second or two, but best not to stop. Better to take sponges and drinks on the run, snatching a cup of water or juice in some cases a special drink from the tables, and pour the water – but not the juice - over your head, wiping head, neck, face, arms and thighs with a well-filled sponge or two.

I got to the top of the hill with an effort, after that my cadence grew more fluent; I was able somehow to run more smoothly and on the downhill my stride lengthened. Gradually the lead over Terry Mitchell, who had moved into second and had been catching me, increased. At the finish it was over three minutes. On the video of the race, made by members of Dundee Road Runners, I look to be flying down from Lochee past the Dundee Royal Infirmary entrance, round the roundabout and round the shops into the finishing straight.

Kieler Gelehrtenschule

Die Ersten Fünfzig Jahre

The First 50 Years

Madras College (South Street)

Kiel Exchange booklet 2007.

The crowds had been out in force round nearly all the route except the areas north of the Kingsway, and thousands thronged the last 300m behind the barriers. A colleague, art teacher Sandy Cuthbert, told me he couldn't believe I had run 26 miles at that speed. I hadn't, but the pace over the last five or six miles was close to 12 miles per hour.

The photo-finish line under the gantry was crossed at between 2:17:23 and 2:17:24, the latter being the official time. It was the fastest time by a veteran in the UK that year. Terry was 2nd in 2:20:50, Rab Heron 3rd in 2:21:26. After the race I was led away in the silver blanket given to all finishers to be interviewed on Radio Tay. They opened a line to Kim in St Andrews and our conversation was broadcast on air. She told me the car wouldn't start. Fortunately I didn't swear – as if! As we discussed what to do other listeners phoned in with helpful suggestions. One man offered to come and start the car but when he did he couldn't and left the bits on the pavement. Soon another listener brought the family over and we were reunited for photographs of the four of us, Kim with Mikey nestling in our "Kangourou" pouch, and me holding Rosie and the winner's cup. I wear a striped woollen hat that Kim had knitted in rather Rasta-like colours. Marjorie Thoms won the women's race in 3:02:08, leading home a very good field, and I was also photographed with her.

The prize, cup apart (what do you do with cups?) was a £50 sports voucher, and all in all it was a pretty successful excursion for all of us who had trained together or were friends. Charlie Robertson of Newport, Scottish marathon champion in 1948 and 1952, won the over-65 title with around 3:20. Ian Grieve was 12th in 2:32, and there were many more personal bests from our club. Murray McNaught ran 2:23:34, and Sam Graves 2:23.57 and Angus Mackintosh around 2:50.

There were a couple of other marathons that year, including Glasgow when I was 7th in 2:19:34. That was the occasion when the family had a chat with the gold lamé-suited Jimmy Savile in the hotel lift, and Rosie was most impressed. Her "bragging rights" with her friends were secure for a long time after that. Bob Dalgleish, Glasgow's event supremo and SCCU general secretary, may have been grateful to me for providing a home win in 1980 at Bellahouston, and invited the family to stay in the race HQ every year, which we did several times.

I'll skip over these and other races to give an account of the 1984 Dundee Marathon. I had been contacted by the Courier after winning in 1983 and asked to write a weekly series of training advice articles to appear weekly. Then George Mackintosh of Radio Tay had the idea of recording rather similar advice as a series of 26 four minute talks to be broadcast on Radio Tay on Saturday mornings.

I wrote them in longhand and he then had them typed – it was before the computer age – then I recorded them at breakneck speed, or so it seemed, and they went out to who knows how many listeners munching their breakfast cereal. The next step was a small book, Don Macgregor's Marathon Manual. George for some reason had the broadcasts transcribed again, put in a brief biographical sketch and some ads, as well as a good photograph taken during the 1983 race by David Greig from Newport, whom I cannot trace.

The book was launched before the press, and over 2000 were sold at £1 each. I have since photocopied or given away a few dozen of the books and have only one left. In theory there is another in St Andrews University Library, but it may have been stolen as I can't find it. The University Library contains a number of years of Athletics Weekly volumes, donated by Ron Morrison and myself, which are a good resource.

The 1984 Dundee Marathon was again in the cruellest month, April. Again I was favourite, but Charlie Haskett, 7th the previous year in 2:26:31, was 20 years younger and in very good form. His father had been a good cross-country runner and so was his sister Christine Price, an SWCCU champion.

The field was smaller, only around 2000, and other male entrants included Don Ritchie from Lossiemouth, a multi-world record holder for events like 100 miles and 24 hours and whose marathon best was 2:19:35, Alistair Macfarlane from Lenzie, the 1979 Scottish champion, and Terry Mitchell, Sam Graves and Craig Ross. Kim had entered too, and we both looked forward to her running well.

The weather was a bit colder, but again not too windy. The pack ran together for the first few miles as before, until Terry Mitchell and then Charlie pulled away from me along the outer roads from 15 miles onwards. I did not think I would be able to catch Terry, but somehow reeled him in, then went after Haskett. I passed him as we started downhill, and he couldn't respond sufficiently to stop me building up a slight lead. I didn't look back until the bottom of the hill. He wasn't far away, but far enough. I crossed the line considerably less fresh than in 1983, 25 seconds to the good: 2:18:16 to 2:18:41. Charlie was obviously disappointed, but I was relieved rather than exultant.

Murray McNaught was third in 2:19:44 : Macfarlane and Ritchie also ducked under the 2:20 "barrier", with Terry Mitchell 26 seconds faster than his 1983 run in 6th (2:20:24). Kim was pleased with her time of 3:25:04 – rather faster if you deduct the time taken to cross the line in those days before "chip" timing where all runners' times can be taken individually from start to finish line.

Soon after the race I decided that I would not try for a treble but find a marathon offering more than a £50 sports voucher. In 1985 I would confine myself to commentating. Eventually I settled on the Wolverhampton "Millennium" marathon on 31st March. I was beaten into third place over the last mile or two, but came away with a total in "subventions" of £500 in total, and £330 in vouchers. That was good for our family budget and well worth the trip.

The vouchers were for a sports shop in Liverpool. We visited it on the way home from staying with Kim's parents in Bournemouth, and it was hard trying to buy sports stuff for all the family that everyone either needed or wanted. Lucky us to have such choices to make!

The race commentary at Dundee went quite well the next month, but I attracted the ire of one of the Dundee Tory councillors by making a joke about literacy standards. He came storming over and I had trouble mollifying him. I don't suppose the Labour administration politicians worried too much. In the end it all passed over peaceably.

These things gave me an entrée to commentating on the visitors' and childrens' races at St Andrews and then Cupar Highland Games, and more recently I have taken over all the commentating and announcing at St Andrews, thanks to Ian Grieve, who has become not just a Chariots of Fire extra celebrity but with others started the Games, held on the last Sunday in July and has been Games Secretary since their inception.

Hans-Werner Suhr and Rainer Schöneich 2007.

In 1986 there was a competition to find the "Voice of Radio Tay": entrants had to submit a cassette, and I recorded one about St Andrews. Somehow I was adjudged the winner, the prizes being £600 of travel vouchers from Thomas Cook and, even better, the chance to host a 2 hour long programme of chat and records on Radio Tay – in the late evening of the 30th December as it turned out, but no matter.

I decided the best way to approach it was to have a semi-scripted conversation with my friend John di Folco, a local historian and cultural expert. We sat in the studio near Tannadice Stadium, home of Dundee United FC, alone except for a technician behind the glass. My role was to pose the questions, chat with John, who provided most of the expertise, and to play our own choice of records at intervals. It was a little like "Desert Island Discs", and great fun even though I doubt if many listened on the evening before Hogmanay.

In the summer of 1986 the family was on holiday in Normandy in a big Eurocamp tent. At one stage I was badly bitten by insects that fell from a tree, and my ankles swelled up quite badly. I may say that my daughter is also the target of midges and other bugs but that Kim and the two boys are not. The best preventative against midges is the Avon product "Skin So Soft" which the winged hordes fly away from. Another considerably more expensive remedy is to buy one of the machines that emit carbon dioxide, so that the bugs think it is a large mammal, fly towards it and get sucked in by a sort of vacuum cleaner, to be parcelled up in disposal bags. Hotels and guest houses in the Highlands have used these with advantage.

Whether the bites had anything to do with it or not, I started having attacks of rapid heartbeat soon after, diagnosed by Dr Tom Clark as hyperventricular tachycardia. I found later it was quite common and affected a number of friends and acquaintances. After I wrote about it in the Scottish Marathon Club newsletter, a number of correspondents wrote to me, such as Charlie Robertson of Dundee 1983 fame.

I was affected to the extent that I thought I was going to die – i.e. imminently. A Norwegian lady called Greta Thompson helped me immensely by teaching me how to put myself into a relaxed state by concentrating on each area of my body from scalp downwards. I recorded a script and put it into practice so effectively that I could send myself to sleep. I later lent the tape to a friend who had similar problems. Happily the tachycardia stopped after about six months and has never returned. I decided however that I should perhaps stop trying to compete at such a high level. I was nearly 47.

The 1986 SAAA marathon championship, held over a course that went through the old town and then out to Silverknowes and back by Granton, finishing in a side-street beside Meadowbank to save the organisers money, was my last marathon. It was one of the slowest, 2:27:30. I set off quite relaxed, though after a disturbed night in the George Hotel where I couldn't sleep and felt feverish. I was well beaten by Brian Carty of Shettleston Harriers who came past me at Cramond (17 miles). Later I wrote to Colin Youngson, for the book by Fraser Clyne and himself "A Hardy Race" (2000) – both of them were Scottish champions – that at the finish I crawled in and "looked like

317

an escapee from some 15th century Dürer woodcut (one of the victims of the Four Horsemen of the Apocalypse) as I was led away to the shelter of the stadium shower room." Unfortunately my father and stepmother had come to see me run in person for the first and only time – they had watched the big races on television. That was my last SAAA marathon.

It took me a while to recover, that afternoon and later. Although I narrowly won the Scottish over-50s cross country title at St Andrews in 1990 from Mel Edwards, and my last outright win was in the Cupar Games 8-miler when I got up from the commentators' table and left the work to my colleague Peter Mason, I have gradually reduced my competitive outings. I still train most days, though usually at a slow pace but with occasional fartlek or speedwork, and with Ron Morrison coach a group of talented senior athletes – students and FAC members. If you're a real runner, you never stop.

Chapter 23
Of families, paintings, marriages, of books
and journeyings…

Throughout the 1970s and 80s I had of course regularly visited and stayed with my father and stepmother, but as I lived in St Andrews and had so many family, work, running and other commitments, I was not constantly visiting them, nor they me. Their attitude to the telephone was that it was only to be used in emergencies, and I too had long been infected by parsimony at least as far as spending money on frivolities like phone calls and clothes was concerned. To my discredit I remember being reluctant to stop at a café for a cup of tea when out with Kim on an early date.

On one occasion, when the children were five or six, I was sent to Cupar to buy a big red plastic tractor as a Christmas present that they could sit on and pedal. For some unaccountable reason I returned with a model made of metal but which could only be pushed and not ridden. Kim showed remarkable self-control and just drove through to get what was in fact required. The only excuse I can offer is these were the last vestiges of the lack of money which I had experienced as a teenager and as a student. It wasn't that money was important to me – on one occasion I omitted to collect one of my monthly salary cheques, then handed out over a desk, until reminded by a colleague who had been in the office and noticed my cheque was still there. Nowadays I am much more generous and this too can be ascribed to being happier with myself, though it is hard for anyone to notice such changes in behaviour unless they look back from a distance at life's patterns.

My stepmother Jean and father Forbes were married for over 52 years. I know little of their relationship. What I observed was that they helped each other, she typing his books and illustrating some. Jean was a talented amateur artist and skilled in the domestic arts of sewing, knitting and so on that have largely gone out of fashion among a younger generation. My brother Forbes lived at Kaimes Road most of the time, though he and his partner have other properties. In the latter years of our father's life, which ended in 1991, and then over the next twelve until our stepmother died in 2003, he was the more regular supporter of the two of them, and it was only right and proper that he should inherit the house, whereas I was given a sum of money just at the

*Anstruther 13 miles road race, 1981: relaxing after win with Rosie,
John di Folco, Angus Mackintosh.*

right moment, when mortgage rates were very high, by my stepmother after
our father's death.

Forbes Macgregor continued to write and publish books until just a few
months before he left us. Sadly, he had suffered a stroke in 1989, aged 85,
and was initially left paralysed down the left side. His speech and mental
powers were not affected, for he was able to continue to write as I have
indicated. He had always preferred to use pencil or occasionally ballpoint
pen and to support his manuscript on a wooden board as he sat at the table
or in his armchair. His handwriting was clear and firm. On a good day mine
is not dissimilar. Originally he was left-handed, or "corry-handit", but the
educational theory of the early 1900s was to force such children to use their
right hands. In the 1950s Forbes junior was permitted to write "round the
corner", having inherited this as well as his bent towards engineering and
technology from at least one of his ancestors.

Gradually our father lost the use of his legs. It was decided that there should be a double amputation. "What choice did I have?" he said to me after he had come home and was installed in a wheelchair. He confronted this terrible operation with the stoicism he had demonstrated throughout his life in the face of tragic events, and continued to be cheerful and act as normally as possible in the circumstances, supported fully by his wife and by Forbes and by the neighbours and medical services, and of course I visited regularly as well with his grandchildren and daughter-in-law.

In late 1991 he was transferred to the Royal Victoria Hospital in Craigleith Road, near Inverleith Park, where he had taken me as a child to sail a wooden yacht across the pond. Forbes, Jean and I went to visit him for the last time on Sunday December 16th, and it was obvious that he could not live much longer. We sat around the bedside, until his wife could bear it no longer, and Forbes took her home. I stayed and held his hand. We talked as we should have talked years before. I will always remember all that he said to me, but one short sentence in particular comes into my mind whenever I am tempted not to embark on things: "I have done so little". I told him that was far from true, that he had written all these books, fathered three children, helped countless pupils, had a wide array of friends. He had not done so little, but so much. Those were his last words.

He slipped into a coma and the nurse suggested that it might be best if I left, as he would not wake up. I went to inform the others, and we sat for a while in the house that already seemed empty and waited for the phone call. It came soon after I had left to get back to my own wife and children in St Andrews, so that I heard the inevitable news, which was still a great shock, as we were sitting in the Dempster Terrace living room.

The funeral was a strange event. It was held in a crematorium and conducted by a minister whom our father did not know. That was perhaps not surprising as he had not attended any church save for weddings and funerals for most of his life. There were quite a few people there, but when you die at 87 many of those who might have attended have gone before you. After the service Jean was too upset to do more than sit in the car, but Forbes and I decided to go and thank the people who had come to pay tribute to our father. I am glad we did, as we should otherwise not have seen again several of the figures of our childhood whom we recognised despite the passing of the years.

Some months later I wrote a poem about my father and the editor of Fife Lines was kind enough to publish it in the 2001 edition. In the closing lines I am on my way back from the hospital and stand at the exit from Corstorphine Woods looking out across the valley at the hills where in the Twenties he had hiked and camped:

"I don't know them as he did: Cairketton, Allermuir…

I've looked them up, a sort of piety

But far too late to honour him. Piety usually is."

Our stepmother survived him by twelve years. I am pleased to say that once I had established my own household relations between us were much better, and both my father and stepmother were delighted when the grandchildren came along. I suspect they thought it might never happen.

My father was brought up on the Authorised Version and on authors who are no longer much read by the general public, such as Thomas Carlyle and David Hume. He had a wide-ranging knowledge of Scottish and English literature and was no enthusiast for some of the worshippers of Hugh MacDiarmid, including the poet himself. In my father's own obituary, by his publisher Gordon Wright in The Scotsman, his sense of humour, and generous, kind-hearted spirit were remarked on and his poetry praised for its readability although he himself would not have claimed to be in the first rank. He was a researcher, populariser and anthologist as well as an educator, essayist and writer of letters and magazine articles, but he also wrote a lot of verse, completed one novel and half-finished a second, nearly all his work being on Scottish themes.

Tastes differ and change from decade to decade. Through my own youth I was also exposed to the Authorised Version but not in the same measure as my father. I mentioned earlier that I was well read in Dickens, Hardy and Scott before leaving school, but after that I preferred a large variety of modern authors. Among my favourites are Kurt Vonnegut, Brian Aldiss, Kingsley Amis, and among contemporary writers Tim Parks, Henning Mankell, Louis de Bernieres, Barbara Trapido and Robert Harris. There are many more. As far as twentieth and twenty-first century poetry is concerned I don't read a great deal but am moved by many of the poems of John Betjeman and especially Philip Larkin, whose late poem "Aubade" I think a masterpiece. Recently I quoted and (briefly) explained the context of the last line to our postman: "Postmen like doctors go from house to house." Unlike my brother, I read a lot of newspapers, at home or in the library, being more interested in the way news is presented than in its content, which is similar the world over: just change the names.

In recent years I have developed an interest in painting, though my own artistic talent is very limited. The walls of the family house in Dempster Terrace and even more in Kinkell Terrace have many photographs and reproductions on them, some prints, especially those of the East Neuk by Jan Fisher of Pittenweem, and a few original artworks, notably by Morag Muir who lives in Newport on Tay opposite Dundee. Morag's big, colourful and beautiful painting of objects associated with the family and growing up adorns the cover of this book. I don't suppose I will ever be a collector on a large scale, but I enjoy making the occasional purchase.

Because my career was in modern language teaching, I had and have many contacts abroad, and in addition to the periods spent as a very young man in Germany and France and the various trips to New Zealand, Japan and Eastern Europe that I was lucky enough to make as an athlete, there were visits and exchanges with which I was involved for many years. The longest lasting of those was the Kiel Exchange, started in the 1950s by Dr John Thompson and Ian Hendry in Madras College, with the Kieler Gelehrtenschule in Schleswig-Holstein. In 1975 I took over the organisation on the Scottish side and was very grateful for all the help the exchange received from parents, colleagues, local authorities and others in Fife and I know the same was felt by our German colleagues, several of whom remain friends. In 2007 the exchange celebrated fifty years, and a ceilidh was held in the Madras College South Street Hall for 200 people, including exchange members past and present. I wrote a booklet about the history of the exchange which is accessible on the Madras College website.

Another venture was the "alliance" between St Andrews and Loches-en-Touraine, an unspoiled medieval town in one of France's richest and loveliest regions. I first went there as community council chairman in 1997, though the Lochois described me as "le maire de Saint-Andrews", an office which would have conferred on me much greater powers, those of chair of the community council being negligible. As the Alliance developed, its counterpart in France being "La Nouvelle Alliance" and one of the leading lights a keen royalist and enthusiast for Mary Stuart and the Auld Alliance, many close friendships were forged and a programme of reciprocal visits established. An agreement to formalise "cultural links" was signed by officers of both alliances and by the Provost of Fife in 2006. I am proud to have helped in establishing these links.

Encouraging different nationalities to know each other better is one of my interests. When the Soviet domination of Eastern Europe relaxed around 1990 and Germany reunited, at least in name, we were always keen to welcome teachers from the eastern regions such as Saxony and Mecklenburg-Vorpommern to come on exchange visits to St Andrews and to stay with our family. The "Ossis" were more eager to sample Scottish life, whereas the "Wessis" came from a more affluent society and had in a sense seen it all before. In the same spirit I encouraged my Kiel exchange colleague Hans-Werner Suhr to include visits to Schwerin and Wismar in the programme for our students. Although the West German government had promoted visits to the "Potemkin village" of West Berlin in the 1950s and 60s, we had only once been able to afford to go to West and East Berlin after that (in 1982). In 1990 we crossed the border east of Lübeck on the very day that the first British visitors were permitted to venture into the DDR without a visa. I persuaded the frontier guard that it was all right by showing him a cutting from the Kieler Nachrichten newspaper, and he waved us through.

Relative to my father's generation, I have travelled a lot. Our children have ventured even farther, whether on business or for pleasure. Apart from travel delays caused by natural, industrial or bureaucratic obstacles, flying has become both more everyday and, it has to be said, unpleasant in some ways. Security and waiting around are tiring and frustrating. In the present economic situation we are told that more and more people are having a "stay-cation" though I see not much evidence of it at the airports. I hope we don't go back to the post-Second World War restrictions on money exchange and travel, and in the internet age that seems unlikely but you never know.

Chapter 24

Tilting at Windmills

In 1986 the St Andrews Citizen ran a front page story saying the Community Council was about to fold. Although I had occasionally gone along to the Town Council meetings and occasional Community Council meetings out of curiosity mixed with amusement, I had not contemplated getting involved until then. It may have been motivated by the tachycardia attacks and the need to find something different to occupy my free time – although I had a full time job as Principal Teacher of German and was happily married with a young family of two. I decided to put my name forward for election. As a result of the headline, there were about 24 applicants for 20 places, and so there was an election. A former colleague, Miss Ann Cantley, ex-Assistant Rector and PT Geography at Madras, topped the first past the post poll, and I was 4th.

At the first meeting in the beautiful Town Hall Council Chamber with its decorated ceiling and padded chairs for Provost and Bailies, all now abolished, I was proposed as chairman by Ann Cantley and seconded. The only other person nominated was a Tory – I had no allegiance, won by 10 votes to 8 and took the chair.

Halfway through the meeting, one of the District Councillors, all of whom sat at the other end of the long table, interrupted the meeting on a point of order. This was the Tory councillor for St Andrews West, whom I had never met. "I have in my pocket a piece of paper", he said, "which says that you are going to be chairman – it is a Liberal plot." (or words to that effect). As I only knew one Liberal, Cllr Derek Barrie, who was also present, I was shocked by the allegation and said that if members felt there had been a plot, I would resign and they could vote again. "No no", chorused some of the members led by Mrs Yvonne Stuart-Meiklejohn, herself a keen and elegant Tory of a certain age.

After the meeting the councillor rang to apologise, saying he could see from my reaction that there had been no plot. But I should have asked to see that surely imaginary bit of paper. In any event I determined at that moment that if I ever joined a political party it would not be the Conservatives.

After a few months I realised that the Royal Burgh of St Andrews Community Council, established as a Community Association in 1974 following the local government reform that foolishly swept away a thousand years of tradition in the shape of Town Councils, Provosts, magistrates, robes and so on, not to mention locally accessible services, was relatively impotent. If I wanted to influence people's lives more positively – which I hoped I was doing in teaching – I would have to move up a rung. One evening after the CC I spoke to Derek Barrie in his car outside the Town Hall in South Street and said I wanted to join the Liberals and stand for the District Council. And so I did, against the same man who had accused me of having been foisted on the CC by the Liberals.

My campaign, in March/May 1988, was not inspired. I went from door to door in the rain, wind and sun, but then as now while canvassing support, was shy in my approach. I should have done what the next candidate did four years later, which was to put newsletters in the pigeonholes of all the students in halls, telling them that only a few votes could get the Tory out. I lost by around 25, my opponent at the count saying in the generosity of relief that I had done much better than he had expected.

I retired to lick my wounds, but Fate had a hand to play. The local paper, the St Andrews Citizen, had printed a story in which it mistakenly referred to "Councillor Macgregor". I took that as a portent. Three months later the Chairman of the North-East Fife District Council, Derek Barrie, had to resign because of an incident that had resulted in a conviction and fine. I went to see him and his wife and try to cheer them up.

The local Liberals decided that I should be the candidate for the by-election in September 1988, and I campaigned hard with lots of support, with much better results on the doorsteps. A lady called Peggy MacGregor (no relation) whose late husband had been called Donald, gave me a golden-coloured pin with his name on it, which I wore on a "lucky" golden Nike T-shirt (Nike being the goddess of Victory) which bore an N on a winged wheel.

The Conservatives had put up author Raymond Lamont-Brown, and they were optimistic, assuming that there would be an anti-Liberal reaction. But they were wrong. Derek Barrie had been a very active and popular councillor, and I had some supporters of my own, so that when the result was declared I had more votes than Barrie had had in May, just over 1100, and Lamont-

Brown had fewer than 800. The champagne the Tories had reportedly ordered remained on ice.

At the first Council meeting I was put forward to be a member of the St Andrews Links Trust, established by Act of Parliament in 1974 to run the golf courses, which in St Andrews belong to "the local authority for the time being" and must be maintained as "a public place of resort and recreation". It's not just for golfers, and use of the links is normally free to non-golfers, though the Trust and Links Management Committee can close the courses and charge entry for special events like The Open.

Well! The St Andrews opposition councillors were all a-tremble. Appoint such a novice, not even a proper golfer, to such an important position? In fact I played occasionally and had for a few years been a member of the New Golf Club until affronted by some right-wing exchanges I had heard in the bar during the Rhodesian UDI crisis. I was appointed and soon found the work of the Trust riveting and that I could "make a difference" down at the Links.

I took a good two years to find my feet on the Council, so much so that fiery Independent/Scot Nat Jimmy Braid (for whom I voted in 1974 when he almost put out Sir John Gilmour (Con) at the General Election) remarked I was not living up to my promise. He was right.

Re-elected in 1992, I became chair of Housing and chair of the Licensing Board, as well as vice-chair of the Links Trust. Suddenly I was a better councillor, more active and quicker thinking. The Housing meetings went well, and under the Director, Mike Stanley, and his Depute, Derek Muir, we had introduced an "HED" scheme (Heat-Efficient Dwelling) which, had the life of the District Council not run out in 1996, would have ensured that every council property in NE Fife would have had loft insulation, double glazing and efficient heating by 2000. More than half of the housing stock had been bought under "Right to Buy" legislation – the better half – which made the HED work necessary. My main objection to RTB was that while councils could if they chose build new properties, these in their turn would have to be sold off at much below their value to the next tenants in a few years. It made no sense.

The Licensing Board had the status of a court, so that members in particular had to be careful what they said. The first clerk of the court to hold office

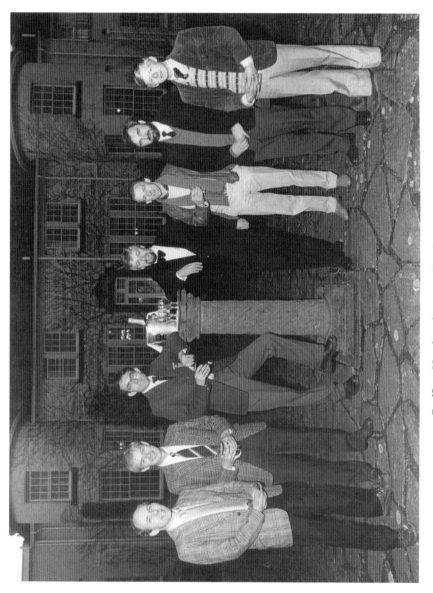

Rufflets Hotel : relay team drinks to success.

in my time would swivel in his chair to stare at the chairman and members as if challenging them to come out with some idiotic or offensive comment. I became chairman in my second term after four years of learning what the board did, and managed to introduce ways of reducing the interminable reading out loud of every detail of every single application for extended hours etc, for which I hope the applicants, all of whom had to wait in a crowded County Hall until their case came forward, were grateful.

A high point was a case where an Edinburgh-based QC had lodged an objection to an application near his holiday house on the Fife coast. He did not like the way the case was proceeding and advanced more than once up the central aisle towards me as chairman. I had to tell him politely but forcibly to sit down. He did.

The St Andrews Links Trust was a revelation. Established some 14 years before I became a Trustee, it had a small office near the public toilets set into the hillside across the road from the Royal and Ancient Clubhouse. The secretary operated with one assistant, recently appointed. Fees to play the courses had to be paid in cash or by cheque, and no credit cards were accepted. There were very limited changing facilities even for the Old Course. The whole set-up required an update.

It was not the fault of the employees, but because of old-fashioned attitudes and shortage of finance that things remained so low-key. There are those in St Andrews and elsewhere who spend their time praising the practices of the past and excoriating anything new. "It's aye been" attracts a sizeable vote anywhere, and I have a certain sympathy with that too.

My first action as a Trustee was to vote in the annual election for Chairman in January 1989. The Trust has eight members, three nominated by the Royal and Ancient Golf Club, three by the local authority (successor to the Town Council), one is the sitting MP, and the eighth a nominee of the Secretary of State for Scotland. A former leading light in the legal profession, Lord Mackay, had drawn up the Act, over whose every paragraph and comma there has been regular wrangling ever since.

It was a difficult choice, as Sir John Carmichael, who was an R&A nominee and had vast experience, was challenged by Ian Smith, the Secretary of State's nominee. I didn't really know the background, and voted for Mr

Smith, who was elected. Over the next year and a half the Trustees developed a plan to build a new changing facility on the ground near the West Sands, close to the first tee of the New Course. This was very controversial locally in St Andrews, and the Trustees and Links Management Committee (LMC) agreed to hold a public meeting to defuse concerns about the proposal to build. There had been a previous public meeting about a proposed change in the yearly tickets and the doing away with the country member category on which the clubs had expanded dramatically. This second meeting promised to be a stormy one, and Ian Smith, a former civil servant, decided on the late afternoon of the meeting that he did not wish to chair it. Nowadays I would probably have offered to chair it myself, but I did not have sufficient confidence or knowledge, and so I phoned first Air Marshall Sir Peter Bairsto, who was out, and then the Hon J.M. Lindesay-Bethune, who lived near Elie and was in.

John Lindesay-Bethune, a former Guards officer and old-style Tory, saved the day. With imperturbable politeness and masterly efficiency he defused the critics' attacks and all ended relatively peaceably. The following January, 1991, he was elected chairman and stayed in post for two years, being succeeded by Peter Bairsto, who chaired the Trust until 1995, when his second term as R&A nominee ran out, and local government changes meant that I too was forced to leave both Council (which was being abolished in favour of a unitary Fife Council for which as a teacher and hence employee I was ineligible) and the Trust, both to my regret.

Soon after arriving at the Trust, I wrote to the Secretary, asking if a reference in the scanty minutes to a public relations sub-committee being set up had ever been acted on. Answer: No. I asked the Trustees if one could be established; it was, and I chaired it. We appointed consultants after interview. The successful applicants were called Chasquis, made up of a running friend Peter Mason – who had started training with our group at Tentsmuir and ran the London Marathon with a toadstool hat in 2 hours 40 minutes – and his business partner (and later wife) Lesley Brocklebank. This reads as if the appointment were fixed, but it wasn't. The only other applicant arrived late and made a poor impression on the sub-committee.

The chasqui were the relay runners of the Inca, though Peter Bairsto didn't realise this and pronounced the word chas-quis. That became irrelevant, however, as Peter Mason was soon appointed to a full-time position as

Berlin 1998: Liz Higgins, DFM, Patricia, Tom and Sinead Esler, Craig Walker.

External Relations Manager. With him I worked on the early editions of the glossy yearbook "A Year at St Andrews", for which I wrote a few historical articles about the town. I also persuaded the Trustees to help finance long-time journalist Tom Jarrett's definitive work "St Andrews Links – the First 600 years". Tom, Peter and I worked together to edit the manuscript down to about half its original length. It was published by Mainstream in 1995. My original copy (signed by Tom Jarrett) was stolen but Peter has since given me a copy of the 2005 edition in which he features as co-author. Sadly it could not be signed by Tom, who passed away before it came out, but it is signed by Peter Mason!

The Links Clubhouse working party was chaired by Peter Bairsto, and others on it included the well-known golfer Marigold Speir, Cllr Douglas Hamilton, Robert Burns, chair of the LMC and me. The architects were Fife-based Hurd, Rolland. After much negotiation and hard work, the "white elephant", as it

331

was described by opponents, was opened on June 29th 1995 by Ryder Cup captain Bernard Gallagher. It has proved a great success, being open to the public and not just golfers. I am proud of the part I played in its development and in laying down the original conditions for its use by the public, e.g. no formal dress code, though no bare feet either.

One set of issues has caused controversy since the Links have been played over, and that is ownership and access. Tom Jarrett deals with the historical aspects in his book, but in the 1990s the spectre of St Andrews people losing their rights on the golf courses raised its head again, this time because of imminent local government reform which would replace the district councils by one Fife Council. Representatives of the outgoing Fife Regional Council, sought to look again at the 1874 Links Act with a view, it was feared by many locally, to wresting control of access from the Trust with its new-found financial success and handing it to the new council. In the absence of action, the Links Act would lapse in 1999, all statutory rights under it would disappear, and the Links would be run by the new Council. A small committee was set up, which I chaired, to undertake the onerous task of consultation with all and sundry who considered themselves interested parties and to report back to the Trustees and then to a public meeting in the St Andrews Town Hall.

Local critics included a new group calling itself the Golf Heritage Society of St Andrews. The Golf Heritage Society crossed swords with me after I wrote an article for the St Andrews Citizen, completely off my own bat but checked over for accuracy at my request by Tom Jarrett, outlining the history of the Links and criticising the GHS views that (inter alia) local rights were being eroded, that R&A members enjoyed inappropriate privileges that should be reduced, that the Links Trustees should be directly elected in some way or reconstituted as a limited company with each St Andrews resident having a share entitling him or her to vote on all material Trust matters. These views were voiced at a public meeting held by the GHS in the Town Hall in May 1994. The chairman of the GHS had written on 10th April 1994 to the Secretary of State for Scotland, Ian Lang MP, asking if he would convene a public inquiry "into some of the more disquieting aspects of the running of the Links Trust", and issued a statement.

In July the GHS wrote to North East Fife District Council seeking financial support from the St Andrews Common Good Fund for a referendum whose question was to be "Do you agree that the administrative, managerial and financial control of St Andrews Golf Links should be returned to the citizens of the town by allowing direct elections to a new controlling body by the electorate of St Andrews?"

The request was turned down by the Council.

After two public consultations, at one of which I was amusingly described as "MacGoebbels", the public meeting was held in November 1994. Two newspapers, one green and one blue, had been thrust through every St Andrews front door before the meeting. These outlined the current arrangements, the realistic options for the future and the advantages and disadvantages of each.

Most of the responses from the very large number of meetings and written communications with and from interested parties were against any tampering with the Act, though not all had finished their discussions before the date of the meeting. The FRC said it sought further discussion and consultation before taking a final view of the matter. It is hardly necessary to say that St Andrews people thought that their view – if a common one could be established - was the one that should count.

I asked during the meeting if the GHS had received a reply from the Secretary of State in relation to their wish for a public inquiry and if it would be published. I knew the request had been turned down. Instead of replying directly, the GHS spokesman went off at a tangent. Case closed, and the chairman of the meeting moved on to serious consideration of the points at issue.

The conclusion was that the majority wished for no changes to the Links Act – it was too risky. Looking back now, I am sure that the Golf Heritage people were very genuine opponents of the direction the Trust was taking, but in my view misguided and in some respects ill-informed. I bear them no ill-will – it is all water under the bridge. In retrospect I find the whole episode instructive, rather sad and also in a sense amusing.

At the District Council, it was the plenary meetings, held in the evening, that I liked least. It was an opportunity for opposition (numbering 4 plus a supposed independent) and administration (13) to have a go at each other, one or two in a most unedifying way.

Every budget debate could have been scripted, in Cupar as in every similar body from the House of Commons up or down, depending how you look at it: administration makes costed proposals, seconded more briefly; opposition castigates the proposal and rubbishes the administration, putting forward usually unrealistic and uncosted alternatives ("take 5% off all areas"). There is then a debate in which points are scored and a couple of people plead for moderation, before the summing up and division with the predictable result. The press representative puts down his or her pen or closes the laptop in relief, unless he or she is already asleep or at home with a good book, glass in hand.

This description could be applied to the corresponding Fife Council meetings too, so I don't need to repeat it later. I liked and like being one of the moderates.

Sadly I had to leave local government in late 1995, and returned to the the Community Council, where over the period 1997-2007 I served as ordinary member, vice-chair and two more terms as chair.

In 1998-99 my life went into crisis. At home, things were no longer so happy, as my wife and I drifted apart. I had encouraged her to study at the University (Social Anthropology) rather than train to be a primary teacher. I suspected that the College of Education would treat her as if she were 17. University was much more fun than life at home with a tired and increasingly frustrated teacher. I couldn't cope with all the changes in methodology and approach, and thought them mostly regressive.

Following a referendum, a Scottish Parliament was to be set up for the first time since 1707. I put my name forward as a candidate to the local Liberal Democrats, but did not survive the first sifting through. The party chose Iain Smith narrowly over Andrew Arbuckle, whom I thought a better choice. Some members believed there had been dirty work at the crossroads and for some crazy reason I decided to cut myself adrift and stand as an independent. Menzies Campbell and Andrew met me in the Madras College staffroom to try to persuade me not to go ahead with it, but I was determined, quoting Nelson's statement "I claim not to have controlled events, but confess plainly that events have controlled me." I was messianic, in other words off my rocker.

Andrew refused to shake hands as I left to stride along South Street telling all my acquaintances of my decision. I hired an employee, Lesley Moffat, whom I had known though not taught at school and whom I met now during the Lammas Market when she had just lost her job. Several former and present councillors came "on board", and I campaigned vigorously, launching my challenge in Madras College where Eric Liddell had spoken to the pupils in 1923 after taking part in the Inter-University Sports. What I forgot was that the hall he had spoken in was now the Library, the present Hall having been built in 1955-56. Thus I got off unwittingly to a false start.

Simultaneously I was writing huge volumes of verse, most of it rubbish but some of it not too bad (in my later judgement). In 2004 I made a selection and aided by my ex-Madras student and friend Sheila Perry, an employee of the Scottish Gallery of Modern Art who lives in a house on the site of Corstorphine railway station, published it as "Stars and Spikes" under the imprint of "Nutwood Press", Rupert Bear being a childhood favourite of my children. I used to knock under the kitchen table and pretend that Raggety – a creature made of twigs who has no friends and likes digging up bulbs – was responsible. They were not fooled.

The hustings meetings went well. Jimmy Braid from St Monans had a spy at the first one near Newburgh who reported that I had wiped the floor with my rivals. These included Ted Brocklebank (Con), a successful ex-TV producer whom I thought a natural Liberal. He had been a Madras pupil and one of his sons had been in my register class once.

I won't go through the campaign. In April my energy was beginning to flag, and on the eve of polling day I was worn out. My agent, Malcolm Black, a Regional councillor and former parliamentary candidate for the SDP, was not optimistic. A second independent from Falkland had been also nominated.

The result was predictable: Iain Smith won easily from Ted Brocklebank, with the SNP and Labour nowhere. I received about 1500 votes, not nearly enough. A second year pupil who stopped me in the corridor at Kilrymont had been right: "Not enough publicity".

I went into a depressive phase, and had to be referred to a psychiatrist. My moods darkened, and I could hardly run at all. I was unable on occasion to leave my chair in the modern languages base and go to class. The doctor signed me off for a week or so and I was put on lithium.

Happily I slowly recovered and have not experienced any further bi-polarity, though I did speak to a renowned expert in the field, a sufferer herself, Professor Kay Redfield Jamison, when she came to St Andrews where in the 1950s she had spent a happy year as a student on an exchange programme.

The Liberal Democrats had been obliged to expel me for standing against Iain Smith, but after about a year I said sorry and was allowed back in. Nobody seemed to harbour resentment, though Derek Barrie, the campaigns manager but who had no official role at the meeting, stopped my attempt to become candidate in a St Andrews by-election by in my view quite improperly addressing the local Liberal Democrat members after Bill Sangster, the other candidate, and I had left the room.

Fate smiled on me again later when I was chosen to fight incumbent Tory Mike Scott-Hayward in the Elie, St Monans and Pittenweem Fife Council Ward in 2003. Perhaps it was more of a simper, since I went down by a couple of dozen votes after a hard-fought campaign. The result was announced on the day of my stepmother's death. I retreated to the CC to lick my wounds, but quite unexpectedly Fate started smiling again in 2007.

There was to be a new system of multi-member wards. Election was to be by Single Transferable Vote. Cllr Bill Sangster had put his name down for St Andrews and for the East Neuk and Landward ward, which included a vast swathe of territory from just outside St Andrews round to Boarhills, Dunino, Kingsbarns, Crail, Arncroach, Carnbee, Kilrenny, Cellardyke, Anstruther, Pittenweem, St Monans, Colinsburgh, Kilconquhar, Elie and Earlsferry and then inland to Peat Inn, New Gilston and Largoward. Peter Douglas, who had married Kim and me, was the retiring councillor for the eastern part of the ward.

Bill had been selected to fight St Andrews along with Frances Melville and a new man, Robin Waterston, who had been head of mathematics and temporary Depute Rector at Madras. Euan Jardine from Falkland and Jane Ann Liston, who had been member for St Andrews South East, had not been selected, in Euan's case because of boundary changes and in Jane's because she had lost out to Robin. In the ballot to select candidates Euan was just behind me on first preference votes and well ahead of Jane Ann. However after reflecting a while Euan decided there would be too much driving involved if he got elected, and withdrew. Thus I soon found myself rolled out as the fellow-nominee of Lib Dem leader Cllr Elizabeth Riches for the new ward, and after a hard campaign the newly elected member with Elizabeth and Mike Scott-Hayward who both got in easily. The SNP candidate had been ahead of me on first preferences but I picked up enough in subsequent rounds of counting to get in on the 7th count. Ouf!

With some relief I could give up the chair of the St Andrews Community Council. During that last three year period the St Andrews – Loches Alliance was finally signed by the Fife Council Provost, Cllr John Simpson, by Mary Freeborn and Virginia Fowler on behalf of St Andrews and by Jean-Jacques Descamps, Maire de Loches, on behalf of la Ville de Loches. That was a good moment.

In the previous year, 2005, occurred the most embarrassing episode in the history of the Community Council. It concerned Jack Nicklaus. A proposal was put forward to make the golfer an Honoured Citizen of St Andrews, a distinction the CC was able to bestow on a few individuals who had performed meritorious services to the former Royal Burgh. However an earlier council had ruled that such nominations had to be agreed by a minimum of all but three of those voting.

The council met, and the result of the postal ballot was read out. Four votes had come in against the proposal, though the vast majority were in favour. The press representative, freelance Dougie Miller who conscientiously sat through almost every CC meeting in the hope of a few crumbs, grabbed the chance of a big brioche loaf. I was aghast when the story broke the next day and cursed the anonymous nay-sayers (though I now know who they were).

What should I have done as chair? The error I made was not to ask for the matter to be considered in private, as the CC had the right to do for confidential matters. But nobody in that room would have believed that St Andrews Community Council was going to refuse such an honour to Jack Nicklaus, especially as the council had honoured him on another occasion previously. [One may ask why he had to be honoured again.]

The full force of the storm broke in the Courier, and a second wave smashed the frail vessel Community Council into the rocks when the Scotsman, whose reporting staff had been asleep at the periscope for a fortnight and more, suddenly fired a torpedo. There was international coverage, for the press had gone mad. Letters flowed in like sewage down the Kinness Burn in spate, accusing us of being a mixture of Lucretia Borgia and John Balliol. The only thing I could do was to write a letter of apology to Jack Nicklaus, which I handed in to a contact in the R&A. Nicklaus wrote a courteous reply to say he considered the matter closed. In fact some members of the St Andrews Golf Club were not too unhappy at the council decision, as Nicklaus had accepted honorary membership of their club on the Links Road decades before and hadn't been back since.

In 2005 the Royal Bank of Scotland – yes, that one – issued a special Jack Nicklaus fiver, of which signed copies continue to change hands for ridiculous amounts of money.

I still have his letter, typed and signed – also one from JRR Tolkien. That will never be sold, but I would consider offers for the Jack Nicklaus letter. After all, he may have an honorary degree, but he's not an Honoured Citizen of St Andrews. And I certainly won't be!

Chapter 25

Fife Athletic Club

My participative career in athletics continued after 1976 in the colours of Fife – a white vest with the words Fife AC in blue. It was designed by Norman Brook and Ron Morrison, modelled on the Californian West Coast Striders and had the Cupar AAC red band.

In the beginning there was little in the way of athletics in north east or central Fife. On the Highland games circuit a young Terry Mitchell was already showing a clean pair of heels to the opposition at places like Ceres, Strathmiglo, Thornton and Newburgh. There was also, for those who had the bridge toll money, a team from Dundee called Hawkhill Harriers. Pitreavie in Dunfermline was already a very successful club.

In the early 1970s a number of little clubs started up in the area. In Cupar, a youthful John Hendry, who in the 1950s had been a promising miler, along with a few others, such as Norman Brook, later to be a major figure in the UK coaching scene, and Bill McCallum, later a district councillor, started Cupar and District AAC, who competed for a couple of years in various Scottish leagues including Division 2 of the Track & Field League.

In St Andrews Colin Mitchell, a former Scottish schools half mile champion, P.E. teacher Elspeth Wallace, retired business man Archie Pagan, Ian Docherty, and Eleanor Gunstone met to set up a club, St Andrews AAC, in that seat of learning. They asked me to join as treasurer, a post for which I was ill-qualified, but I declined at that point to run for them first claim. In Glenrothes Bill Melville, John Christie, Andrew Arbuckle and a few others set up Glenrothes AC who competed with no great distinction for a couple of years.

Also training in the area but running for other clubs were Sam Graves, and students Paul Kenney and Phil Hay. Ron Morrison, a long time member of Shettleston Harriers like his father and also latterly of St Andrews University where he was doing research, also agreed to join a new club, a matter we often discussed on our runs.

And so in late 1975 Fife Athletic Club was formed after many meetings, most of them in a wooden hut in the Fluthers car park that served as the Cupar headquarters. The first annual subscription was £5. It was important that the Club got off to a good start. Initially it was a Club for seniors and they achieved some good performances in the first year.

The success of Fife has not been due solely to competitive success, but also to the work behind the scenes. The stamina of a secretary such as David Cowieson, who looked after Fife AC for its first twelve years, or of Mel Scobie, book-keeper for many a year, typified the tremendous effort that has gone into making Fife what it has become. It is the same for all successful clubs.

Other names feature regularly throughout the past decades in the support team. Frank and Margaret McLaren even moved house so that they could be geographically in the centre of Fife. Elspeth Wallace and Anne McFarlane, the multi-talented Graham "Scoop" Bennison and Eleanor Gunstone are among many others who have given long service to the club.

Our young athletes owed their development to an enthusiastic and persistent team of coaches, of whom Dave Francis and Elspeth Wallace are the most long-lasting (though eternally youthful). Dulcie Graham, David Hamilton, John Linton, the Allisons, Brian Hughes, Ian Gordon, Sheena Christie and John Hendry are among many others who feature in the list. It testifies to the many hours voluntarily given to teach the rudiments of athletics. As everyone knows coaching proceeds in all weather conditions.

I hope others will not be offended if I omit all their names – there are just too many. Dave Francis has brought through the ranks and age-groups nearly all of Fife AC's best athletes of both sexes. One of the prime examples of progression to international level has been Penny Gunstone (Rother), whom I first saw as a skinny little 11-year old winning the Fife Schools cross-country at Madras College Kilrymont, where she was at school. Her mother Eleanor became an official in order to support her three children Doug, John and Penny, who all throve in the running world. Penny later became a top cross-country and road runner and duathlete, and is a GP in a doctor/dentist marriage with her ex-high jumper husband Rob Rother.

Then there is Andrew Lemoncello, who went from promising schoolboy to Olympic steeplechaser and has now transformed himself into a marathon runner. He started with Elspeth and then Dave, who passed him on in his teenage years to Ron Morrison. Andrew is now coached in America by a local coach but is still advised by Ron, who travels to most of his big races, at his own expense – MEPS, MPs and MSPs please note.

Fife AC has supplied its share of timekeepers, referees and judges at big events. Alan and Kathleen Findlay officiated at the Commonwealth games. Sam Taylor has carried his watch for several decades and richly deserves a gold-plated long service version. Liz and Allan Faulds have helped all along the way. Eleanor Gunstone and Ron Morrison have also carried out numerous refereeing duties, in Ron's case including at the IAAF World Championships at Holyrood in 2008. Ron had previously become Fife's first ever Scottish Athletics Federation president. Eleanor Gunstone's stints at the top included that of treasurer of the SWAAA and SWCCU.

Colin Mitchell, a local farmer and former Scottish Schools 880 yards champion, was the first president, followed by Cllr Bill McCallum and Ron Morrison. Andrew Arbuckle, another farmer, councillor, journalist and athletics all-rounder (like Ron Morrison ready to have a go at everything from hammer to pole-vault to hurdles to cross-country) had a strawberry-picking bus in which we travelled to distant races – the 1977 trip to a British Cup in Liverpool being a classic. Pushing the bus when it broke down was an added incentive. But it was much better than the trips I had made with Edinburgh Southern when the team manager, Jim Smart, would phone up and say in a persuasive voice things like: "Donald, would you fancy a wee trip to Southampton at the weekend to run a 10,000?" Sometimes I went.

Most of the FAC races were local, but we did compete in the national Scottish events throughout the year and occasionally ventured into England, Wales or to Northern Ireland. From Inverness to London was the scope of my own journeying to compete in an FAC vest, though I had a few years as a member of Thames Hare and Hounds when visiting the Bryants in New Malden and later Kingston sur Tamise.

For some years I took over the editorship of "Relay", a regular club magazine of which I wrote nearly everything myself. It was produced by photocopying, leading Ron Morrison's son David to remark on looking at an archived issue that "desk publishing has moved on a bit since then". Nowadays Relay, until recently under Graham Bennison, is available on the Fife AC website.

Our teams were there or thereabouts but were rarely quite up to the strength of the strongest clubs such as Shettleston, Edinburgh AC and Southern, Edinburgh Racing Club under its various sponsorship guises, however we could mix it with the likes of Aberdeen, Falkirk, Bellahouston, Cambuslang, Victoria Park and Spango Valley. There were occasional dashes of brilliance from young athletes like John Ness and Wendy Allison. The women's teams were sometimes stronger, especially in the older age groups where inter alias Jocelyn Scott, Caroline Brown, Margaret McLaren and Kim Macgregor won national awards.

Stars of the club include Caroline Innes, now Caroline Baird MBE, who went on to win four Paralympic Gold Medals and should if there was any justice be in the Scottish Sporting Hall of Fame along with Liz McColgan, Jim Alder, Lachie Stewart, Ian Stewart and Allan Wells and a couple of others. It was on the hills that FAC produced more real talent in Neil Martin, man of mystery Tony Stapeley (or was it Stapley?) from Springfield via the North of England, and later Owen Greene, Andrew Lemoncello, "Chunky" Liston, Graham Bee et al..

At home our road running squad was one of the best around, with Terry Mitchell the reinstated professional from Star of Markinch, Doug Gunstone once he left EAC and moved to Broughty Ferry, Dave Lang who had come to Cupar to manage the Bradford and Bingley at the Crossgate, Alan MacIntosh the quiet steeplechaser from Warout, Glenrothes, Ian Duncan who had been at university in St Andrews and sometimes came up to join our Edinburgh to Glasgow team. Fife's best position ever was 2nd in 1998, and we won the most meritorious award in 1976, 1982 and 1997.

Paul Kenney (Dundee University) ran for us second claim – he was later the father of GB international Laura Kenney. Craig Ross and Sam Graves came from the Hawks. I even got Ian Stewart of Birchfield and Scotland, my Munich and Christchurch room-mate, to agree to join us after one Edinburgh-Glasgow relay where he had whizzed past me in Aberdeen colours, but he never put pen to paper.

It is impossible to include all the stories about Fife AC and about athletics in those years. For a period I went into athletics administration, becoming President of the Scottish Cross Country Union in 1980-81. The job involved presiding at regular meetings in Glasgow with consequent late returns home. I do not enjoy night driving and so it was best when Ron Morrison took over that chore. At one meeting we managed to complete a re-write of the constitution in about two hours – which I thought a good achievement. Athletics officials can be just as argumentative and petty-minded as politicians or poets (according to my dad), and the SCCU, SAAA and SAF were no exception to that.

A couple of times I was asked to be team manager for British or Scottish small teams, once to Elgoibar in the Basque country, and once to the Marathon de l'Essonne near Paris. When we got to Elgoibar it was snowing so heavily that the race was cancelled. The "Equipe G-B" for Essonne 1982 was made up of three women led by Caroline Rodgers. They seemed to need little looking after so I entered as well. Caroline finished 1st woman in 2:48:09, while I was 9th, second Briton and first veteran in 2:21:40. Britain was second in both men's and women's races, to North Korea, who had the first four, and France respectively. Caroline and I shared a delicious moment of illicit delight when the organiser handed over brown envelopes full of francs – 3000 each, about £300. At last! I thought – to hell with the canteens of cutlery and the tokens for luncheon for two at the Café Superbe. I'm sure it was still against the rules, but I dare anyone to disqualify me in retrospect. The same incidentally goes for the drugs test I was asked to take following the SAAA marathon in 1981, when Colin Youngson (Aberdeen) beat me. I tried and tried to produce a urine sample, but it was impossible – so I just went home!

In 1980 and 1981 I had taken the Scottish Veterans' Cross Country title at Irvine (with Andy Brown second) and Aberdeen, then ten years later I squeezed home at St Andrews up a tough little hill next to James Stirling's quasi subterranean/submarine Andrew Melville Hall just ahead of my old friend and rival Mel Edwards, to whom Roger Bannister had written in the 1950s to advise him to eat more.

Since 1986 coaching has become more important, along with easy running Van Aaken style with the two Rons Morrison and Hilditch and Susan Gourlay the "Duracell Bunny". Until recently a BA Purser, Sue exhibits permanently the dynamic behaviour I recognise from my own on return from a long air trip to Australia.

Fife continues to flourish, with a new generation headed by our women's training squad of Helen Sharpe, Hester Dix, Megan Crawford (both St Andrews University), Sarah Cullen, Alison McGill, Morgan Murphy and Amie McKimmie, plus athletes like Halina Rees and others. If you are an athletics fan and read the results, watch out for these names! As long as they don't overtrain …

Chapter 26

The Fringe of Gold

Views from friends were canvassed before I decided to call this book "Running My Life". I have also pondered alternative endings as in "The French Lieutenant's Woman", set in the town of Lyme Regis, home of fossils, pensioners, surfers and second hand bookshops, where I picked up a small 1946 Italian dictionary while helping John Bryant research "The Marathon Makers". It involved quite a lot of information from Dorando's contemporaries in Carpi near Modena, and I managed to quarry the main facts out of the chunks of Italian that I was presented with.

You can't write about things until they are remote enough for you to feel they happened to somebody else, and that's what I have tried to do. This last chapter covers the ten years, and a little bit before that, since I retired from Madras College in the summer of 1999. The highlight of the previous year had been the visit to Berlin the school made by coach in the Easter holidays. My friend Patricia Esler, who teaches Drama and puts on wonderful productions in school and in local theatres, had suggested that the school organise a trip somewhere, "I'll go if you go", I replied, and so it came to pass. Four members of staff were in charge: Liz Higgins, our librarian, a Canadian English teacher called Craig Walker, Patricia and me, Patricia being accompanied by her two younger children, Tom and Seonaid, both of primary school age.

We travelled by coach, a long journey via Hull and Rotterdam, then overnight to Berlin. Our booking was in the Jugendgästehaus on the Wannsee, not far from the site of Himmler's infamous conference of 1942 that decided on the annihilation of Europe's Jewish people. The area is quietly residential, and the only swine I saw were wild boar during an early morning run. The warden of the hostel was very strict – no noise after 10pm – except that a French group came two days after us and wanted wine on the tables. "Sie wollen Wein auf den Tischen? " he kept repeating. "So was gibt es nicht!"[That's ridiculous!]

We had had problems with one pupil, who came from a troubled background. He had drunk beer on the ferry, despite our all-night patrols, and in the morning explained the presence of empty bottles in the waste basket by saying "some English boys" had dumped them. As on the Kiel Exchange trips, I have always believed it is best to let any potentially naughty people show their true colours in the closed environment of the ship going out, one of the reasons I preferred slow to fast travel.

That lad had very low horizons back home, but when we took the group to the Pergamon Museum we couldn't get him out of the place. The Pergamon is one of four that stand on the Museumsinsel in the River Spree and contains part of a Babylonian processional way ornamented with blue and yellow lion tiles, as well as an entire Greek temple. The visit was a triumph of culture. The same could not be said for four 15 year old girls who refused to get out of the coach at the Olympic stadium as they wanted to carry on playing cards. You can lead a horse to water…

A striking feature of the expedition was the moving visit to the KZ Sachsenhausen to the north of Berlin. There the NS guards, of both sexes, had tormented, tortured and killed thousands, then collected the remains and hoarded shoes, gold fillings and hair. It was unspeakably sinister. "Arbeit macht frei" stood over the gates: a cliché now, but testimony to a terrible barbarism that sporadically breaks out all over the world; and the Western countries are not immune from charges of involvement.

In 1998 Berlin was in course of reconstruction, and I have been back several times since, mostly to see or work with my friend Volker Kluge and his wife Gabi. I first wrote to him with questions about his book on Otto Peltzer, and now I have translated so many articles that I am beginning to know about a tenth of what he does about the Olympic movement and international sport. Berlin is built on sand, and has been reconstructed many times. Let us hope that there will be no more major reconstructions for a long long time.

After leaving Madras College in 1999 and surfacing from the depression that accompanied the triple crises of break-up, retirement and electoral meltdown on a small scale, I wasn't sure what to do. I sought advice from a job centre consultant who said I would be sure to find something. He was right. To add to the income stream I started with supply teaching.

Supply teachers stand in for absent members of staff on a daily or longer term basis. Students on the whole do not want to have a supply teacher and often act up. In one school I entered the French classroom to find the pupils chucking the French dictionaries out of the windows! In another, which considered itself rather superior, I returned to my classroom after lunch to find that a pupil had torn up my library book and defenestrated it as well. Such a thing had never happened to me in almost forty years of teaching.

These things paint a false picture. Nearly all the pupils I taught were reasonably attentive, and as ever I enjoyed teaching the youngest ones and the oldest, but not those in between. Pupils should be out of the classroom more doing active things – it's like factory farming to keep them penned up. The choice of subjects even now is too restricted and some of them are irrelevant.

I dropped supply teaching when I was lucky enough to obtain a part-time job as French and German tutor at the University of Abertay Dundee Business School. The colleagues were friendly but one or two a bit suspicious until I had proved myself, and I too had a lot to learn. When two colleagues left, I took over all the French and German teaching at all levels up to Honours, which was great fun. The best students I had were Polish, plus the odd German or Irish student, the French, whose education system does not encourage spontaneity, somewhere in the middle, and I have to say that with some exceptions the English and Scottish students, however willing, were in terms of language skills the weakest. The best UK language students did not on the whole go to Abertay. To make matters worse the University had taken the decision to phase French and German out – incredible in a business school – so I had to give up that employment in 2006.

I also had a chance to teach a few evening classes at Dundee University. Again that was enormously rewarding. The classes had an interesting mix of traditional evening class students of the kind I had taught in Madras in the 1960s, and a wide range of international students of all ages from 17 to 70 and countries from Kazakhstan to Nigeria. Students from Lagos tried to persuade me that their capital should be preferred to Glasgow as the host city for the Commonwealth Games in 2014. Sadly the University of Dundee also began to reduce language provision around this time.

For four years, from 1996 to 2000, I sat on the University Court at St Andrews, elected as a General Council Assessor. I enjoyed involvement in such things as interview panels and committees. The serving Rector, elected by the students, chaired the regular Court Meetings. In my period as an Assessor the Rector was Donald Findlay QC, with his distinctive mutton-chop whiskers and whose term was spoiled near its end by an incident involving the singing of inflammatory football songs. He was succeeded by Andrew Neil, said to detest the nickname "Brillo Pad" bestowed on him by Private Eye. Andrew was regularly called away to answer his mobile by the window, as he cultivated his important pressman about town image. He once advised me to "put my pennies together" and buy a house in the Alpes Maritimes. I might have been his neighbour.

The Principal of the University at that time was Struther Arnott, who had just received a CBE to add to his FRS and FRSE. I liked him, for he was friendly (at least to me), clever and interesting to talk to. He hailed from a small town in Lanarkshire and had attended the University of Glasgow. A molecular biologist, he was particularly adept at recruiting top class members of staff to join the University structure. His relationship with Donald Findlay QC, who chaired the Court meetings, could be described as prickly; and in the university he was liked by about as many as disliked him – the fate of most principals.

Members of Court were of course unpaid, but I had other jobs that brought in some money. Occasionally I was asked to be a "Group Leader" for an organisation based in Boston, Massachussetts called Elderhostel. It caters for students aged from 55 upwards, the only barriers to joining the courses or programs being finance and the ability to move around without assistance, though a few people choose to ignore that. With Elderhostel I visited places in the UK, as well as London and Brussels to the British and European Parliaments and to London and Paris for an Art History tour.

The State Opening of Parliament coincided with one programme, and the Americans were delighted to be standing about six feet away from the Queen's State Coach on its way to Westminster. We followed that evening and listened to the most pathetic debate I have heard in my life. ("This rotten government…")

On the Art programme everyone was looking forward to our visit to the Louvre except me, because two of the group, despite the rules, needed wheelchairs.

To procure these took time and I needed to stay with the wheelchair users and the rest of the group. As usual, visitors to the Palais du Louvre made a bee-line for the Vénus de Milo and the Mona Lisa and ignored practically everything else.

The Edinburgh Festival was also popular. It gave Group Leaders a chance to attend art exhibitions, concerts, theatre, dance and film performances of the highest standard. Elderhostel is very much a Good Thing.

The first tour was based at Sir John Lister-Kaye's Georgian/Victorian mansion on the estate called "Aigas", near Beauly, which is part of an environmental field centre where John and his wife Lucy run a series of programmes, assisted by a staff of rangers who are enthusiastic and hard-working, characteristics of the proprietors also.

That first programme started hesitantly on my part as I was far too polite to the American seniors on the way up from Glasgow Airport. On the first evening I was out for a run and came across a dead deer by the side of the road that had obviously just been hit by a vehicle. When I got back to the house I reported this, saying it was about a mile away on the south side of the road. Later that evening Sir John came over, having collected the deer (which would be used in the kitchen), and asked "How did you know it was a mile?" I explained that I knew because I was a runner.

After that the ice was broken and we got on well. We were all waiting to leave, when John again came over to the group and said to me "Donald, whaur's yer troosers?", to which I replied that the remark was as original as it was amusing. For once, not esprit de l'escalier!

I was back at Aigas several times, visiting Orkney on one occasion with a group. The job of the Group Leader is not really to lead, but to look after the Elderhostellers, making sure the programme is adhered to and trying to solve problems without causing more. On 11th September 2001 a group was about to go back to the States the next day when the news of the terrorist attack came over. The Aigas staff brought a television down to the dining room and I contacted London. After the obvious delays the entire group got away on schedule, but I was accused by one gentleman of panicking. I didn't, it was just that there was initially no flight information available.

After 9/11 and in recent years due to exchange rates the number of Elderhostel programmes in the UK has been reduced, but in 2004 I had a chance to become a tour guide for German-speaking groups touring Scotland in a week. The entrepreneur who had pioneered this is Klaus Frömmel, who with his father-in-law runs Rob Roy Tours from his home in North Berwick. Tragically, his young wife died in 2006 leaving three young children, but somehow Klaus and Richard and their enthusiastic staff kept the firm operating and it seems to be going from strength to strength.

I had to be trained for the job, and although I am not a Blue Badge guide, all the years of taking foreign groups and individuals round has given me an understanding of what to do and how much to say. Klaus took me on a tour of Edinburgh indicating where the coach should stop and why. I used notes but after a few turns you know what information should be given out. I especially like the visit to Calton Hill where within a couple of hundred yards (on a clear day) you have just about all of Scotland's history to talk about, the especial favourite of most visitors being the sad queen Mary Stuart and her poor choice of men.

For two summers I did nine tours per year, each of about a week. The route took us from Edinburgh on the anti-clockwise route through Fife, Dundee, up to Inverness, over the sea (or the bridge depending on direction) to Skye, south again to the Argyll capital of Inveraray, and finally via the western shores of Loch Lomond to Glasgow.

I used to sing in the bus, the only tour guide for Rob Roy Tours to do so, and tell jokes and anecdotes, mainly from my father's collections "Macgregor's Mixture" and its successors. The only snags were the waits at the airports, the need to keep to schedule and still allow photo stops and toilet stops without appearing to rush, and the arrival at that night's hotel where there were invariably problems to be sorted out. A very few of the guests were over-ready to complain to Klaus about something – anything – that might result in a refund, for the tours were not cheap. On the whole the guests enjoyed the tours and showed their appreciation of drivers and tour guides in various ways. (This is a euphemism in the case of one driver in particular.)

When I was elected to Fife Council in May 2007 I just did not have the time or the energy to do more than the occasional day tour, but I keep in touch with Klaus and wish him and his team and family well. I'm not going to say anything much about Fife Council as I'm still trying my hardest to help the citizens along the Fringe of Gold that is the East Neuk and its hinterland. I am a member of the Liberal Democrat/Scottish National Party administration. My Fife Council colleague Elizabeth Riches and her husband David and I share many a cup of tea or glass of wine away from meetings, and in the council itself and in our communities I'm not aware of having any real enemies, though of course they could be lurking ready to pounce. As time goes on I grow ever more independent-minded.

Other occasions worth noting, among many, were the celebrations for the Kiel-Madras 50th exchange, mentioned elsewhere, where I met up with Hans-Werner Suhr and Barbara, and my friendship with Volker and Gabi Kluge. In St Andrews, along with Terry Mitchell and a lot of others, I was inducted into the University's Sports Hall of Fame, or Hall of Shame as Ron (who introduced me) and I call it. It's not that I am ungrateful for the honour, and of course most people were delighted to have their achievements recognised – Terry bought his first-ever suit for the occasion – but I feel that it's somehow not quite right to have people in your Sports Hall of Fame if they haven't at least studied there or been on the staff. Chris Hoy started his studies at St Andrews – he left because there were no cycling facilities – but honorary graduates like Sir Alex Ferguson don't in my view belong in that group. But that's only my view. I would like to see much more community access to the University playing fields. In Queensland towns I visited in 2010 people were constantly running, walking, cycling and playing games, whereas on beautiful June evenings after term ends the expanse of grassy University playing fields lies practically deserted.

I made a joke at the ceremony. Ron had said "Somehow, they awarded him a degree" and I blurted out without really meaning to: "Ah, but a degree was worth something in those days." The audience, including numerous senior people including Chancellor and Principal, erupted – it was like a Bateman cartoon, "The Man Who Called the Quality of Degrees into Question".

Honours are a ticklish subject. Our system is nonsensical, and efforts to democratise it by honouring school janitors, cleaners and so on are bound to fail. All those who get honours should be treated equally. How much more difficult or responsible is it to be a nurse than a top civil servant waiting for his "K"?

If I were in charge of it I would have a single honour for everybody thought to deserve one. A touch of Burns would not come amiss:

> Ye see yon birkie ca'd 'a lord'
> Wha struts, and states, an a' that?
> Tho' hundreds worship at his word,'
> He's but a cuif for a' that
> For a' that, and a' that,
> His ribband, star an' a' that
> The man o' independent mind,
> He looks and laughs at a' that.
> (A 'cuif' is a dolt.)

I still enjoy running, the more so because I don't have the pressure any more to perform. I was never really ambitious as a teacher as I was reluctant to move away from St Andrews for too long, but I was ambitious in running, starting, it has to be said, from a very low base and taking a long, long time to move towards the heights. I didn't win any Olympic medals – though I came within 1 min 34 second of one in Munich – or Commonwealth Games medals. I was 8th, 7th and 6th at those big Games, setting a personal best of 2:14:15.6 at Christchurch and I ran 23 miles 971 yards in 2 hours at Pitreavie in 1970. I did win five Scottish titles at 6 miles, 10 miles and marathon, was in two winning Edinburgh-Glasgow teams, won Scottish marathon championship medals over a 21 year period from 1965-86, captured Scottish veteran cross-country titles (2 in the 40-45 bracket, one at 50-55), ran 24 marathons under 2:20 (though only four under 2:17), and two World Veteran titles at 10,000m (30:04.2) and marathon (2:19:23), the last one in my own country, Scotland. That's boasting, but it's also fact, and I can't say I'm not proud of it all.

But I'm prouder of my family and their progress, and enjoy coaching and occasionally racing, as well as more or less daily training with my friends; I enjoy giving talks on athletic subjects, and at last I have produced this, again with a lot of help from others.

Everything proceeds from your upbringing and your genetic background. My childhood was idyllic until our mother died, but that stopped my development as first-born in its tracks. Then a good education, during which I was almost exclusively in male company as well as having low self-esteem, and that took a long time to conquer. It was running and going to St Andrews University that changed me, so that I was able after that period to travel the world to compete, and to enlarge what talents I have in languages, writing, local politics, visits and exchanges, tour guiding and so on and to develop a wide circle of friendships, those with my closest friends, godson, brother and my grown-up children being very strong. Theirs is the happiest Macgregor generation to date, thanks of course also to their mother. We have been very lucky. Long may it remain so.

On July 25th 2009 I celebrated my 70th birthday, two days late, in the Café in the Park in St Andrews Museum, catering by Jim Braid, son of Jimmy Braid, the ex-Provost of St Monans, and his team. The place was full with 32 guests plus a young saxophonist, food was plentiful and the fizzy wine and fruit juice flowed. Ro and Tom were there, Mikey being in South America with his girlfriend Angie, where they had both learned to speak fluent Spanish. We all have it in us to achieve.

It was a bit like Bilbo Baggins's eleventy-first birthday party, though I didn't disappear. I do have a Lord of the Rings mug that shows a gold ring when hot water is poured into it and a T-shirt though, and can if I wish put my gold wedding ring round my neck on a white shoelace and make a wish.

This is it: I hope I die before I get old.

And the alternative ending? I'll steal this from the poet Robert Graves and end with a comma,

Chapter 26.2

Off to the Showers

We have crossed the line now, and here for us to mull over on the weary or exultant way to the showers are some quotations that might apply to running or other aspects of life:

(1) Bewegung ist Leben und Stillstand der Tod (Movement is life and standing still death) – motto of ultra long-distance courier Mensen Ernst (1795 or 1799 – 1842) who ran from Paris to Moscow, Constantinople to Calcutta, Munich to Nafplion and finally from down the Eastern Mediterranean coast into Africa as far south as Syene (Aswan) where he died of dysentery.

(2) The race is not to the swift, nor the battle to the strong, but that's the way to bet. - Damon Runyon

(3) Run slowly, run daily, drink moderately and don't eat like a pig. – advice from Dr Ernst van Aaken, LSD pioneer, Waldniel, Germany

(4) Ihr Racker, wollt ihr ewig leben? [You dogs, do you want to live for ever?] said by Frederick the Great of Prussia to his giant Guards when they seemed reluctant to charge.

(5) Mind is everything – muscles, pieces of rubber. Everything that I am, I am because of my mind. – Paavo Nurmi, the "Phantom Finn", winner of 9 Olympic Gold Medals 1920-28.

(6) Training shouldn't be a gasping grind with one eye on the watch. – Ron Clarke, multiple world record-holder.

(7) My arm is long and my vengeance is total – regular refrain from Ron Morrison (quoting from the film Billion Dollar Brain) when trying to get fit after injury.

(8) Train, don't strain – Fred Wilt and many others

(9) Go for grass – Donald Macgregor

(10) If any day you're too busy to run, you're too busy. – John Bryant. London Marathon director, journalist and author, long time member of Thames Hare & Hounds (founded 1875).

(11) If you lead, I won't follow. If you follow, I won't lead. – Gandhi to political parties

(12) Every day one should read a poem, make some music, look at a beautiful picture and if possible say something sensible – J.W. Goethe (tr.)

Three useful phrases for visiting Tibet:

(13) Lama loung-gom-pa tschig da – that looks like a running monk in a trance over there.

(14) Kaleh peb! – Go gently (addressed to those departing)

(15) Kaleh jou! – Sit softly (addressed to those remaining)

(16) Good enough is rarely good. – my brother Forbes Macgregor, roads engineer, DIY and car expert

(17) Five things to do every day, all to be taken in the widest context:

Run a mile, play some music, write a poem, drink a glass of wine, make love…(could be 20 miles, listening to Classic FM, writing this, opening a bottle of red, taking a romantic interest some flowers.)

(18) Without toil there have triumphed a very few. (Pindar)

(19) Le coeur – organe de gauche (motto of French socialist party)

(20-26) The whole of "Pedestrianism" (1813) is crammed with maxims about training along similar lines, though injunctions against over-indulgence in alcohol and any sex during training went out with Dunky Wright. It's all relative – athletes in Captain Barclay's time were allowed up to three pints of beer with meals daily and half a pint of red wine after dinner, at a period when the water supply was unhealthy. And like the pedestrians, Ron Hill doesn't drink milk.

(26.2) Water is best. (Pindar again)

We've arrived at last:

A poem on hot showers

> I don't know who invented hot showers
> But to them every blessing should flow
> We can stand there for minutes or hours
> When we've been out in rain, frost or snow
> After running or sailing or biking
> Whether sweating or taking things slow
> A hot shower's to everyone's liking
> For it leaves every body a-glow.

© D.F.Macgregor 2010

Appendix I - Marathons 1965 onwards

Year	Date	Event	Location	Time	Position
1965	12 June	SAAA	Westerlands/Dumbarton	2:22:24	2
1966	11 June	AAA Poly	Windsor/Chiswick	ret 20mls	dnf
1967	26 Aug	AAA	Baddesley Colliery	2:17:19	3
1967	10 Oct	Košice	CSSR	2:24:54.2	11
1969	10 May	Karl-Marx-Stadt	GDR2:18:51	5(5)	
1969	5 Oct	Košice	CSSR	2:17:33.2	2
1970	16 May	SAAA	Meadowbank	2:17:14	2
1970	23 July	Commonwealth Games	Edinburgh	2:16:53	8
1971	6 April	Marathon – Athens	Greece	2: 26:05	5
1971	8 May	Edinburgh-N.Berwick	Edinburgh	2:19:00	3(10)
1971	13 June	AAA Maxol	Manchester	2:19:34	19
1971	26 June	SAAA	Meadowbank	ret 23 mls	dnf
1971	30 Oct	Westdeutsche Regional Champ	Köln	2:19:00.2	1(a.K)
1972	15 April	Waldniel	Germany	2:25:18	3
1972	4 June	AAA Maxol	Manchester	2:15:06	3(15)
1972	10 Sept	Olympic Games	München	2:16:34.6	7
1972	4 Dec	Fukuoka	Japan	2:14:15.4	6
1973	23 June	SAAA	Meadowbank	2:17:51	1
1974	31 Jan	Commonwealth Games	Christchurch NZ	2:14:15.4	6
1974	22 June	SAAA	Meadowbank	2:18:08	1(20)
1974	26 Oct	Harlow Marathon	Harlow	2:17:46	3
1975	1 June	AAA Michelin	Stoke	2:20:50	15
1975	28 June	SAAA	Meadowbank	ret 15 mls	dnf
1976	8 May	AAA (OG trial)	Rugby	2:21:27	12

Year	Date	Event	Location	Time	Position
1976	26 June	SAAA	Meadowbank	2:24:12	1(25)
1978	7 May	AAA	Sandbach	2:22:45	40
1978	3 June	SAAA	Meadowbank	2:23:33	2
1978	15 Oct	Cleveland County	Middlesbrough	2:19:19	2
1979	26 June	SAAA	Meadowbank	2:19:15	2
1979	2 Aug	IGAL World Champs	Hannover	2:22:50	2(30)
1979	22 Sept	RRC	Milton Keynes	2:18:30	6
1980	12 April	Westland Marathon	Nederland	2:22:33	4
1980	20 Aug	IGAL World Veterans Champ	Glasgow	2:19:23	1
1980	28 Sept		Aberdeen	2:26:43	7
1981	11 April	Westland Marathon	Nederland	2:38:15	36(35)
1981	20 June	SAAA	Edinburgh/Cramond	2:21:31	2
1981	27 Sept		Aberdeen	2:21:52	3
1982	4 March	Essonne	France	2:21:40	9
1982	9 May		London	2:20:42	36
1982	17 Oct	Peoples nr 1	Glasgow	2:22:06	10(40)
1983	24 April	Peoples Health nr 1	Dundee	2:17:24	1
1983	26 June	Loch Rannoch		2:26:51	3
1983	11 Sept	Peoples nr 2	Glasgow	2: 19:34	7
1984	29 April	Peoples Health nr 2	Dundee	2:18:16	1
1984	30 Sept	Peoples nr 3	Glasgow	2:19:01	10(45)
1985	31 Mar	Wolverhampton Millennium		2:23:00	3
1985	23 June	Loch Rannoch		2:25:00	1
1985	22 Sept	Peoples nr 3	Glasgow	2:19:36	10
1986	20 April		London	2:22:05	66
1986	1 June	SAAA	Edinburgh/Cramond	2:27:30	2(50)
1988	24 April	People's Health Nr 7	Dundee	dnf	ret 15

Colour Plates

St Andrews from St Rule's Tower(chapter 3).

July 1962: the traveller returns.
Forbes and Donald together at 17 Kaimes Road (chapter 5).

Class trip with 1H to West Lomond, Fife 1965 –Duncan Monteith (chapter 6).

Calendar Boys: Macgregor, Wolde, Wade, Košice 1969 (chapter10).

Karl-Marx-Stadt (Chemnitz): Squire Yarrow and DFM in front of the XX Jahre
DDR banner, May 1969 (chapter 11).

Robbed: Arne Andersson and Gunder Hägg 1944 (chapter 12).

Athens 1971: at the Parthenon (chapter 14).

Olympic gear, 1972, Munich village (chapter 17).

Start of Marathon (chapter 17).

DFM leads Hill into last lap (chapter 17).

Lost & found: baggage label on kit bag that was returned form Riem Airport, September 1972 (chapter 17).

World Veteran Championship Marathon, Bellahouston Road, August 1980: DFM and John Robinson (NZ) lead group at end of lap one (chapter 19).

Wedding, Boarhills Kirk, 6 December 1980:
Willie McKane, Rev. Peter Douglas, Kim and Donald Macgregor (chapter20).

Paterfamilias: Rosemary Kim 1981 (chapter 20).

Mikey on tractor, 8 Dempster Terrace 1985 (chapter 20).

Tommy and Whisper on Dempster Terrace veranda 1991 (chapter 20).

Up at last: Tommy reaches out for an Alpine Kuh, 1991 (chapter 20).

Three generations: Ro, Daddy, Granpa, Mikey, 17 Kaimes Road 2003 (chapter 20).

*Gonfannon: DFM with
Royal Burgh of
St Andrews
Community Councillors
Kenneth Fraser
and Ken Crichton
(chapter 23).*

*Her last summer: Jean Macgregor at
17 Kaimes Road 2003 (chapter 25).*

*Volker and Gabi Kluge with Shila, Pritzhagen,
Brandenburg 2010 (chapter 26).*

Ro and Morag Muir, Café in the Park, July 2010 (chapter 26).

Runners and partners in the Lakes (chapter 26).

St Andrews women's team, Allan Scally Relay 2003,
with Ron and Don (chapter 26).

Glasgow University: Rosemary Kim Macgregor, MA (chapter 26).

Glasgow University: Michael Macgregor, MA with parents (chapter 26).

Auld acquaintance not forgot: at DFM's 70th: Agnes McKane,
Ann Morrison (chapter 26).

Two wise men: DFM, Ron Morrison, Ron Hilditch 2008 (chapter 26).

*St Andrews Highland
Games: with Ian Grieve
2007 (chapter 26).*

In the thick of it: Ro in the Bristol half (chapter 26).

Lyme Regis: with John and Carol Bryant (chapter 26).

Guatemala shade: Mikey and Angie 2009 (chapter 26).

Happy Birthday: Tom, Dad, Ro 2009 (chapter 26).

*Cllrs Elizabeth Riches and DFM, Anstruther Duck Race, Easter 2010
(John Kinsman) (chapter 26).*